ACCESS
FRENCH

A FIRST COURSE FOR ADULTS

BERNARD GROSZ with **HENRIETTE HARNISCH**   Series editor: **JANE WIGHTWICK**

McGraw·Hill

New York   Chicago   San Francisco   Lisbon   London   Madrid   Mexico City
Milan   New Delhi   San Juan   Seoul   Singapore   Sydney   Toronto

Library of Congress Cataloging-in-Publication Data
is available from the United States Library of Congress

Originally published by Hodder Arnold, a member of the Hodder Headline Group,
338 Euston Road, London NW1 3BH, UK

10 9 8 7 6 5 4 3 2 1

ISBN 0-07-143080-6 (book component)
ISBN 0-07-142821-6 (book + 2 CD package)

McGraw-Hill books are available at special quantity discounts to use as premiums and sales
promotions, or for use in corporate training programs. For more information, please write to the
Director of Special Sales, Professional Publishing, McGraw-Hill, Two Penn Plaza, New York, NY 10121-
2298. Or contact your local bookstore.

ACKNOWLEDGEMENTS

Pour Annie, Daniel, Rudy, Franz et Ilona.

The author and publishers would like to thank the following for use of their material in this volume:

Accor Hotels for Novotel logo and text p142; © Anite Business Systems Ltd/SeaFrance for booking form p118; Groupe Auchan for web page p39; Sylvain Beauregard, beauregs@celine-dion.net/www.celine-dion.net for text on Celine Dion p31; www.bib.chiroux-croisiers.liege.be for map of Liège on p110; www.boboprevention.com for medicine chest on p164 ; *Site web du réseau canadien de la santé*, http://www.canadian-health-network.ca/customtools/homef.html, Santé Canada, 1999 © Reproduit avec la permission du Ministre des Travaux publics et Services gouvernementaux Canada, 2003: web page on p154; www.cartevisite.com for business cards p25; Carrefour France for food items on p45 (a, d, h, i); www.dakarville.sn for web page on p130; Comité Départemental du Tourisme du Nord for web page on Douai p93; Europcar for logo and text on p125; Groupe Envergure for hotel search site on p136; Gérard Fouilleul, http://perso.clubinternet.fr/gfo/mouroux.fr for architect's drawings p175; www.franceguide.com for web page p67; www.francophonie.org for maps on pp11, 28; Intermedia, The Ministry of Tourism, Daniel Kedar, Jean-Pierre Grasset & Daniel Elie for web page Haïti Tourisme (www.haititourisme.org) on p48; Administration communale de la Ville de Liège, www.liege.be, dessinateur Michel Heusdins, for web page p107 & text p108; www.seloger.com for web page on p173; Merck.fr for Médibronc syrup on p162; www.multimania.com for creole recipes p49; Société Créations Nelson for p176 (photo e); Nestlé France for p44 (b); Société Quicksilver for photo a, p176; www.redoute.fr for fashion images p176 (b, c, d & f), Les Restos du Cœur for text on pp87-88; Hôtel Château Tilques for hotel page p138; Laboratoire UPSA for Upfen packet p163; Laboratoire URGO for Humex pastilles on p162; www.vanuatutourism.com for their home page p165 & *Santé* p166; www.vietnamtravelling.com for texts on Vietnam pp188-9l; VVF Vacances for logo and text on p54; Yahoo France for their web page on p1.

Every effort has been made to trace and acknowledge ownership of copyright. The publishers will be glad to make suitable arrangements with any copyright holders whom it has not been possible to contact.

Photo acknowledgements

Air France p115 (c). Alamy p16 (top), p36 (1, 2 & 4), p149 (bottom, 2nd from bottom), 172 (top, 2nd from top, 2nd from bottom). C. Baldwin p5 (c), p9, p33, p66. S. Baldwin p35, p41 (top), p44 (right), p46 (bottom), p51 (bottom), p54, p55, p56 (top), p61 (bottom), p63 (top), p73 (top), p79, p81, p83, p89 (bottom), p90, p95 (top right, centre right, bottom left, far right: top), p98 (left), p103, p108, p114 (**a, b, d, e, f, g**), p119, p121, p124, p139, p153, p155, p157 (top), p160, p186 (top & bottom left). Corbis p15 (**c, e, g**), p17 (centre right), p19 (bottom), p84 (centre), p149 (top, 2nd from top), p172 (bottom). Das Fotoarchiv p18. Life File p5 (**a & d**), p15 (**a & b**), p17 (far left), p22 (right), p36 (3 & 5), p84 (right), p95 (top left), p114 (**h & i**), p172 (centre). J. Lowe p56 (bottom), p73 (bottom), p89 (top), p141, p145, p154. Rex Features Ltd p31, p84 (left). Still Pictures p15 (**d**). Tografax p45 (**d & j**), p86 (bottom left). C. Weiss p17 (right), p19 (top).

Cover main image: Stone/Getttyimages.

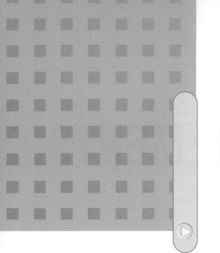

INTRODUCTION

Access French is a refreshing, modern introduction to the French language, culture and people. It is specially designed for adults of all ages who are just starting out learning French or who are returning after a long gap.

The course is ideal for independent study but is also suitable for learning with a partner or in a class. In the coursebook, learners and teachers will find an extended range of activities covering all four skills as well as ideas for group activities.

A further range of ideas, activities, tips and advice is available on our website, www.accesslanguages.com. You don't have to use the site to benefit from the course but, according to your particular needs or interests, you will find a great deal of extra practice, information and links to useful French sites. For more depth in a particular language structure, for example, we have included additional interactive activities and we've even included advice and links for the major examinations and qualifications.

Access French offers a fun and friendly approach to the French language as it is spoken in France and other French-speaking countries today. It will enable you to deal with everyday situations, covering practical topics such as travel, shopping, making a complaint at a hotel or eating in a restaurant and many of the activities are based on genuine French websites. The course is also ideal for those who wish to study French for business purposes and will provide learners with a sound basis of vocabulary and grammar structures.

ACCESS FRENCH

The coursebook is divided into 10 carefully graded units. At the beginning of each, the content and objectives are clearly identified and you can check your progress at various points throughout the unit. Each unit starts with a number of activities relating to the previous one so you can revise topics already covered, giving you the confidence to move on to new areas.

The units offer a wide range of activities which will quickly enable you to start reading and writing contemporary French, and the listening exercises featuring authentic French-speakers are integral to the course.

Each unit consists of:

- a checklist of topics covered in the unit

- review activities (Vous vous souvenez?): these give you the chance to review important points in the previous unit

- listening activities: authentic conversations, passages and exercises to increase your listening skills and to help you acquire confidence

- speaking activities

- reading activities: authentic documents and exercises to extend your vocabulary and comprehension

- writing activities: practical and authentic forms to complete, grammar activities and letter-writing to consolidate key points and to reinforce confidence when travelling to a French-speaking country

- exercises and games to work on with a partner

- exercises and games to work on with a group in order to practise the language through various practical situations

- games to be played with a partner or in a group

- **LANGUAGE FOCUS** Language Focus panels: these offer brief and concise structural and grammatical summaries with related activities

- **LEARNING TIP:** Learning Tip: containing useful linguistic and cultural information

- **READY TO MOVE ON?** Ready to move on: frequent reviews enabling you to check your progress and to feel confident in what you have learnt

- **Découverte de la FRANCOPHONIE** Découverte de la Francophonie: special sections at the end of each unit giving general information and related activities on French-speaking countries around the world

- **GLOSSARY** Glossary: French-English glossaries containing vocabulary used in the unit

- **LOOKING FORWARD** Looking Forward: preparation and dictionary skills ready for the next unit

-  links to our dedicated website www.accesslanguages.com containing extra activities to practise key points, useful links to French sites and advice on further study and qualifications

Answers to the exercises and recording transcripts are available in a separate **Support Booklet** and we strongly recommend that you obtain the **Access French Support Book and Cassette Pack**, which will enable you to develop your listening skills and get used to hearing the French language as it is spoken now.

We hope that working through this course will be an enjoyable experience and that you will find this new approach to language learning fun. Bonne chance!

CONTENTS

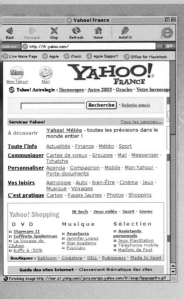

UNIT 1
Bonjour

By the end of this unit you will be able to:

- Say hello
- Introduce yourself
- Understand different ways of greeting and react accordingly
- Ask and understand simple questions
- Say where you live and where you are from
- Learn the French alphabet and numbers

Recognising words or phrases in French is not always as difficult as it seems. The Internet age has hugely accelerated the immigration of English and American into the French language.

You only need a few words to begin with in order to find your way around. Prove this to yourself by starting off straight away listening to a natural French dialogue.

1 On commence? (Shall we start?)

A Listen to the dialogue and pick from the list below the information asked for. Don't worry about understanding every word. Just see if you can get the gist.

- Profession
- Address
- Telephone no.
- Name
- Marital status

B Listen to the same dialogue and put the following questions in the right order:

(QUEL) (NOM) (EST) (VOTRE) (?)

(VOTRE) (QUELLE) (ADRESSE) (EST) (?)

(PROFESSION) (EST) (VOTRE) (QUELLE) (?)

Did you pick out the answers to the questions in the dialogue?

C Now work in pairs and ask your partner what his or her name is. When you are asked, the reply is: **Je m'appelle …**

> Note that there is another way of asking for someone's name: **Comment vous appelez-vous?**

> If you did not catch an answer and want the person to repeat it, say:
> **Pardon?** or **Vous pouvez répéter, s'il vous plaît?**
> (Can you repeat, please?)

D Listen to the dialogue and fill in the gaps using the words below:

(nom – appelle – prénom – je – enchanté)

A Bonsoir, je m'( ) Pierre Jacques.

Mon ( ) est Jacques et mon ( ) est Pierre.

B ( ) m'appelle Laure Boisin.

A ( ).

B Enchantée.

E 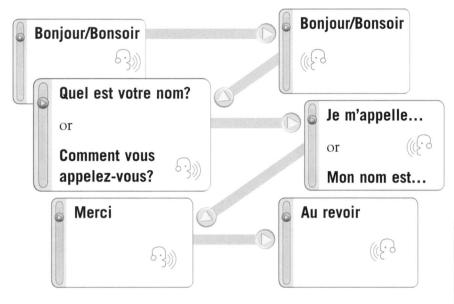 Mix and Match game. Your teacher will give you a card with a name on it. Go round the class and find the person who forms the other half of your pair (for example Adam–Eve). Here are the words to help you:

Bonjour/Bonsoir

Bonjour/Bonsoir

Quel est votre nom?

or

Comment vous appelez-vous?

Je m'appelle…

or

Mon nom est…

Merci

Au revoir

2 La fiche (The form)

A Complete the form below with your own details:

CARTE TRAIN/FAMILLE	50% DE REDUCTION – VALABLE EN EUROPE
PROPRIETAIRE DE LA CARTE:	
Nom de famille:	
Prénom:	
Adresse:	
Ville:	
Code postal:	
Age:	Nombre d'enfants:

LEARNING TIP:
Greetings

Bonjour: literally means *Good day* and should be used during office hours.

Bonsoir: means *Good evening* and should be used after office hours.

Au revoir: means *Goodbye*.

In a more informal way, French people use **Salut!** meaning *Hi!* or *Bye!* However, these days you'll also hear people say **Bye!** or **Ciao!**

Titles

When greeting someone, French people often add a title to their **Bonjour**, especially in shops and other public places.

You will hear:

Bonjour/Bonsoir/Au revoir monsieur to a gentleman
madame to a lady
mademoiselle to a young girl

www.accesslanguages.com **is full of interesting ways to expand your French. There are suggestions for each unit to help you practise and extend what you know, whether for general use, examinations or leisure.**

UNIT **1**

ACCESS FRENCH

Nombre d'enfants?

un	deux	trois	quatre	cinq	six

sept	huit	neuf	dix

B In the previous dialogues, to ask for somebody's name we said:

(**Quel**) (**est**) (**votre**) (**nom?**)

(What) (is) (your) (name?)

You can make many more questions using the same model:

- What is your first name?
- What is your postcode? etc.

Now work with a partner. Ask him or her for the information needed to complete the form in activity 2A.
Quel est votre...?

When you have finished, swap roles.

At this stage, don't worry about answering all these questions in French. You will be able to do this very soon.

You'll find an activity to help you remember the numbers on www.accesslanguages.com

✓

Check that you can...

- ask and answer questions about your name in two different ways
- say 'Please' and 'Thank you'
- count up to 10
- greet someone at different times of day
- say 'Goodbye'.

3 Qui suis-je? (Who am I?)

A [AC] ▶ Look at the sentences below. Can you guess what each of them means?

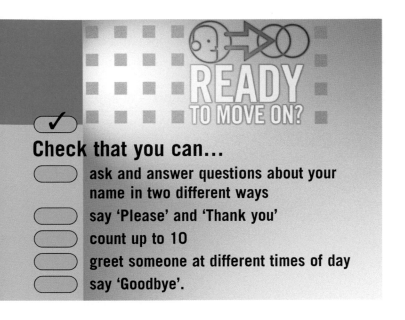

1 Je suis professeur de mathématiques.
2 J'ai deux enfants.
3 Je suis mariée.

4 J'habite à Bruxelles.
5 Je suis née à Montréal.

6 Je suis suisse.
7 J'ai 20 ans.

B ▶ Look at the photos of four people below and listen to them introduce themselves in French. Can you work out who's who?

> Paul – Justine – Jamal – Nathalie

a French mechanic
from Bordeaux
4 children

b English
from London
age 20
lives in Brussels

c Swiss
32 years old
married
2 children

d Canadian
born in Montreal
teacher
lives in France

Bonjour UNIT 1

5

C 🖊 ▶ Have a look at the following sentences and try to fill in the gaps using the words below:

Try the additional activity on
www.accesslanguages.com

> ai – suis – habite – suis – ai – suis – suis – m'appelle

1 Je ⬭ garagiste. **5** Je ⬭ Jamal.

2 J' ⬭ quatre enfants. **6** Je ⬭ de Londres.

3 Je ⬭ célibataire. **7** Je ⬭ anglais.

4 J' ⬭ en France. **8** J' ⬭ 32 ans.

D 🖊 ▶ Complete the sentences below by changing the verb in brackets:

1 Il ⬭ Michel Bourgeois. (s'appeler) **5** Christian ⬭ marié. (être)

2 Je ⬭ de Lille. (être) **6** Il ⬭ deux enfants. (avoir)

3 Brigitte ⬭ à Birmingham. (habiter) **7** Vous ⬭ un téléphone portable? (avoir)

4 Elle ⬭ française. (être) **8** J' ⬭ 55 ans. (avoir)

E 🖊 ▶ Now go back to activity 3C and write the details of each person using **il** or **elle** accordingly.

F 🎧🖊 ▶ Listen to the following numbers.
Are they correct? If not, write the correct answers:

a • 18 ⬭	**e** • 30 ⬭	**i** • 12 ⬭	**m** • 13€ ⬭
b • 25 ⬭	**f** • 41 ⬭	**j** • 6 ⬭	**n** • 21€ ⬭
c • 66 ⬭	**g** • 50 ⬭	**k** • 40 ⬭	**o** • 37€ ⬭
d • 14 ⬭	**h** • 15 ⬭	**l** • 68€ ⬭	

LANGUAGE FOCUS

Encore des nombres

11 • onze	12 • douze	13 • treize	14 • quatorze	15 • quinze
16 • seize	17 • dix-sept	18 • dix-huit	19 • dix-neuf	20 • vingt

20 • vingt	21 • vingt-**et**-un	22 • vingt-deux	25 • vingt-cinq…
30 • trente	31 • trente-**et**-un	32 • trente-deux	36 • trente-six…
40 • quarante	41 • quarante-**et**-un	42 • quarante-deux	47 • quarante-sept…
50 • cinquante	51 • cinquante-**et**-un	52 • cinquante-deux	58 • cinquante-huit…
60 • soixante	61 • soixante-**et**-un	62 • soixante-deux	69 • soixante-neuf…

The missing words in activity **3C** are all verbs:

(**Je suis**) (**J'ai**) (**J'habite**) (**Je m'appelle**)

Many verbs follow regular patterns:

habiter – *to live*

j'habite	*I live*
il habite	*he lives*
elle habite	*she lives*
vous habitez	*you live*

s'appeler – *to be called* (lit. *to call oneself*)

je m'appelle	*my name is*
il s'appelle	*his name is*
elle s'appelle	*her name is*
vous vous appelez	*your name is*

The verbs *to be* and *to have* are irregular:

être – *to be* **avoir** – *to have*

je suis	*I am*	**j'ai**	*I have*
il est	*he is*	**il a**	*he has*
elle est	*she is*	**elle a**	*she has*
vous êtes	*you are*	**vous avez**	*you have*

In French, the word for **I** is **je**.

Je suis *I am*

But note that if the following word starts with a vowel or the letter *h*, **je** becomes **j'**.

J'ai	*I have*
J'habite	*I live*

You can find more practice of these verbs at www.accesslanguages.com

Bonjour **UNIT** **1**

7

4 Et vous?

A    Look and listen.

To make questions to which you expect the answer *Yes* or *No*, simply keep the same word order as in a statement but raise your voice at the end.

You can also add the expression:
Est-ce que...

**(Est-ce que) Nathalie est mariée?
– Non, elle est divorcée.**

Justine habite en France.	Justine habite en France?
Jamal a 4 enfants.	Jamal a 4 enfants?
Nathalie est mariée.	Nathalie est mariée?
Elle a 32 ans.	Elle a 32 ans?
Il est de Londres.	Il est de Londres?

Est-ce que Justine habite en France?	Oui, elle habite à Paris.
Est-ce que Jamal a 4 enfants?	Non, il a 2 enfants.
Est-ce que Nathalie est mariée?	Non, elle est divorcée.
Est-ce qu'elle a 32 ans?	Non, 34.
Est-ce qu'il est de Londres?	Oui, de Greenwich.

B How would you ask for the following information in French?

- Married?
- Children?
- Live in Liverpool?
- From Brussels?

- Address?
- French?
- Nationality?
- First name?

C Listen to three people being interviewed in Lille and complete the table below:

Nom de famille	Lambert		Dupont
Prénom		Julien	
Habite à	Lyon		
Situation de famille		marié	
Enfant	0		
Age	41		
Profession			

D Compare your answers with your neighbour. Did you get all the information?

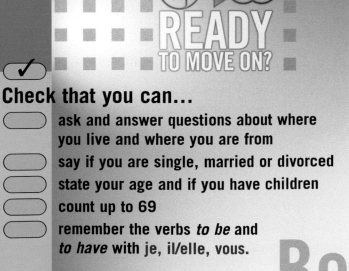

READY TO MOVE ON?

✓

Check that you can...

- ask and answer questions about where you live and where you are from
- say if you are single, married or divorced
- state your age and if you have children
- count up to 69
- remember the verbs *to be* and *to have* with je, il/elle, vous.

Bonjour **UNIT 1**

5 Alphabet

A 🎧 🔊 ▷ Listen to the alphabet and repeat it:

| F L M N S Z | B C D P T V W | G – J |

| H K Q R X Y | A – E – I – O – U |

B 👥 🔊 ▷ Work with a partner. Your teacher will give you a card with a set of words like the ones below. Spell your words to your partner then write your partner's words in the space provided on the card.

Partner A
Durand
habiter
Lyon
Georges

Partner B
Bardot
avoir
Avignon
jardin

C 👥 🔊 ▷ Now work with two other members of your group.

Ask them to spell their names:

– **Comment vous appelez-vous?**

– **Jacques Lebon.**

– **Vous pouvez épeler?** or **Comment ça s'écrit?**

– **L-E-B-O-N.**

Découverte de la FRANCOPHONIE

La Francophonie est une organisation qui regroupe l'ensemble des pays et constitutions dont les habitants utilisent le français comme langue maternelle, officielle ou véhiculaire.

At the end of each unit, we will go round the world and discover other 'francophones' countries…

A What is '**Francophonie**'?

B Look at the map above showing members of **la Francophonie**, then look at the following list of countries. Can you pick the ones that are members?

a	le Canada		**g** • l'Egypte	
b	la Belgique		**h** • l'Inde	
c	le Portugal		**i** • le Vietnam	
d	la Suisse		**j** • le Maroc	
e	le Sénégal			
f	le Royaume-Uni			

Find out more about **la Francophonie** at www.francophonie.org

UNIT **1**

11

ACCESS FRENCH

GLOSSARY

Nouns

nom (m)	name
prénom (m)	first name
numéro (m)	number
famille (f)	family
ville (f)	town/city
enfant (m,f)	child
an (m)	year
étudiant (m)	student (male)
étudiante (f)	student (female)
pays (m)	country
langue (f)	language/tongue

Adjectives

français(e)	French
anglais(e)	English
célibataire	single
marié(e)	married
divorcé(e)	divorced

Verbs

être	to be
avoir	to have
s'appeler	to be called

pouvoir	can/to be able to
habiter	to live
naître	to be born
épeler	to spell

Expressions

oui/non	yes/no
Quel(le) est votre…?	What is your…?
Vous pouvez répéter, s'il vous plaît?	Can you repeat please?
s'il vous plaît	please
Je m'appelle…	My name is…
Enchanté(e)	Pleased to meet you
Bonjour	Good morning/Good day
Bonsoir	Good evening
Bonne nuit	Good night
Au revoir	Goodbye
Salut!	Hi!/Bye!
monsieur	sir/Mr
madame	madam/Mrs
mademoiselle	miss
merci	thank you
de Paris	from Paris
Je suis né(e)…	I was born…

UNIT 2
Les autres et moi

LOOKING FORWARD

In **Unit 2**, we will be looking at jobs, occupations and daily routine. To prepare, look at the jobs listed below. Can you guess what they mean? Is your job listed? Look up any jobs you can't guess in a dictionary, and your own job if it's not listed.

jardinier • boulanger-pâtissier • informaticien • secrétaire • caissier • cuisinier • directrice d'entreprise • serveuse • infirmière

UNIT 2
Les autres et moi

By the end of this unit you will be able to:
- Say what your nationality is
- Say what you do for a living
- Explain briefly what your job consists of
- Count up to 100
- Use the present tense of regular verbs
- Use the negative form
- Ask questions to find out more details about someone

1 Vous vous souvenez?

A Match the following expressions:

1	Pleased to meet you.	**a**	Je suis célibataire.
2	What is your first name?	**b**	Bonsoir, monsieur.
3	Good evening, sir	**c**	Vous avez des enfants?
4	I am single.	**d**	Quel est votre prénom?
5	Do you have any children?	**e**	Enchanté(e).

LEARNING TIP:

When introducing someone to someone else, start with

Voici...

Voici Pierre.

Voici Yasmin.

Voici Sébastien et Alex.

B You are in France with a friend, Mary. You visit your French friend Julien who lives near Calais. Mary does not speak any French.

Work out what you'll say to introduce Mary to Julien in French. Here are some clues:

Mary
28 years old
born in Cardiff
lives in London

2 Quoi de neuf?

A Try to match the jobs with the pictures that describe them.

1 Secrétaire

2 Serveur/serveuse

3 Boulanger/boulangère

4 Infirmier/infirmière

5 Informaticien/informaticienne

6 Cuisinier/cuisinière

7 Jardinier/jardinière

a   b   c

d   e   f   g

Les autres et moi

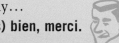

LANGUAGE FOCUS

Ça va? *(How are you?)*

Comment allez-vous?   *formal*

Comment ça va?

Ça va?

Quoi de neuf?   *informal*

Reply…

(Très) bien, merci.

Ça va!

Bof, comme ci comme ça!

Mal!

B Listen to the conversation between Yves Morel and Marianne Blanchard, two people who used to work in the same company some years ago, and pick the correct answer:

Marianne est …

mariée ⬭

célibataire ⬭

divorcée ⬭

Marianne travaille pour …

une grande entreprise ⬭

une petite entreprise ⬭

une entreprise moyenne ⬭

Yves travaille pour une compagnie…

anglaise ⬭

hollandaise ⬭

polonaise ⬭

Yves est…

chef de cuisine ⬭

chef de production ⬭

chef du personnel ⬭

Les genres *(genders)*

French has two genders: masculine and feminine. Everything around you (nouns, such as fruit, furniture, countries, people etc.) is either masculine or feminine. Every word you use to describe these nouns (adjectives, such as nice, happy, green, English) will change its ending accordingly. Generally, an **e** is added to the masculine adjective to make it feminine.

masculine

feminine

Masculine

Yves est **français.**   John est **anglais.**

Feminine

Marianne est **française.**   Mary est **anglaise.**

3 Les genres

A   It's your turn to try the following:

1   Steve est **américain.**

2   Britney est ( ).

3   Patrick est **marié.**

4   Véronique est ( ).

5   Thierry est **petit.**

6   Marie est ( ).

Les autres et moi UNIT 2

B 🗣 ► Can you make up some more examples?
Here are some new words to help you:

1 Angleterre ⟶ anglais

2 Pays de Galles ⟶ gallois

3 Ecosse ⟶ écossais

4 Irlande ⟶ irlandais

4 Quelle est votre profession?

A 🎲 📼 ► Look at the articles in which Mark,
Justine and Thérèse explain what they do for a living.
Don't try to understand every word but look out for the
ones you recognise.

Je m'appelle Mark,
je suis allemand et
je travaille en France.

Mon travail consiste à
accompagner des personnes ou
des groupes dans des voyages,
des visites touristiques de villes,
de lieux et d'établissements
historiques, comme par exemple
des monuments célèbres, des
usines, des cathédrales, etc.
Je travaille pour une grande
compagnie de voyages allemande.

Je m'appelle Justine et je travaille dans un grand magasin en Angleterre.

Nous vendons toutes sortes de choses. Mon travail consiste à enregistrer le paiement des marchandises achetées par les clients.

J'utilise une caisse enregistreuse et un lecteur optique. Je reçois les paiements en espèces, par chèques, cartes de crédit ou débit automatique.

J'emballe les marchandises et je les mets dans un sac. Je commence mon travail à 9h00 et je finis généralement à 17h30.

J'ai 64 ans. Je ne travaille plus mais je suis toujours très occupée…

Malheureusement, je suis veuve, mais j'ai beaucoup d'amis qui me rendent visite, et puis, nous allons souvent au cinéma ou au théâtre.

Je m'occupe souvent de mes trois petits-enfants que j'adore. Je suis aussi étudiante à l'«Université du 3e âge». J'étudie l'anglais et l'allemand, j'adore ça!

Je m'appelle Thérèse Brochet

UNIT **2**

Can you work out who does what? Try to match the pictures and the jobs.

1 Hôte/hôtesse de caisse   **2** Retraité/retraitée   **3** Guide

a

b

c

LANGUAGE FOCUS

Le présent (*the present*)

Look at these regular verbs and the patterns they follow:

travaill**er** – *to work*	fin**ir** – *to finish*	vend**re** – *to sell*	se laver – *to have a wash*
je travaill**e**	je fin**is**	je vend**s**	je **me** lav**e**
tu travaill**es**	tu fin**is**	tu vend**s**	tu **te** lav**es**
il/elle travaill**e**	il/elle fin**it**	il/elle vend	il/elle **se** lav**e**
nous travaill**ons**	nous fin**issons**	nous vend**ons**	nous **nous** lav**ons**
vous travaill**ez**	vous fin**issez**	vous vend**ez**	vous **vous** lav**ez**
ils/elles travaill**ent**	ils/elles fin**issent**	ils/elles vend**ent**	ils/elles **se** lav**ent**

Note that the verb **se laver** (*to have a wash*) is called a **reflexive verb**. These verbs can be recognised by the word **se** at the front. This extra word works like a mirror reflecting the subject of the verb. **Je me lave** literally means *I wash myself*.

Here are some examples:

se marier	**Je me marie.**	*I'm getting married.*
s'appeler	**Il s'appelle Julien.**	*His name is Julien.*
se brosser	**Nous nous brossons les dents.**	*We're brushing our teeth.*

B Vrai ou faux (*True or false*)

		Vrai	Faux
1	Mark est français mais il habite en Allemagne.		
2	Thérèse aime beaucoup aller au cinéma.		
3	Justine travaille dans un supermarché.		
4	Thérèse étudie deux langues étrangères.		
5	Justine s'occupe des clients à la caisse.		
6	Mark voyage beaucoup.		

5 Le présent

A Complete the following sentences by using the right form of the verbs in brackets. Don't forget to identify what group each verb belongs to before you conjugate it.

1 J' _____ le français et l'italien à l'université. (étudier)

2 Nous _____ les marchandises des clients. (emballer)

3 Vous _____ les touristes à l'hôtel? (accompagner)

4 Elle _____ un souvenir de Paris. (choisir)

5 Les enfants _____ vite. (grandir)

6 Ils _____ visite à Chantal régulièrement. (rendre)

7 Je _____ les escaliers. (descendre)

8 Normalement, je _____ à 7h00. (se réveiller)

9 Nous _____ dans le parc chaque dimanche. (se promener)

Look at our website for further practice.

Les autres et moi UNIT 2

B 🎲 ✏️ ▶ Now try to translate the sentences in activity A into English.

Notice that French has one form of present tense whereas English has two:

J'étudie le français means *I study French* or *I am studying French.*

LANGUAGE FOCUS

Not all verbs follow the patterns on page 20. Those that don't are called 'irregular verbs' and must be learned individually. Here are two examples:

aller – *to go*	**faire** – *to do/to make*
je vais	je fais
tu vas	tu fais
il/elle va	il/elle fait
nous allons	nous faisons
vous allez	vous faites
ils/elles vont	ils/elles font

C 🔊 🎧 ▶ Work with a partner. Choose one article from activity 4A on page 18 and explain to your partner what Mark, Justine or Thérèse does for a living, using **il** or **elle** accordingly. When you have finished, swap roles.

✓

Check that you can...

- say how you are
- say what your nationality is
- say what you do for a living
- say where you work
- use some verbs in the present tense.

Search for your ideal job. Our website provides links to French recruitment sites.

6 Compagnie internationale

A  Listen to Daniel Garaud talking about his company.

Here is a list of words. Can you pick out the ones you hear in the interview?

compagnie
usine
Directeur Général
supermarchés
mi-temps
hypermarchés
Europe
employez
ouvriers
décembre
personnes

B Listen to the interview again and answer the following questions:

1 Of what kind of chain is Daniel Garaud the managing director?

2 The company has outlets around the world (**dans le monde**) but in how many countries (**pays**)?

3 What European countries does Daniel mention?

C  Here are some extracts from the interview. Have a look at them. Can you pick the French for the following words or expressions?

office
I know
busy
shops
full time
it's difficult
it depends

Interviewer: Monsieur Garaud, bonjour et merci de me recevoir dans votre bureau; je sais que vous êtes très occupé. Pourriez-vous vous présenter et me parler de votre compagnie?

Daniel Garaud: …Comme je vous l'ai dit, nous avons des supermarchés et des hypermarchés, mais aussi des petits magasins: en tout, il y a a 28 hypermarchés. Nous avons 55 supermarchés en France, 31 en Allemagne… C'est très difficile à dire, car ça dépend de la situation géographique des magasins. Par exemple, au Canada, notre hypermarché à Québec-City emploie 89 personnes plein temps, celui de Boston aux Etats-Unis emploie 72 personnes plein temps…

UNIT **2**

23

7 Des nombres…

A 🎲 ▶ Look at the following numbers. You know all the words but can you work out what number they represent by matching them to the figures?

1	soixante-huit	**5**	quatre-vingt-neuf	**a**	99	**e**	92
2	soixante-dix	**6**	quatre-vingt-dix-neuf	**b**	80	**f**	71
3	soixante-quinze	**7**	soixante-et-onze	**c**	68	**g**	89
4	quatre-vingts	**8**	quatre-vingt-douze	**d**	70	**h**	75

▶ **LANGUAGE FOCUS**

En résumé…

60 • soixante	61 • soixante-**et**-un	62 • soixante-deux…
70 • soixante-**dix**	71 • soixante-**et-onze**	72 • soixante-**douze**…
80 • quatre-vingt**s**	81 • quatre-vingt-un	88 • quatre-vingt-huit…
90 • quatre-vingt-**dix**	91 • quatre-vingt-**onze**	96 • quatre-vingt-**seize**…
100 • cent		

B 🔊 ✏️ 👥 ▶ Work with a partner. Select six numbers between 60 and 99 and write them in a grid like the one below, but don't show them to your partner. Try to guess your partner's numbers by suggesting in turn a number in French. The first person who guesses all six numbers wins. **Bonne chance!**

C 🎧 ▶ Now listen to the interview in activity 6A again, and complete the following table:

Nombre d'employés

Québec-City		Boston	
Valenciennes		Rouen	

8 Encore des questions?

A  Look at the following business cards. Listen and answer the questions using the information on the cards.

1
a
b
c
d
e

Patrick NADLER, D.C.

Chiropracteur - Ostéopathe

Diplômé l'institut Franco-Européen
de Chiropratique, PARIS

CHIROPRATIQUE
M A N U S   V I T A   E S T

Immeuble Tinirouru - 1er Etage
Rue Nansouty (derrière la Brasserie de Tahiti)
Papeete - Tahiti

Tél : 42.23.30

2

buronline.com

LE PORTAIL DE LA BUREAUTIQUE
ET DE L'INFORMATIQUE

Laurent Greber | Webmaster

76, rue de la Tour d'Auvergne - 77185 Lognes - Tél./Fax : **01 70 00 11 77**
E-mail : **laurent.greber@buronline.com** - site : **www. buronline.com**

a
b
c
d
e

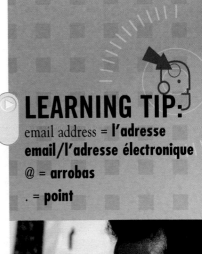

LEARNING TIP:
email address = **l'adresse
email/l'adresse électronique**
@ = **arrobas**
. = **point**

Les autres et moi UNIT 2

B Listen to Sandrine Muller interviewing people in the street in Lille and fill in the gaps in the dialogues using the words below:

> tous les jours – ménage – le soir – étudiant –
> infirmière – qu'est-ce que – mercredi – jeudi –
> à quelle heure – vers – quelquefois

Dialogue 1:

Sandrine: Bonjour monsieur, quelle est votre profession?
Homme: Je suis ⬭.
Sandrine: Et ⬭ vous étudiez?
Homme: J'étudie l'Histoire de France à l'Université de Lille.
Sandrine: Vous allez à l'université ⬭?
Homme: Oh non, seulement lundi, ⬭ et vendredi.

Dialogue 2:

Sandrine: Bonjour madame, qu'est-ce que vous faites dans la vie?
Femme: Je suis ⬭.
Sandrine: Et vous commencez ⬭ en général?
Femme: En général, à 7h00, et je finis ⬭ 15h00.
Sandrine: Qu'est-ce que vous faites ⬭ normalement?
Femme: Et bien, ça dépend. Je m'occupe de mes enfants, mais ⬭, je vais au cinéma avec des amis ou au restaurant. Je ne travaille pas le ⬭ et le samedi, je fais donc le ⬭, les courses…
Sandrine: Et le week-end?
Femme: Le week-end? C'est difficile parce que je travaille le dimanche à 11h00, c'est donc mon mari qui va régulièrement à la piscine ou au parc avec les enfants.

LEARNING TIP:
Qu'est-ce que *and* Quel(s)/Quelle(s)

Both expressions mean *what*.

Quel is used to refer to a noun:
Quel est votre nom? *What is your name?*

Qu'est-ce que is used to refer to an action (verb):
Qu'est-ce que vous faites lundi soir? *What are you doing on Monday night?*

La forme négative (The negative)

To make a sentence negative in French, you need to use two words: **ne** and **pas.**
Look at the following examples:

Je travaille à Nice ⟶ Je **ne** travaille **pas** à Nice

Je vais à la banque ⟶ Je **ne** vais **pas** à la banque

C ✎ ▷ It's your turn. How would you say…?

1 I don't smoke. (fumer)

2 I don't speak Italian. (parler italien)

3 I am not married. (être marié(e))

D ▷ **Et vous?**

Work with a partner and make up a similar dialogue in French using your own details. Here are some suggestions:

> Name
> What you do for a living
> What it consists of
> What time you start/finish
> What you do in the evening/weekend/on Monday night

READY
TO MOVE ON?

✓ Check that you can…

- say more about your job
- count up to 100
- find out somebody's details
- ask for their email address
- ask people what they do after work or at weekends
- use the negative form.

UNIT **2**

27

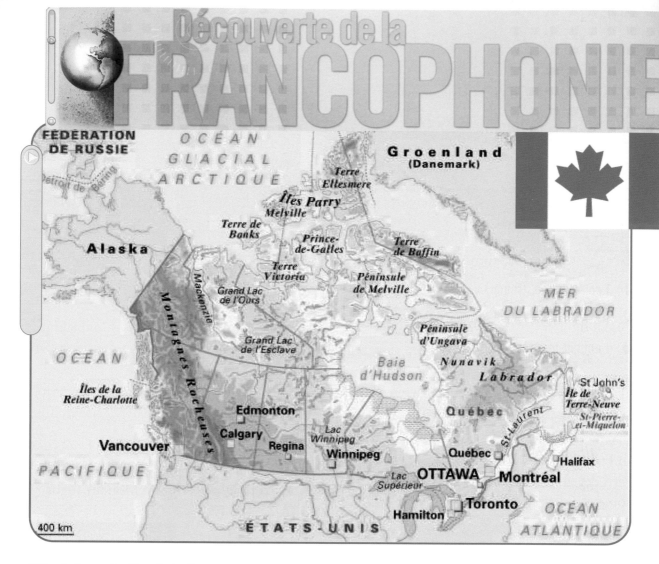

Découverte de la FRANCOPHONIE

FÉDÉRATION DE RUSSIE

OCÉAN GLACIAL ARCTIQUE

Groenland (Danemark)

Détroit de Bering

Terre Ellesmere

Îles Parry
Melville

Terre de Banks

Prince-de-Galles

Terre de Baffin

Alaska

Terre Victoria

Péninsule de Melville

Grand Lac de l'Ours

Mackenzie

MER DU LABRADOR

OCÉAN

Montagnes Rocheuses

Grand Lac de l'Esclave

Péninsule d'Ungava

Baie d'Hudson

Nunavik

Labrador

St John's
Île de Terre-Neuve
St-Pierre-et-Miquelon

Îles de la Reine-Charlotte

Edmonton

Québec

St-Laurent

Calgary

Lac Winnipeg

Vancouver

Regina

Winnipeg

Québec

Halifax

PACIFIQUE

Lac Supérieur

OTTAWA

Montréal

Toronto

OCÉAN ATLANTIQUE

400 km

Hamilton

ÉTATS-UNIS

L'Amérique du Nord, le Canada

A Look at the information about Canada on pages 29–30, then try to work out in English what each of the following details represents.

a • Ottawa

b • 780 000

c • 30 600 000

d • 24.1%

e • 1.4%

f • 3.4%

g • français

h • 1.2%

i • 100 cents

Fiche pays

Généralités

Nom officiel	Canada
Nom courant	CANADA
Code ISO	CAN
Continent	Amérique du Nord
Superficie	9 976 139 km^2
Fête nationale	1er juillet
Fête nationale (événement célébré)	Création de la Confédération du Canada (1867)
Capitale	Ottawa
Population de la capitale (agglomération)	780 000 habitants

Population

Généralités

Population (estimation)	30 600 000 habitants
Nom des habitants	Canadiens

Répartition ethno-linguistique

Amérindiens et Inuits	1,8 %
Origine allemande	3,4 %
Origine britannique	40,0 %
Origine chinoise	2,1 %
Origine française	24,1 %
Origine italienne	2,9 %
Origine néerlandaise	1,4 %
Origine ukrainienne	0,7 %
Autres	23,6 %

Les autres et moi UNIT **2**

Langue

Langue officielle (1)	anglais
Langue officielle (2)	français

Pratiques religieuses

Catholiques	45,7 %
Chrétiens orthodoxes	1,5 %
Juifs	1,2 %
Protestants	36,5 %
Sans religion	12,4 %
Autres	2,7 %

Économie

Généralités

Unité monétaire	dollar canadien
Code monétaire	CAD
Subdivision monétaire 1 dollar canadien =	100 cents

Politique

Statut	Etat fédéral, membre du Commonwealth britannique. Monarchie parlementaire: le chef de l'Etat est la reine d'Angleterre, représentée par un gouverneur général.

B  **Céline, une passion!** Look at Céline Dion's biography and try to complete the summary on page 32 in English.

@ Passion Céline Dion: Biographie

Back Forward Stop Refresh Home AutoFill Print Mail

Address: @ http://www.celine-dion.net/biographie/cd_bio_f.htm

@ Live Home Page @ Apple @ iTools @ Apple Support @ Apple Store @ Microsoft MacTopi

Favorites | History | Search | Scrapbook | Page Holder

Fiche rapide:

Nom: Céline Dion

Date de naissance: 30 mars 1968

Lieu de naissance: Charlemagne, Québec, Canada

Signes astrologiques: Bélier, ascendant Lion (et Singe dans l'horoscope chinois)

Statut civil: Mariée, avec René Angélil

Agent: René Angélil

Couleur des yeux: Noisette

Taille: 1,71 m (5'7.5")

Qualités: Autodétermination, professionnalisme et discipline. Pour ceux qui en doutent, elle a déjà passé trois semaines sans émettre le moindre son, pour reposer ses cordes vocales. Elle ne consomme aucune drogue, elle ne fume pas et ne prend de l'alcool qu'occasionnellement

Défauts: Elle est gourmande et quelquefois impatiente, surtout au lever du lit

Chiffre chanceux: 5 (elle garde précieusement dans un sachet de plastique une pièce de 5 cents de 1968 trouvée par terre)

Parfum: Chanel no. 5

Couleurs préférées: Noir, blanc et rouge

Collections: Elle dépense une fortune pour des souliers, elle en a plus de 600 paires

Sports pratiqués: Golf

Autre choix de carrière: Mannequin de mode

Chanteurs préférés: Stevie Wonder et Michael Jackson

Chanteuses préférées: Natalie Cole, Barbra Streisand et Ginette Reno

Instrument de musique: Piano

Internet zone

Les autres et moi

Summary:

- Céline was born on 30th of ( ) 1968 in ( ).

- Céline is ( ) to René Angélil, who is also her ( ).

- The colour of her ( ) is hazel.

- Her main qualities include ( ), ( ) and ( ).

- Although she occasionally ( ) ( ), she does not take any ( ) and does not ( ).

- Her favourite colours are black, ( ) and ( ).

- Célion Dion spends a fortune on ( ), she actually has more than 600 pairs.

- Stevie Wonder and Barbra Streisand are some of her favourite ( ).

GLOSSARY

Nouns

ami/amie	friend	Ecosse (f)	Scotland
Angleterre (f)	England	espèces (fpl)	cash
boulanger/boulangère	baker	étudiant/étudiante	student
bureau (m)	desk/office	Europe (f)	Europe
caisse (f) (enregistreuse)	till	hôte/hôtesse de caisse	cashier
carte (f) de crédit	credit card	hypermarché (m)	hypermarket
chef (m, f)	manager	infirmier/infirmière	nurse
chèque (m)	cheque	informaticien/informaticienne	IT Consultant
chose (f)	thing	Irlande (f)	Ireland
comptable (m, f)	accountant	jardinier/jardinière	gardener
cuisinier/cuisinière	chef/cook	jeudi (m)	Thursday
dimanche (m)	Sunday	langue (f)	language/tongue
directeur/directrice	manager	lieu (m)	place
		lundi (m)	Monday

GLOSSARY

magasin (m)	shop	**grand(e)**	big/tall
marchandises (fpl)	goods	**hollandais(e)**	Dutch
mardi (m)	Tuesday	**irlandais(e)**	Irish
matin (m)	morning	**moyen(ne)**	medium
mercredi (m)	Wednesday	**occupé(e)**	busy
monde (m)	world	**petit(e)**	small
nombre (m)	number	**polonais(e)**	Polish
paiement (m)	payment	**tout(e)**	all
pays (m)	country	**veuf/veuve**	widowed
Pays de Galles (m)	Wales		
Pays-Bas (mpl)	Netherlands		
petits-enfants (mpl)	grandchildren		

Verbs

piscine (f)	swimming-pool
Pologne (f)	Poland
sac (m)	bag
samedi (m)	Saturday
secrétaire (m, f)	secretary
serveur/serveuse	waiter/waitress
soir (m)	evening
supermarché (m)	supermarket
travail (m)	work
usine (f)	factory
vendredi (m)	Friday
vie (f)	life
ville (f)	town

accompagner	to accompany
acheter	to buy
adorer	to love
aller*	to go
choisir	to choose
commencer	to start
consister à	to consist of
descendre	to go down
employer	to cmploy
enregistrer	to keep records of
étudier	to study
faire*	to do, to make
finir	to finish
fumer	to smoke
grandir	to grow up
mettre*	to put
parler	to speak
recevoir*	to receive
rendre visite à	to visit (someone)
s'occuper de	to look after/ to deal with
travailler	to work
vendre	to sell

Adjectives

allemand(e)	German
américain(e)	American
anglais(e)	English
célèbre	famous
écossais(e)	Scottish
étranger/étrangère	foreign
français(e)	French
gallois(e)	Welsh

*** irregular verbs**

UNIT **2**

33

GLOSSARY

Others

beaucoup	a lot
bien	well
comme	as, like
donc	so, consequently
maintenant	now
mais	but
mal	badly
parce que	because
puis	then
seulement	only
toujours	always
très	very

Expressions

Comment allez-vous?	How are you?
Comment ça va?	How is it going?
Ça va?	All right?
Quoi de neuf?	What's up/What's new?
Ça va!	All right!
Bof!	So, so (informal)
Comme ci, comme ça!	So, so (formal)
par exemple	for example
à mi-temps	part time
à plein temps	full time
Qu'est-ce que…?	What…?
A quelle heure…?	(At) what time…?
Voici…	Here is/are…
Ça dépend!	It depends!

🎧 LOOKING FORWARD

In **Unit 3**, we will be shopping for food and buying drinks in a café.

To prepare, have a look at the following words and pick out the items you need to buy on your next shopping trip:

du fromage • du dentifrice • du thé • du jus d'orange • du pain • du beurre • de l'huile • du jambon • du savon • de la confiture

UNIT 3
Le cybermarché

UNIT 3
Le cybermarché

▶ **By the end of this unit you will be able to:**

- Shop for food
- Explain what you buy and what you need to buy
- Understand and use the articles 'the' and 'a/an'
- Use 'some' and 'any'
- Buy drinks in a café
- Count beyond 100

1 Vous vous souvenez?

A 🎧 👥 ▶ Work with a partner and ask the following questions. Note down the answers in English.

1   Quel est votre prénom?

2   Vous êtes marié(e)?

3   Quelle est votre nationalité?

4   Quelle est votre profession?

5   Où travaillez-vous?

6   Vous commencez le travail à quelle heure?

7   Qu'est-ce que vous faites en général le week-end?

ACCESS FRENCH

B Here are five jobs. Can you match each of them to the brief descriptions below?

1 Etudiant(e)

2 Secrétaire

3 Réceptionniste

4 Avocat(e)

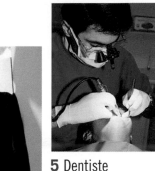

5 Dentiste

a Je travaille avec des touristes et des professionnels. Je m'occupe des clients qui arrivent dans l'établissement et je vérifie les réservations. Je réponds au téléphone et je m'occupe aussi des paiements.
Je suis…

b Je travaille avec des juges, et je défends des personnes qui, quelquefois, sont des criminels.
Je suis…

c J'apprends le français. Je vais à mon cours toutes les semaines. J'adore le français.
Je suis…

d Je travaille pour une grande compagnie internationale. Je travaille directement pour le Directeur. Je l'aide dans ses tâches administratives et je réponds au téléphone.
Je suis…

e Je travaille dans la bouche de mes clients. En général, les gens ne m'aiment pas beaucoup!
Je suis…

C From the answers in activity **1A**, write a short summary in French about your partner using **il** or **elle**.

PETITS SABLÉS
NORMANDS
AU BEURRE

Poids net: 160g ℮

2 Avant tout!

A 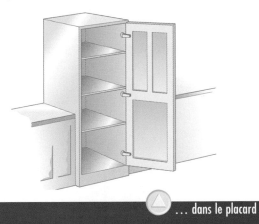 Here is a list of goods that you would find either in your fridge or in your cupboard. Working with a partner, can you sort out what goes in the fridge (**le réfrigérateur**) and what goes in the cupboard (**le placard**)?

la bière	le café
le thé	le sucre
le lait	la crème fraîche
les fruits	les pâtes
la limonade	le pâté
le vin blanc	

... dans le placard

... dans le réfrigérateur

Un croissant, deux croissants ...

For the plural form of nouns, the French generally add an **-s** at the end of the noun, but unlike English the **-s** is never pronounced.

There are exceptions. For example, most words ending with **-eau**, **-au** and **-eu** in the singular form take an **-x** in the plural. But believe it or not, there are exceptions to this too!

Le cybermarché UNIT 3

LANGUAGE FOCUS

Les articles (the)

Look at the following words:

le poulet (*masculine*) **la** moutarde (*feminine*) **les** petits pois (*plural*)

le, la, les mean *the*. In French, *the* varies according to the gender and the number of the word referred to.

Note that **le** and **la** change to **l'** when the following noun begins with a vowel or a silent **h**: **l'eau** (*the water*), **l'huile** (*the oil*).

Les articles (a/an)

In French, there are two ways of saying *a/an*:

un croissant (*masculine*) – *a croissant*

une bouteille (*feminine*) – *a bottle*

For the plural form, use **des**:

des frites – *chips*

Note that **des** is often not translated in English.

LEARNING TIP:
S'il te plaît!

Only use **s'il te plaît** when you know the person you are talking to very well. If you don't know him or her well, use **s'il vous plaît**.

You will find more practice on using French genders and articles at www.accesslanguages.com

B Imagine that you're having a meal with your French friends. You keep asking them to pass you something. Complete the following requests using **le, la, les** or **l'** (to help you, the gender of the word is given in brackets).

1 Franz, passe-moi () salade (f), s'il te plaît!

2 Nordine, passe-moi () eau (f), s'il te plaît!

3 Daniel, passe-moi () huile (f) et () vinaigre (m), s'il te plaît!

4 Annie, passe-moi () sauce (f), s'il te plaît!

5 Rudy, passe-moi () sucre, s'il te plaît!

6 Nelly, passe-moi () légumes, s'il te plaît!

7 Ernest, passe-moi () limonade, s'il te plaît!

3 En route pour le shopping!

A [A C] ▷ Vrai ou faux (*True or false*). Have a look at the Pribas hypermarket sign and decide whether the statements below are true or false:

	Vrai	Faux
1 You can buy petrol at 3.00 am.	⬭	⬭
2 There is a crèche.	⬭	⬭
3 The hypermarket is open on Sundays.	⬭	⬭
4 There is a bottle bank.	⬭	⬭
5 There is a newsagent.	⬭	⬭

BIENVENUE...

VOTRE HYPERMARCHÉ PRIBAS VOUS ACCUEILLE:
DU LUNDI AU SAMEDI DE 8H30 À 22H00

■ Distributeur Automatique de Billets
■ Boîte aux lettres
■ Pharmacie
■ Presse

■ Garderie
■ Station-Service Essence 24h/24
■ Récupérateur Textile
■ Récupérateur Piles

B [A C] ▷ Look at the picture below showing departments (**les rayons**) in Auchan hypermarket, then have a look at the shopping list. Can you tell which department you would get these items from?

Auchandirect

Vos courses | Inscription | Services
Accueil | Magasin | Les Promos | Nouveautés

Parcourir nos rayons

Pain... | Petit déjeuner | Fruits, Légumes | Bio-Diététique... | Produits laitiers
Boucherie... | Charcuterie... | Conserves | Epicerie salée | Condiments...
Surgelés | Saveurs d'ailleurs | Epicerie sucrée | Boissons... | Vins, Alcools
Apéritifs | Produits bébés | Soin, Hygiène... | Maison... | Animaux

1	fresh chicken	→	Rayon...
2	rice	→	Rayon...
3	tin of tomatoes	→	Rayon...
4	fresh courgettes	→	Rayon...
5	cream	→	Rayon...
6	bread	→	Rayon...
7	cheese	→	Rayon...
8	wine	→	Rayon...
9	toothpaste	→	Rayon...
10	washing-up liquid	→	Rayon...
11	fruit juice	→	Rayon...

Le cybermarché

C A C ▷ Here are five departments in a store. For each, pick out the item that you would not find in that department.

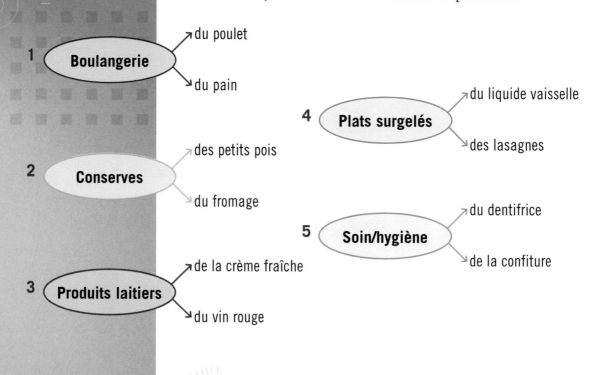

1 **Boulangerie** → du poulet
→ du pain

2 **Conserves** → des petits pois
→ du fromage

3 **Produits laitiers** → de la crème fraîche
→ du vin rouge

4 **Plats surgelés** → du liquide vaisselle
→ des lasagnes

5 **Soin/hygiène** → du dentifrice
→ de la confiture

Go to www.accesslanguages.com to learn more about French shopping on the Internet.

D 🎧 ▷ Listen to three people who are just about to go shopping and have a look at their shopping lists. Try to spot the errors and correct them.

3
tea
frozen chips
toilet paper
butter
roast chicken
apple tart

1
sausages
oil
ham
carrots
beer

2
1 bottle of wine
bread
2 kg of oranges
1 lemon
shampoo

Du pain, du vin…

Have a look at activity 3C again. Did you notice that the articles used with the nouns were not **le**, **la** or **les**?
Du, **de la**, **des** are used to translate the English *some* and *any*.

Note that sometimes these words are not translated in English:
Vous mangez **du** fromage? *Do you eat cheese?*
Vous voulez **de la** crème? *Do you want (some) cream?*

Here are some examples:
de la moutarde (*feminine*)   **du** vin (*masculine*)   **des** frites (*plural*)

du and **de la** become **de l'** in front of a vowel or a silent **h**:
de l'eau (*feminine*)   **de l'**argent (*masculine*)

When using the negative form, **du**, **de la**, **des** and **de l'** are replaced by **de** or **d'**:
Je n'ai pas **de** vin, **de** pain, **de** soupe, **de** frites. *I don't have **any** wine, **any** bread, **any** soup, **any** chips.*

E ✏ ▷ Try to fill in the gaps using either **le**, **la**, **les** or **l'** (*the*) in the left-hand column or **du**, **de la**, **des** or **de l'** (*some*) in the right-hand column:

1 **le** jambon   ◯ jambon

2 ◯ salade   **de la** salade

3 **les** chips   ◯ chips

4 ◯ shampooing   **du** shampooing

5 **la** viande   ◯ viande

6 ◯ huile   **de l'**huile

Le cybermarché UNIT 3

41

F Now look at this trolley (**le chariot** or **le caddie**). Work with a partner; in turn, say aloud what's in it using the expression **Il y a + du**, **de la**, **des** or **de l'…** (*There is/There are some…*).

If your sentence is correct – right article, right gender – your partner will give you one point; if you make a mistake, you don't get a point. Follow the example **et bonne chance!**

(**A**) Dans le chariot, il y a du poulet.

(**B**) Bien! Un point.

LANGUAGE FOCUS

J'ai besoin de… / Il me faut… (*I need…*)

J'ai besoin de lait, de vin et de confiture.	*I need some milk, some wine and some jam.*
Il me faut **du** lait, **du** vin et **de la** confiture.	*I need some milk, some wine and some jam.*
J'ai besoin de vitamines.	*I need some vitamins.*
Il me faut **des** vitamines.	*I need some vitamins.*
J'ai besoin d'un coup de main.	*I need a hand/help.*

READY TO MOVE ON?

✓ Check that you…

- can say what's in your fridge
- can say what you need to buy
- know the difference between le, la and les
- know the difference between un, une and des
- know the difference between du, de la, des and de.

4 On prend un verre?

A [AC] ⊙ You are in a café in France. Look at the menu. Can you work out the meaning of most of the drinks?

Café de la place

Apéritifs

Cocktail maison	6€
Kir *(vin blanc et crème de cassis)*	4€
Coupe de Champagne	7€
Kir Royal *(Champagne et crème de cassis)*	8€
Américano	6€
Ricard, Pastis	4€
Martini blanc ou rouge	4€
Suze, Campari, Picon	5€
Porto blanc ou rouge	5€
Whisky	6€
Gin Tonic	7€

Sodas

Coca-Cola, Orangina, Schweppes	3€50
San Pellegrino	3€50
Diabolo *(1/4 limonade et sirop)*	3€50
Sirop *(1/4 eau minérale et sirop)*	3€50
Jus de fruits *(ananas, pamplemousse, orange, pomme, tomate)*	3€50
Eau Evian, Vittel	2€50
Badoit, Perrier	2€50

Bières

Kronenbourg 1664	4€
Heineken	4€
Bière «Choulette» brune	4€

Vin «Cuvée du Patron»

rouge, blanc, rosé	
le verre	3€
la ½ bouteille	7€
la bouteille	12€
Café, café-crème	2€50
Thé, infusion	3€50
Chocolat	3€50
Digestifs, eaux de vie	6€

Taxes et service compris.

B ⊙ Listen to a group of people about to place their orders in the café. Look at the menu above and note the drinks you hear.

LEARNING TIP:

Commander...
To order...

To reply to the question:
Qu'est-ce que vous désirez?
or **Vous désirez?** (*What would you like?*), start your answer with:

Je voudrais... I *would like...*

Je prends... I'll *have* or I'm *having...*

Pour moi... For *me...*

Payer... *To pay...*

To ask for the bill in a café or in a restaurant, just say:

L'addition, s'il vous plaît!

If you are in a shop and want to pay, say:

C'est combien? or **Ça fait combien?**

C Listen to the conversation in activity B again and try to fill in the gaps in the following conversation, choosing the words from the list below:

> voudrais – prends – désirez – addition –
> jus – soif – combien – avec – verre –

Daniel: Monsieur, s'il vous plaît!
Serveur: Messieurs-dame, bonsoir. Vous ⟨＿＿＿＿＿＿⟩?
Annie: Pour moi, un grand Diabolo menthe ; je meurs de ⟨＿＿＿＿＿＿⟩!
Serveur: ⟨＿＿＿＿＿＿⟩ des glaçons?
Annie: Oui, s'il vous plaît! Et vous Nordine, qu'est-ce que vous prenez?
Nordine: Moi, je ⟨＿＿＿＿＿＿⟩ un crème.
Franz: Et pour moi, un ⟨＿＿＿＿＿＿⟩ de tomate, s'il vous plaît!
Serveur: Et pour monsieur?
Daniel: Je ⟨＿＿＿＿＿＿⟩ une bière, s'il vous plaît; oh non, je préfère un ⟨＿＿＿＿＿＿⟩ de vin rouge.
Serveur: Merci messieurs-dame...

Later...

Daniel: Monsieur, s'il vous plaît, l'⟨＿＿＿＿＿＿⟩!
Serveur: Alors, ça fait 12,50€, monsieur.
Daniel: Pardon, c'est ⟨＿＿＿＿＿＿⟩?
Serveur: 10€.
Daniel: Voilà.
Serveur: Je vous remercie. Au revoir messieurs-dame.

D Work in small groups. Imagine that you are in a café in France. One of you plays the waiter/waitress, the others are the customers. Look at the menu in activity 4A and prepare a conversation similar to the one in activity 4B. The expressions in the Learning Tip will help you.

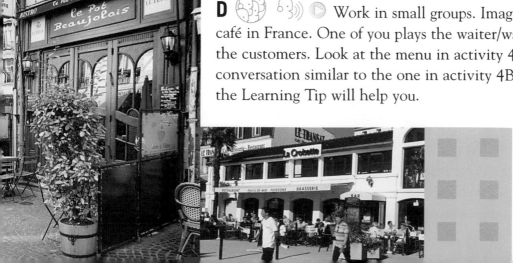

5 Les quantités

A  Here is a list of quantities. Can you match each quantity with a food item?

1 250 g (grammes)   **2** 1 kg (kilo)   **3** 750 g   **4** 1 l (litre)   **5** 1 paquet

6 1 tranche   **7** 1 morceau   **8** 1 pot   **9** 1 plaque   **10** un peu

a chocolat   **b** sauce   **c** jambon   **d** confiture

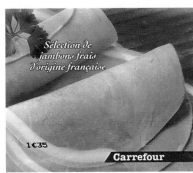

e beurre   **f** pommes de terre   **g** oranges

h huile d'olive   **i** biscuits   **j** gâteau

Le cybermarché UNIT 3

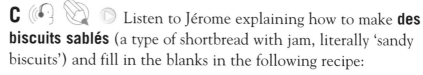

B ✎ ▷ Following the examples in activity 5A, rewrite the 10 correct phrases using **de** or **d'** (*of*) accordingly.

Example: une tranche **de** jambon *a slice **of** ham*

C 🎧 ✎ ▷ Listen to Jérome explaining how to make **des biscuits sablés** (a type of shortbread with jam, literally 'sandy biscuits') and fill in the blanks in the following recipe:

Pour 12 biscuits sablés, il faut:

- (⬭⬭⬭⬭⬭⬭) de farine
- (⬭⬭⬭⬭⬭⬭) de sucre
- 120 g de (⬭⬭⬭⬭⬭⬭)
- 4 jaunes d' (⬭⬭⬭⬭⬭⬭)
- (⬭⬭⬭⬭⬭⬭) de sucre glace
- (⬭⬭⬭⬭⬭⬭) de confiture de framboises
- une pincée de (⬭⬭⬭⬭⬭⬭)

Sélection de jambons frais d'origine française

1€35

Carrefour

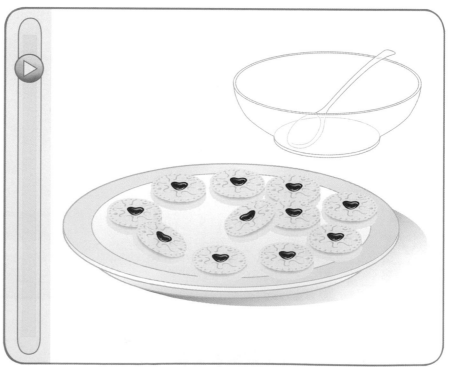

Encore des nombres!

100 • cent	101 • cent un	110 • cent dix	199 • cent quatre-vingt-dix-neuf

200 • deux cents   232 • deux cent trente-deux

300 • trois cents   362 • trois cent soixante-deux

500 • cinq cents   900 • neuf cents

1000 • mille   1001 • mille un   2010 • deux mille dix

1000000 • un million

En résumé

	the	*some/any*	*any (negative)*	*of*
Masc.	le, l'	du, de l'	de, d'	de, d'
Fem.	la, l'	de la, de l'	de, d'	de, d'
Plur.	les	des	de, d'	de, d'

READY TO MOVE ON?

✔ Check that you can...

- ⬭ order drinks in a café
- ⬭ count up to 100 and beyond
- ⬭ give and understand quantities.

Le cybermarché UNIT 3

Découverte de la FRANCOPHONIE

HaïtiTourisme

La Secrétairerie d'Etat au Tourisme

"Haïti est internationalement reconnue pour sa culture, sa peinture, sa musique et l'accueil réservé à ses visiteurs.

L'apport culturel des entités indiennes, africaines et françaises, lui confère une forte personnalité et une position privilégiée parmi les pays de la Caraïbe."

Langues: français et créole

Religions: catholique, protestante et vaudou

Statut politique: république

Capitale: Port-au-Prince

Superficie: 27 750 km² (kilomètres carrés)

Economie: construction, agriculture, pêche, art, services, mines d'or et de marbre

Climat: tropical

Monnaie officielle: la gourde

Production agricole: café, maïs, riz, haricots, bananes, cacao, canne à sucre, mangues, ananas, papayes, mandarines, fleurs, épices, etc.

L'Amérique Centrale, Haïti

A Look at the facts on Haïti. Study them carefully for three minutes and memorise as many details as you can, then cover with a piece of paper and try to answer the questions on page 49 in English.

Go to our website for more links to
sites about French-speaking America.

Unit 3

1 What are the three religions in Haiti?

2 Apart from French, what is the other official language in Haiti?

3 What is the climate in Haiti?

4 What is the capital city of Haiti?

5 What is Haiti internationally renowned for?

6 Can you name at least five types of fruit and vegetables that

Haiti produces?

7 Apart from gold mines, what other mine can you find in Haiti?

B [A C] ✏️ ▶ You have decided to cook a créole meal. Here are three créole recipes
(starter, main course and dessert). They are all in French, but try to prepare your shopping
list in English using a dictionary where necessary. Make sure you don't forget any important
ingredients. **Bon appétit!**

LA BONNE CUISINE CRÉOLE

AVOCATS AU CRABE
Catégorie: Entrée

Ingrédients: pour quatre personnes

- 2 avocats
- 1 boîte de crabe émietté
- quelques brins de ciboulette
- 1 petite échalote
- 1 petit piment
- le jus d'un citron vert
- 3 cuillerées à
  soupe d'huile
- sel, poivre

THON AU VIN BLANC
Catégorie: Poisson

Ingrédients:
pour 4 personnes

- 1/2 litre de
  vin blanc
- 2kg de thon
- 2 tomates
- 1 oignon
- 2 citrons
- thym, persil,
  ciboulette,
  poivre, sel
- piment en
  morceaux
  (selon
  convenance)

CHOCOLAT MARTINIQUAIS
Catégorie: Dessert

Ingrédients:
pour six personnes

- 1 litre de lait
- 3 cuillerées à soupe de
  cacao en poudre
- 1 œuf
- 150g de sucre
- 1 bâton de cannelle
- noix de muscade râpée
- 1 cuillerée à soupe
  de maïzena
- 1 gousse de vanille
- 150g de cacahuètes grillées
  ou d'amandes effilées grillées

41•••••

•••••40

Le cybermarché UNIT 3

GLOSSARY

Nouns

ananas (m)	pineapple
avocat (m)	avocado
avocat (m)	solicitor, lawyer
boîte aux lettres (f)	post box
bouteille (f)	bottle
cacahuète (f)	peanut
cacao (m)	cocoa
café (m)	coffee
cannelle (f)	cinnamon
cassis (m)	blackcurrant
chips (mpl)	crisps
ciboulette (f)	chives
citron (m)	lemon
citron vert (m)	lime
confiture (f)	jam
conserves (fpl)	canned food
cours (m)	course
crème (f)	cream
crème (m)	milky coffee
cuillère (f)	spoon
dentifrice (m)	toothpaste
distributeur (m) **automatique**	vending machine
épice (f)	spice
framboise (f)	raspberry
frigo (m)	fridge
frites (fpl)	chips
fromage (m)	cheese
garderie (f)	creche
glaçon (m)	ice cube
haricot (m)	bean
huile (f)	oil
infusion (f)	herbal tea
jambon (m)	ham
jus (m) **de fruit**	fruit juice
lait (m)	milk
liquide (m) **vaisselle**	washing-up liquid
maïs (m)	corn
marbre (m)	marble
morceau (m)	piece
moutarde (f)	mustard
muscade (f)	nutmeg
or (m)	gold
pain (m)	bread
pamplemousse (m)	grapefruit
pâtes (fpl)	pasta
persil (m)	parsley
pile (f)	battery
placard (m)	cupboard
plat (m) **surgelé**	frozen meal
poisson (m)	fish
poivre (m)	pepper
pomme (f)	apple
pomme (f) **de terre**	potato
poulet (m)	chicken
réfrigérateur (m)	fridge

GLOSSARY

riz (m)	rice		
sel (m)	salt		
semaine (f)	week		
shampooing (m)	shampoo		
sirop (m)	syrup		
station-service (f)	petrol station		
sucre (m)	sugar		
tâche (f)	task		
thé (m)	tea		
thon (m)	tuna		
tomate (f)	tomato		
tranche (f)	slice		
verre (m)	glass		
viande (f)	meat		
vin (m)	wine		

Expressions

Bonne chance!	Good luck!
Ça fait combien?	How much does it come to?
C'est combien?	How much is it?
Il me faut…	I need…
J'ai besoin de…	I need…
Je prends…	I'll have, I'm having…
Je voudrais…	I would like…
l'addition!	the bill!
Passe-moi…	Pass me… (informal)
Passez-moi…	Pass me… (formal)
s'il te plaît	please (informal)
s'il vous plaît	please (formal)

Verbs

coûter	to cost
défendre	to defend
répondre	to reply
vérifier	to check

LOOKING FORWARD

In **Unit 4** we will be talking about leisure time and the activities you do during your spare time.

To prepare, look at the following activities and pick out those you are most likely to do as a leisure activity (use a dictionary if you are not sure):

jouer du piano • **faire de la natation** • **faire la vaisselle** • **repasser** • **jouer au badminton** • **faire collection de timbres**

UNIT
4
La vie de famille

Le cybermarché

UNIT 4
La vie de famille

By the end of this unit you will be able to:

- Understand holiday brochures
- Talk about your leisure activities
- Explain what sport or activity you do during your spare time
- Talk about your family
- Understand and use possessive adjectives

1 Vous vous souvenez?

A Look at the pictures on page 53. Can you write down what they are in French? Don't forget to use **du, de la, de l', des** or **de, d'**. Here is an example:

du vin or **une bouteille de vin**

B Brainstorm. Work with a partner. You have one minute to take it in turns to say the names of drinks in French. Don't allow your partner to think for more than a couple of seconds after you've said your drink. **Vous êtes prêts? Alors c'est parti!**

2 On y va...

A Have a look at the advertisement on the following page for VVF Auvergne (Village Vacances Famille) and pick out the leisure activities available within the Chambourguet complex.

La vie de famille UNIT 4

AUVERGNE / Super-Besse «Chambourguet»

Votre village-club en demi-pension ou en pension complète

Ce site est ouvert
du 08/06 au 14/09.

- 92 logements répartis en petits bâtiments avec vue sur la montagne, à 1350 m d'altitude, au cœur du Parc naturel régional des Volcans d'Auvergne.

- Petit déjeuner en buffet. Déjeuner et dîner en buffet avec soirées à thèmes en vacances scolaires et buffet ou service à table (autres périodes).

- Restaurant enfants de 3 mois à 5 ans en vacances scolaires.

- Réception, espace montagne et tourisme, bar, restaurant, salons de jeux et de télévision, bibliothèque, salle de spectacles.

- Mini-golf, mur d'escalade, terrain de volley, de pétanque, aire de jeux pour enfants.

- Accès gratuit à la piscine (avec toboggan) et à la patinoire (hors location de patins) de la station à 800 m.

Côté loisirs

Au village-club:
Rencontres info-tourisme, gymnastique, tournois, découverte de la volcanologie et de l'environnement, et en juillet août, découverte de l'escalade et du tir à l'arc. Jeux, spectacles, cinéma, soirées musicales et dansantes.

Balades familiales à la découverte des lacs, de la flore, visite de fermes dont une en journée (avec pique-nique*); possibilité d'approche en voiture. Randonnées* sportives avec accompagnateur de moyenne montagne.

Semaines à thème: «L'Auvergne insolite et gourmande» du 29/06 au 06/07 et «Histoire et traditions en Auvergne» du 6 au 13/07.

A proximité:

Nombreux sentiers de randonnée entre lacs et volcans (le lac Pavin, la vallée de Chaudefour et sa réserve naturelle). Location et sorties VTT.* Tennis,* bob-luge* et planche à voile* à la station, à 800m. Promenades à cheval* à 3km, canoë* à 20km, parapente* à 50km. Nombreux cours d'eau et lacs pour la pêche.*

* Payant.

B 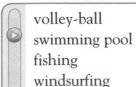 Which of these activities or facilities are free of charge?

volley-ball	ice skating
swimming pool	paragliding
fishing	canoeing
windsurfing	

3 Mon temps libre

A  Juliette is asking people what they do during their spare time. Listen to them and try to complete the sentences by choosing the right ending from the right-hand column.

However you like to spend your leisure time, you're sure to find an Internet group dedicated to it. www.accesslanguages.com has links to French lifestyle websites.

1 Quand je ne travaille pas,…

2 Et le week-end, et bien…

3 Nous allons quelquefois…

4 Je suis plutôt sportif: …

5 Le curling?…

6 J'ai deux enfants…

7 Nous regardons la télévision…

8 Je suis aussi musicien…

a …et je joue de la guitare et de la batterie.

b …et bien, je m'occupe de la maison.

c …C'est comme la pétanque, mais sur glace.

d …mais j'aide aussi ma femme dans les tâches ménagères.

e …je fais du football, de la musculation.

f …et j'aime rester avec eux.

g …au cinéma et ensuite, nous allons au MacDo.

h …nous allons à la piscine le samedi matin.

LANGUAGE FOCUS

Nous allons au MacDo

When going somewhere, the French use the verb **aller à** (*to go to*).
The preposition **à** changes according to the gender of the place:
Je vais **au** cinéma. (*masculine*)
Je vais **à la** piscine. (*feminine*)
Je vais **aux** Galeries Lafayettes. (*plural*)

Note that if a word starts with a vowel, **au** and **à la** become **à l'**.

But remember that when visiting people or going to someone's place, the French use the verb **aller** followed by **chez:**

Nous allons **chez** Martine.	*We are going to Martine's*
Vous allez **chez** le boucher?	*Are you going to the butcher's?*
Je vais **chez** elle.	*I'm going to hers.*

La vie de famille UNIT 4

55

B Listen to the three people again and read the following extracts. Can you spot eleven factual mistakes?

Interview 1

Femme: Ouh, quand j'ai du temps libre, quand je ne travaille pas, et bien je m'occupe du jardin car j'ai quatre enfants et croyez-moi, il y a du travail… Alors, je fais le ménage, et j'adore faire le ménage…

Interview 2

Homme: Et bien, je suis plutôt sportif: je fais du football, de la danse et depuis quelques années, je fais du curling.
Juliette: Du curling? Qu'est-ce que c'est?
Homme: Le curling? C'est comme la pétanque, mais sur glace. Je vais à la piscine une fois par semaine, le samedi matin et je n'aime pas beaucoup ce sport.

Interview 3

Homme: Je suis aussi chanteur et je joue du piano et de la batterie. Ma femme déteste quand je m'exerce à la batterie, je ne sais pas pourquoi…

C Try to make French sentences using the verbs **faire** or **jouer** as in the example:

Je / faire / le basket   *Je fais du basket.*

Je / jouer / le ping-pong

Nous / faire / les mots croisés (*crosswords*)

Je / faire / la plongée sous-marine (*scuba diving*)

Elle / jouer / le hockey

Il / jouer / le violon

Vous / faire / le sport?

Tu / jouer / les jeux électroniques (*electronic games*)?

Il / faire / la peinture (*painting*)?

Je fais du foot, je joue aux cartes et je joue de la guitare

When talking about leisure activities, the French often use the verb **faire** (*to do*). **Faire** is usually followed by **de**, but note how **de** changes according to the gender of the activity.

Masculine: **du**
Je fais **du** football
Je fais **du** saut à l'élastique (*bungee jumping*)
Je fais **du** vélo (*cycling*)
Je fais **du** tricot (*knitting*)

Feminine: **de la**
Je fais **de la** natation (*swimming*)
Je fais **de la** peinture (*painting*)
Je fais **de la** voile (*sailing*)
Je fais **de la** marche (*walking*)

Note that if an activity starts with a vowel,
du and **de la** become **de l'**:
Je fais **de l'**équitation (*horse riding*)
Je fais **de l'**aviron (*rowing*)
Je fais **de l'**escalade (*rock climbing*)

When talking about playing games, the French also use the verb **jouer** (*to play*). **Jouer** is always followed by **à**, which changes in the same way as **aller à**:
Masculine: Je joue **au** badminton, je joue **au** tennis
Feminine: Je joue **à la** marelle (*hopscotch*), je joue **à la** belote
Plural: Je joue **aux** cartes, je joue **aux** fléchettes (*darts*)

For musical instruments, use **jouer** followed by **de**:
Je joue **du** piano, je joue **de la** guitare, je joue **des** castagnettes

LEARNING TIP:
**le rugby et
le basket**

English words used in French are generally masculine:

**le football, le bobsleigh,
le kayak, le rafting,
le snowboard,
le patchwork,** etc.

Check that you can...
- ☑ **say what you do during your spare time.**
- **use the verbs faire de, jouer à... and jouer de**
- **ask others what they do during their spare time.**

Practise your French verbs on
www.accesslanguages.com

4 A la maison

A Look at the pictures. Work in pairs and try to match each picture with the activity it represents.

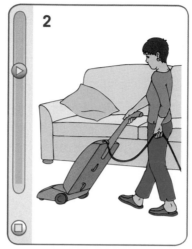

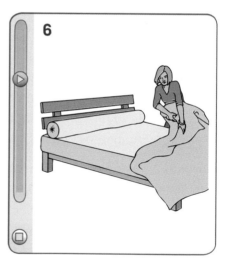

a faire la cuisine   **b** faire le lit   **c** faire le repassage

d faire les courses   **e** passer l'aspirateur   **f** faire la vaisselle

B (🎧 ▶) Now Juliette is interviewing a married man. She asks him who does all the housework. Listen to what he says and try to fill in the gaps by choosing the missing words from the box:

> quelquefois – voiture – poussières
> – maison – journée – aide –
> rien – lessive – fois – chance

Juliette: Excusez-moi, monsieur, vous êtes marié?

Homme: Oui, ma femme est là-bas, elle gare la (⟶).

Juliette: Alors pouvez-vous me dire qui fait le ménage à la maison?

Homme: C'est moi! Je fais la cuisine et je fais la vaisselle tous les soirs. Et puis dans la (⟶), je fais le lit, je fais la (⟶), je passe l'aspirateur une fois par semaine et je fais le repassage aussi.

Juliette: Mais votre femme a beaucoup de (⟶). Tiens, la voilà! Bonjour madame, mais quelle chance d'avoir un mari qui vous (⟶) dans les tâches ménagères!

Femme: Comment? Un mari qui m'aide? J'aimerais bien! Il ne fait (⟶) à la maison! Moi, je travaille, et quand je rentre, je fais la cuisine, la lessive, le repassage, je fais les (⟶) et je fais aussi les courses. Un mari qui m'aide?

Homme: Mais ma puce, ne t'énerve pas, je fais la vaisselle (⟶).

Femme: Quelquefois? Une (⟶) par an, pour mon anniversaire! Allez, on rentre à la (⟶) et je ne suis pas ta puce!

La vie de famille UNIT 4

C 🎲 ▷ Here is a list of words used to express frequency (how often something happens). Have a look at them and try to sort them in order from the most frequent to the least frequent:

rarement   quelquefois   toujours
jamais   souvent   occasionnellement

D ✏️ ▷ How would you say the following? Remember that in French, the frequency words come just after the verb. *Example:*

Je joue **souvent** au tennis.   *I often play tennis.*

1 I rarely do the washing-up.

2 I always make the bed.

3 Do you sometimes go clubbing? (aller en boîte)

4 I always watch soaps. (regarder les feuilletons)

5 I occasionally go to the gym. (aller à la gym)

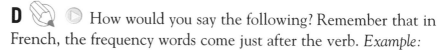

LANGUAGE FOCUS

Au fil des jours et des mois... *(As days and months go by...)*

Monday 15th February	lundi 15 février
Tuesday 20th March	mardi 20 mars
Wednesday 5th July	mercredi 5 juillet
Thursday 19th September	jeudi 19 septembre
Friday 2nd June	vendredi 2 juin
Saturday 3rd October	samedi 3 octobre
Sunday 1st August	dimanche 1er (premier) août

Days and months in French do not have capital letters.
For **on** Monday, **on** Wednesday, just say **lundi, mercredi**
For **on** Monday 5th June, say **le lundi 5 juin**
For Mondays, say **le lundi** or **les lundis**
For **on the** 5th of October, say **le 5 octobre**

E A C ▷ Look at the French Bank Holidays below. Can you match the dates on the left with what they represent on the right? Use a dictionary if you get stuck on the last few.

Les jours fériés en France

1	1er janvier	**a**	Jour de l'an
2	avril	**b**	Noël
3	1er mai	**c**	Assomption
4	8 mai	**d**	Ascension
5	mai	**e**	Fête du travail
6	juin	**f**	Fête nationale
7	14 juillet	**g**	Toussaint
8	15 août	**h**	Fête de la Victoire 1945
9	1er novembre	**i**	lundi de Pentecôte
10	11 novembre	**j**	Armistice 1918
11	25 décembre	**k**	lundi de Pâques

LEARNING TIP:

Je fais le pont...

When a Bank Holiday falls on a Thursday or a Tuesday, French people usually **font le pont** (*make the bridge*). This means that they take Friday or Monday off as well.

F A C 🔊 🎧 ▷ Work in pairs and ask each other the exact date of the following events in the UK. Use the model:

– La Saint Patrick, c'est quel jour exactement?

– C'est le 17 mars.

le lendemain de Noël (26th December)

la Saint Georges (23rd April)

la Saint André (30th November)

la Saint David (1st March)

la Fête des Mères (10th March)

la Fête des Pères (16th June)

la Saint Valentin (14th February)

votre anniversaire?

La vie de famille UNIT 4

It's fun to look at websites of French family trees and histories. Check out the links on www.accesslanguages.com

5 Ma famille

A Four people (Nelly, Pascale, Thierry and Aïsha) are describing their family photos. Look at the list of family members below then listen and note each word you hear.

grand-père	⬭	fils	⬭	nièce	⬭
grand-mère	⬭	fille	⬭	cousin	⬭
grands-parents	⬭	enfants	⬭	cousine	⬭
père	⬭	oncle	⬭	frère	⬭
mère	⬭	tante	⬭	sœur	⬭
parents	⬭	neveu	⬭		

B Listen to the four people again then try to work out which photo each of them is describing. Match their names with the correct picture.

1 Nelly   **2** Pascale   **3** Thierry   **4** Aïsha

a

c

b

d

Mon frère, ma sœur…

In French, the words for *my*, *your*, *his*, *her*, *its*, *our* and *their* agree with the noun that follows and change according to the gender and the number of this word.

the father – **le** père
    (*masculine*)
my father – **mon** père

the mother – **la** mère
    (*feminine*)
my mother – **ma** mère

the parents – **les** parents
    (*plural*)
my parents – **mes** parents

	père (*masc.*)	mère (*fem.*)	enfants (*plur.*)
my	mon	ma	mes
your	ton	ta	tes
his/her/its	son	sa	ses
our	notre	notre	nos
your	notre	votre	vos
their	leur	leur	leurs

Note that **son jardin** can therefore mean *his*, *her* or *its garden*.

C Look at the following sentences. Try to fill in the gaps using the right form of the possessive adjective in brackets.

1 Le père de (⎯⎯⎯⎯) mère est (⎯⎯⎯⎯) grand-père. (my)

2 La sœur de (⎯⎯⎯⎯) mère est (⎯⎯⎯⎯) tante. (your)

3 Les enfants de (⎯⎯⎯⎯) oncle sont (⎯⎯⎯⎯) cousins. (our)

4 La fille de (⎯⎯⎯⎯) mère est (⎯⎯⎯⎯) sœur. (your)

5 (⎯⎯⎯⎯) maison (*fem.*) et (⎯⎯⎯⎯) jardin (*masc.*) sont magnifiques. (her)

6 (⎯⎯⎯⎯) chien (*masc.*) est tellement mignon. (his)

7 (⎯⎯⎯⎯) petit-ami est anglais, il habite à Londres. (her)

8 Julien est de Paris, mais (⎯⎯⎯⎯) sœur est née à Nice. (his)

You'll find more practice on possessives at www.accesslanguages.com

La vie de famille UNIT 4

LEARNING TIP:
Ma belle-mère…

You might think that the French love their in-laws since to talk about them, they place the word **beau** or **belle** (*beautiful*) in front of father, mother, sister, etc.

Here are a few examples:

ma belle-mère   *my mother-in-law* (also *stepmother*)

mon beau-père   *my father-in-law* (also *stepfather*)

ma belle-sœur   *my sister-in-law*

mes beaux-parents   *my parents-in-law*

mes belles-sœurs   *my sisters-in-law*

For *step-brother* and *step-sister*, say **demi-frère** and **demi-sœur**.

D 🔊 👥 ▶ Your teacher will give you a card with Julien Legrand's family tree on it. Apart from Julien himself, only two names appear on the tree. Can you find out the names of all the members of his family? Go round the class asking questions using the following model:

(A) **Comment s'appelle la sœur de Julien?**
or
Comment s'appelle sa sœur?

(B) **Elle s'appelle…**
or
Je suis désolé(e), je ne sais pas.

6 Et pour finir…

A 🔤 🔊 ▶ **Vrai ou Faux**. Here is an extract from the agony column of «Belle famille» magazine in which Dr Virginie Moreau, psychologist, gives advice to people with family problems. Have a look at it and decide whether the statements on page 65 are true or false:

VIRGINIE MOREAU

Chère Docteur,

Je suis maman de 4 enfants: trois fils de 13, 11 et 7 ans et une fille de 18 mois. Mon mari est routier et il voyage partout en Europe. Je suis donc souvent seule à la maison pour m'occuper de ma famille. Afin de gagner un peu d'argent, je fais le ménage chez des personnes âgées dans le voisinage, mais je me rends compte que travailler tous les jours pour 6,70€ de l'heure n'en vaut pas la peine. Lorsque je rentre, je dois alors m'occuper de la maison et des enfants. Heureusement, ma mère et ma belle-sœur m'aident un peu, surtout le mercredi et le samedi lorsque les enfants ne sont pas à l'école. Alors, elles les emmènent au parc, ils jouent avec leurs cousins, font du vélo ou regardent la télévision ensemble.

Mais les autres jours, après le travail, je dois faire le dîner, le ménage, la vaisselle, la lessive, le repassage, vérifier les devoirs, les leçons… je suis à bout de souffle. Pouvez-vous me donner quelques conseils?

Martine M. (Neuville sur Escaut – 59)

	Vrai	Faux
1 Martine's daughter is 18 years old.		
2 Martine's husband is a lorry driver.		
3 She works as a nurse for elderly people.		
4 Fortunately, her mother and sister help her.		
5 Her children don't have school on Wednesdays and Saturdays.		
6 Martine checks her children's homework.		

La vie de famille UNIT 4

ACCESS **FRENCH**

Many French magazines have online sites. Start by looking at the ones suggested on our website.

B Read the letter again, then try to write the following sentences in French:

1 I am the father of three children.

2 My wife is a businesswoman.

3 She travels all round France and Great Britain.

4 I realise that working for €6.70 per hour is not worth it.

5 My mother-in-law helps me a lot.

6 I have to prepare dinner and do the washing-up.

READY TO MOVE ON?

✓

Check that you can...

- talk about housework activities
- say how often you do these activities
- remember days, months and dates
- talk about your family
- use possessive adjectives (mon, ma, mes).

Découverte de la FRANCOPHONIE

Voyage à la carte

zoom map

Où
Quoi
Comment
Mot clé

Suivez le guide
Affaires
Art de vivre
Fêtes et manifestations
Jeunes
Montagne hiver
Nature
Outremer
Patrimoine culturel
Remise en forme
Infos pratiques
Le magazine
Réservation en ligne
Mieux nous connaître

Maison de la FRANCE

Favorites | History | Search | Scrapbook | Page Holder

bonjour! C'est franceguide.com   Votre valise

- Superficie totale: 551 100 km^2

- 3120 km de côtes (en tenant compte des sinuosités)

- 1600 km (en ligne droite)

- La plus grande plage d'Europe: La Baule (Loire Atlantique, Pays de la Loire) – 12 km

- La dune la plus haute: Dune du Pilat (Gironde, Aquitaine – 105 m)

- Le point le plus haut de France: Le Mont-Blanc (Savoie, dans les Alpes) – 4807 m d'altitude

- La commune habitée la plus haute: Saint-Véran (Hautes Alpes) – 2200 m

- Environ 6000 especes végétales (dont 200 spécifiques à la France)

- 340 sortes de fromages, presqu'un pour chaque jour de l'année

- Environ 450 vins d'appellation d'origine contrôlée!

Internet zone

La France

A 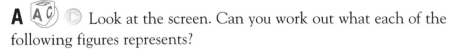 Look at the screen. Can you work out what each of the following figures represents?

a   3120 km.

b   12 km.

c   4807 m.

d   6 000.

e   340.

ACCESS FRENCH

B 🎲 ▶ Have a look at the general information about France, then try to find 12 words from the text which are hidden in the grid (horizontally and vertically only). **Amusez-vous bien!**

VOICI LA FRANCE

POPULATION

60,7 millions d'habitants

Densité : 107 hab/km^2

ORGANISATION ADMINISTRATIVE

La République française comprend :

◆ *la **métropole** (divisée en 22 régions et 96 départements)*

◆ *ainsi que 4 **départements** d'outre-mer (DOM) – Guadeloupe, Martinique, Guyane, La Réunion*

◆ *s'y ajoutent 4 **territoires** d'outre-mer (TOM) – Polynésie Française, Nouvelle-Calédonie, Wallis et Futuna, les Terres australes et antarctiques françaises*

◆ *les collectivités territoriales à statut particulier: Mayotte et Saint-Pierre-et-Miquelon.*

NIVEAU DE VIE

Salaire net moyen par salarié: 19 938 € par an.

CONSOMMATION (PART DU BUDGET DES MENAGES):

24,4 % **logement**, éclairage, **chauffage**

18,1 % **alimentation**, boissons, **tabac**

15,2 % **transports** et communications

11,6 % **loisirs** et culture

6,5 % équipement et entretien du logement

5,3 % habillement

3,6 % **santé**

15,3 % autres **biens** et services (restaurants, voyages, etc.)

a	m	e	t	r	o	p	o	l	e	f	u	b	a
t	t	e	b	s	c	n	o	r	t	y	q	v	h
e	r	s	i	u	h	o	v	o	u	x	u	i	o
r	a	d	e	p	a	r	t	e	m	e	n	t	s
r	n	a	n	i	u	h	f	f	e	t	n	a	o
i	s	y	s	a	f	i	s	a	n	t	e	b	e
t	p	i	d	n	f	e	t	t	e	a	r	a	t
o	o	z	a	i	a	n	m	c	i	u	t	c	s
i	r	e	l	o	g	e	m	e	n	t	o	u	e
r	t	t	o	r	e	r	l	o	i	s	i	r	s
e	s	a	l	i	m	e	n	t	a	t	i	o	n
s	a	l	a	i	r	e	e	t	p	m	a	i	p

C The table below shows the main leisure activities the French take part in during their spare time. Using the vocabulary in the table and the following phrases, make up 12 questions to ask your partner:

Est-ce que vous faites...?

Est-ce que vous vous occupez de...?

Est-ce que vous utilisez...?

Est-ce que vous jouez...?

Est-ce que vous tenez...?

Est-ce que vous écrivez...?

66%	utilisent un appareil photo
23%	s'occupent d'une collection
16%	font du dessin
14%	utilisent une caméra ou un caméscope
13%	jouent d'un instrument de musique
10%	font de la peinture, de la gravure ou de la sculpture
10%	font du chant ou de la musique en groupe
9%	tiennent un journal intime
7%	font de la danse
6%	écrivent des poèmes, des romans ou des nouvelles
4%	font de l'artisanat d'art
2%	font du théâtre

D Now write down the 12 questions using the **tu** form.

La vie de famille UNIT 4

GLOSSARY

Nouns

aire de jeu (f)	playground
alimentation (f)	food and drink
anniversaire (m)	birthday/anniversary
août	August
argent (m)	money/silver
aspirateur (m)	vacuum cleaner
aviron (m)	rowing
avril	April
balade (f)	walk
bâtiment (m)	building
batterie (f)	drum
bibliothèque (f)	library
bien (m)	good
boisson (f)	drink
chance (f)	luck
chauffage (m)	heating
cheval (m)	horse
cœur (m)	heart
côte (f)	coast
courses (fpl)	shopping
cuisine (f)	kitchen/cooking
décembre	December
déjeuner (m)	lunch
devoirs (mpl)	homework
dimanche (m)	Sunday
dîner (m)	dinner
éclairage (m)	lighting
entretien (m)	maintenance
escalade (f)	rock climbing
famille (f)	family
femme (f)	wife/woman
femme (f) **d'affaires**	businesswoman
ferme (f)	farm
février	February
fille (f)	daughter/girl
fils (m)	son
fois (f)	time
frère (m)	brother
garçon (m)	boy
habillement (m)	clothing
janvier	January
jardin (m)	garden
jeu (m)	game
jeudi (m)	Thursday
jour (m)	day
journée (f)	day
juillet	July
juin	June
lendemain (m)	the following day
lessive (f)	washing
location (f)	hiring/rent
logement (m)	accommodation/housing
lundi (m)	Monday
mai	May
maison (f)	house

GLOSSARY

marche (f)	walking	santé (f)	health
mardi (m)	Tuesday	sentier (m)	path
mari (m)	husband	septembre	September
mars	March	sœur (f)	sister
ménage (m)	housework	tabac (m)	tobacco
mercredi (m)	Wednesday	tante (f)	aunt
mère (f)	mother	terrain (m)	ground/pitch
mois (m)	month	tir (m) à l'arc	archery
montagne (f)	mountain	tournoi (m)	tournament
mots (mpl) croisés	crossword	vaisselle (f)	washing-up
mur (m)	wall	vendredi (m)	Friday
musculation (f)	body–building	voiture (f)	car
natation (f)	swimming		
neveu (m)	nephew	**Adjectives**	
nièce (f)	niece	droit(e)	straight
novembre	November	fermé(e)	closed
octobre	October	grand(e)	big
oncle (m)	uncle	gratuit(e)	free of charge
parapente (f)	paragliding	haut(e)	high
patin (m)	skate	nombreux/euse	numerous
patinoire (f)	icerink	ouvert(e)	open
pêche (f)	fishing	payant(e)	not free of charge/to be paid for
peinture (f)	paint/painting	seul(e)	alone/lonely
père (m)	father		
petit déjeuner (m)	breakfast	**Adverbs**	
piscine (f)	swimming pool	comme	as/like
plage (f)	beach	ensemble	together
planche (f) à voile	windsurfing board	heureusement	fortunately
pont (m)	bridge	jamais	never
poussière (f)	dust	plutôt	rather
randonnée (f)	hiking	quelquefois	sometimes
rencontre (f)	meeting	rarement	rarely
repassage (m)	ironing	souvent	often
routier (m)	lorry driver	toujours	always
samedi (m)	Saturday		

La vie de famille

GLOSSARY

Verbs

aider	to help
aimer	to like/to love
comprendre	to understand/to include
détester	to hate
faire	to do/to make
gagner	to earn/to win
garer	to park
jouer	to play
passer l'aspirateur	to vacuum
regarder	to watch
savoir	to know
s'énerver	to get annoyed
s'occuper de	to look after

Expressions

Il n'y a pas de…	There isn't/There aren't any…
Il y a…	There is/There are…
J'aimerais bien!	I wish!
Pouvez-vous me dire…?	Can you tell me…?

LOOKING FORWARD

In **Unit 5**, we will be talking about food and restaurants.

To prepare, have a look at the following sentences and note the ones that apply to you (use a dictionary if you're not sure):

Je n'aime pas le fromage • **Je préfère la viande saignante** • **Aujourd'hui pour déjeuner, je prends un sandwich au thon** • **Je suis végétarien(ne) mais je mange du poisson** • **J'invite souvent mes amis à manger à la maison**

UNIT 5
A table!

UNIT 5
A table!

> **By the end of this unit you will be able to:**
> - Understand restaurant guides and brochures
> - Invite somebody for lunch or dinner
> - Accept or refuse an invitation
> - Understand menus
> - Place an order in a restaurant
> - Explain what's in a dish or ask for an explanation
> - Complain in a restaurant

1 Vous vous souvenez?

A Regardez les mots suivants. Can you match the masculine words with their feminine forms?

père	sœur
oncle	nièce
mari	mère
frère	femme
neveu	tante

B

Travaillez avec un partenaire. Look at the family tree. Take it in turns to say who these people are and what they are doing, as in the following example:

Lucas, le frère de Lucie, joue de la guitare.

Josiane – Roger

Bernard – Marie

Nathalie – Joussef

Lucas

Lucie

Nathan

2 On va au resto?

A [ABC] ✏️ ⏺ Regardez l'extrait du guide restaurants suivant. Try to answer the questions which follow on page 76:

	Le Tutti Frutti	**La Petite Faim**	**A Cloche-Pied**
	Spécialisé en jus de fruits frais et salades.	Ambiance zen. Restaurant macrobiotique. Plats bio.	Bel emplacement face au jardin du manoir qui propose une carte convaincante renouvelée tous les deux mois à des tarifs imbattables. Réservation conseillée.
Genre de restaurant:	café-restaurant	restaurant classique	Restaurant classique
Cuisine:	végétarien	végétarien	France – cuisine traditionnelle
Prix à la carte:	22 €	23 €	26 €
Adresse:	1, rue du Bois joli	9, rue du Pont Neuf	1, chemin du Manoir
Téléphone:	02 45 78 36 87	02 45 82 14 77	02 45 97 01 54
Services:	déjeuner, dîner	déjeuner	déjeuner, dîner
Horaires:	dernier service 1h00 du matin	11h00 – 23h00 sans interruption	dernier service 23h30
Jour de fermeture:		lundi et vendredi	lundi
Que porter?	Tenue décontractée	Tenue décontractée	Pas de restriction
Cartes de crédit acceptées?	Visa, CB, Switch	CB, Visa	Mastercard, Visa
Autres informations:			climatisation

A table!

	Mi Ranchito	La Grande Brasserie	Le Nectar
	Une cuisine colombienne remarquable dans une ambiance festive.	Une grande brasserie aux influences maritimes, fruits de mer et huîtres en particulier. Service courtois et professionnel. Cadre des années 70.	Une des meilleures tables de la région, installée au cœur d'un décor superbe éclairé aux chandelles. Service remarquable. Cave efficace. Attention cependant, l'exception a un prix... Réservation obligatoire.
Genre de restaurant:	restaurant international	brasserie	gastronomique
Cuisine:	Amérique du Sud	France – fruits de mer	France
Prix à la carte:	19 €	61 €	183 €
Adresse:	21 rue Pasteur	200 rue du Lac	15 place des Montagnes
Téléphone:	02 45 23 47 85	02 45 11 08 32	02 45 46 81 00
Fax:	02 45 23 47 91	02 45 11 08 93	02 45 46 81 00
Services:	à emporter, déjeuner, dîner	déjeuner, dîner	déjeuner, dîner
Horaires:	7/7 jours, 11h00 – 24h00	7/7 jours, 11h30 – 1h30 du matin	dernier service 22h30
Jour de fermeture:			dimanche et lundi
Fermeture annuelle			01/08 au 22/08 et vacances de février
Que porter?	Pas de restriction	Pas de restriction	Costume
Cartes de crédit acceptées?	Aucune	Mastercard, American Express, Visa	American Express, Visa
Autres informations:		climatisation	climatisation

Which restaurant(s) would you go to if…

1 you were vegetarian?

2 you wanted a take-away?

3 you didn't want to dress up?

4 today was Monday?

5 you fancied exotic food?

6 you could only pay with your Visa card?

7 you fancied seafood?

B [ABC] ▷ **Vrai ou faux.** Look at the following statements and decide whether they are true or false:

	Vrai	Faux
1 At the Tutti Frutti restaurant, you must wear smart clothes.	⬭	⬭
2 At La Petite Faim, you can eat at 3.00 pm.	⬭	⬭
3 The A Cloche-Pied restaurant is located by the museum gardens.	⬭	⬭
4 Booking is essential at the A Cloche-Pied.	⬭	⬭
5 The Mi Ranchito accepts all major credit cards.	⬭	⬭
6 La Grande Brasserie specialises in seafood and mussels in particular.	⬭	⬭
7 Le Nectar does not have air conditioning.	⬭	⬭

3 Tu viens prendre l'apéro?

A ▷ Annie téléphone à son amie Pascale. Annie is inviting Pascale and her husband Philippe for an apéritif. Fill in the gaps, choosing the words from the box:

> fais – pouvez – c'est – veux – chez – voulez – peux – adore – soir – dois

Pascale: Allô!
Annie: Allô, Pascale? Bonjour, ⬭ Annie.
Pascale: Ah, Annie, comment ça va?
Annie: Ben ça va! Ecoute, je t'appelle pour savoir si tu ⬭ venir prendre l'apéritif samedi ⬭ avec Philippe.
Pascale: Samedi? Non, Annie, je ne peux pas. Je vais ⬭ ma belle-mère, c'est son anniversaire.
Annie: Ah! C'est dommage; et dimanche?
Pascale: Dimanche, oui, ça va, je ⬭ bien. A quelle heure?
Annie: Vous ⬭ venir pour midi. Et vous ⬭ manger avec nous?
Pascale: Non, Annie, c'est très gentil mais je ⬭ finir mon projet pour lundi.
Annie: Tu es sûre? Je ⬭ un couscous…
Pascale: Et j'⬭ le couscous. Ecoute, d'accord… mais on ne restera pas tard.
Annie: Pas de problème. A dimanche alors!
Pascale: Merci Annie, à dimanche!

A table! UNIT **5**

LANGUAGE FOCUS

Voulez-vous crocheter avec moi ce soir?

vouloir – *to want*
je veux
tu veux
il/elle veut
nous voulons
vous voulez
ils/elles veulent

pouvoir – *can/to be able to*
je peux
tu peux
il/elle peut
nous pouvons
vous pouvez
ils/elles peuvent

devoir – *must/to have to...*
je dois
tu dois
il/elle doit
nous devons
vous devez
ils/elles doivent

B Regardez les phrases ci-dessous.
Can you work out what they mean? Match the
French on the left with the English on the right.

1   Je dois prendre le bus à 7h00.

2   Est-ce que nous pouvons rester chez vous?

3   Est-ce que tu veux prendre un verre avec moi?

4   Je ne peux pas, je vais chez ma sœur.

5   Ils ne veulent pas aller en France cette année.

6   Vous devez apprendre ces verbes par cœur.

7   Si tu veux, on se retrouve où?

8   C'est dommage, il ne peut pas changer son billet.

9   Malheureusement, elle doit réviser son français.

a   It's a shame, he can't change his ticket.

b   Can we stay at yours?

c   I can't, I'm going to my sister's.

d   Unfortunately she has to revise her French.

e   I have to catch the bus at 7.00 am.

f   If you want, where shall we meet?

g   Do you want to have a drink with me?

h   You must learn these verbs by heart.

i   They don't want to go to France this year.

C  Travaillez avec un partenaire. Try to role-play the following conversation using the **tu** form. You will find the vocabulary in activities 3A and 3B.

(**A**) Hi, Michel(le), how are things?

(**B**) All right! How are you?

(**A**) Fine. Listen, do you want to go for a drink with us tonight?

(**B**) Tonight? Unfortunately I can't.

(**A**) What a shame!

(**B**) I have to go to Véronique's, it's her birthday.

(**A**) She can come as well if she wants.

(**B**) OK, where shall we meet?

(**A**) At the Café de la Mairie, at 8.00 pm.

(**B**) OK, see you tonight!

Now swap roles, but use the **vous** form.

4 Tu veux manger au resto?

A Regardez le menu à la page 80. Can you work out what the following words are in French?

starter
main courses
dessert
fish
meat
vegetables
home-made
seafood
chips
included

LEARNING TIP:
Je veux bien

To accept an invitation, you can use the following expressions:

Oui, merci/Oui, s'il vous plaît

Je veux bien

Avec plaisir

C'est gentil

C'est sympa

Volontiers

Un Air d'Italie

Entrées:

Salade de pâtes froides au saumon fumé	6,40€		Gratin de légumes au provolone	7,00€
Carpaccio de viande	9,50€		Aubergines gratinées	7,00€
Pizarella panée et son coulis de tomates	6,40€		Salade au chèvre chaud	5,20€

Plats principaux:

■ LES VIANDES:

Côte de bœuf grillée (350g)   13,20€
avec sa salade aux noix, béarnaise et frites

Gigot d'agneau   11,90€
grillé aux herbes, pommes de terre sautées à l'ail

Escalope de veau   13,90€
aux aubergines et spaghetti

Pavé de rumsteck: 13,90€
à la menthe et tagliatelles

Foies de volailles et tagliatelles: 12,50€
au vin de Marsala, champignons, crème

**Emincés de blancs de poulets
et tagliatelles:**   12,50€
à la moutarde et à l'estragon

■ LES PÂTES FRAÎCHES MAISON:

Tagliatelles: 9,10€
– Marsala, jambon cru, champignons, crème fraîche
– saumon fumé
– bolonaise

Tortiglioni: 9,60€
– aubergines, tomates, oignons, champignons
– quatre fromages
– flambés, vodka, champignons, jambon cru

Spaghetti: 9,20€
– fruits de mer
– pesto, ail, basilic, crème fraîche
– pizzaiola, câpres, tomates, olives, ail

Lasagnes: 9,30€
– bolonaise
– florentine, béchamel, épinards
– saumon et poireaux

■ LES POISSONS SERVIS AVEC TAGLIATELLES:

Méli-mélo de saumon: saumon fumé et frais	11,90€
Filet de saumon à la menthe	11,90€
Darne de saumon rôtie à la crème de safran	11,90€

■ LES DESSERTS MAISON: 5,50€

Tiramisu
Mousse au chocolat
Salade de fruits frais
Crème brûlée
Choix de glaces et sorbets

Taxes et service compris.

Un Air d'Italie

B 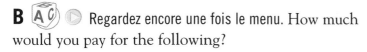 Regardez encore une fois le menu. How much would you pay for the following?

1 Pasta salad with smoked salmon.

2 Goat's cheese salad.

3 Grilled leg of lamb with garlic potatoes.

4 Chicken breast with mustard and tarragon.

5 Fresh pasta with salmon and leeks.

6 Fresh fruit salad.

There is further practice in ordering food and drink in French on our website.

C 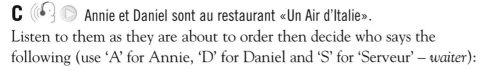 Annie et Daniel sont au restaurant «Un Air d'Italie». Listen to them as they are about to order then decide who says the following (use 'A' for Annie, 'D' for Daniel and 'S' for 'Serveur' – *waiter*):

1 Vous désirez un apéritif?

2 Qu'est-ce que tu veux?

3 Vous avez choisi?

4 Qu'est-ce que c'est 'provolone'?

5 Je n'aime pas beaucoup le fromage.

6 Et comme plat principal?

7 Saignante, à point, bien cuite

8 Je vais prendre les spaghetti.

9 Je suis au régime.

A table! UNIT **5**

81

D How would you answer the following questions?
Choose the most appropriate answers from the right-hand column.

1	Vous désirez un apéritif?	**a**	Oh non, merci, je suis au régime.
2	Vous avez choisi?	**b**	Je vais prendre un steak-frites.
3	Qu'est-ce que c'est 'provolone'?	**c**	Oui, alors comme entrée, je voudrais des crudités.
4	Vous prenez du fromage?	**d**	C'est un fromage italien.
5	Et comme plat principal?	**e**	Oui, un kir, s'il vous plaît.
6	Vous voulez votre steak saignant, bien cuit…?	**f**	Non, je n'aime pas beaucoup le fromage.
7	Vous désirez un dessert?	**g**	A point, s'il vous plaît.

LEARNING TIP:
Il m'aime beaucoup, passionnément, à la folie, pas du tout…

To say what you like or don't like,
use the following expressions:

J'adore le chocolat	*I love chocolate*
J'aime beaucoup les enfants	*I like children very much*
J'aime bien cette musique	*I like this music*
J'aime assez l'art moderne	*I quite like modern art*
Je n'aime pas le fromage	*I don't like cheese*
Je n'aime pas du tout cet homme	*I don't like this man at all*
J'ai horreur de la soupe	*I hate soup*
Je déteste les poireaux	*I hate leeks*

Au chocolat et à la vanille

Look at the following extracts from the dialogue in activity 4C:

Annie: Je voudrais les tortiglioni **à la** vodka, **aux** champignons et **au** jambon.

Daniel: ...non, je vais prendre les spaghetti **à l'**ail, **au** basilic et **à la** crème.

Serveur: ...nous avons aussi un sorbet **aux** fruits rouges.

In French, flavours and fillings are introduced by **à**.
à changes according to the gender and number of the following noun:

les tortiglioni **au** jambon (*masc.*)   *ham tortiglioni*
les spaghetti **au** basilic (*masc.*)   *spaghetti flavoured with basil*

les tortiglioni **à la** vodka (*fem.*)   *tortiglioni flavoured with vodka*
les spaghetti **à la** crème (*fem.*)   *spaghetti with cream*

les tortiglioni **aux** champignons (*plur.*)   *tortiglioni with mushrooms*
un sorbet **aux** fruits rouges (*plur.*)   *red fruit sorbet*

Note that if the flavour or filling starts with a vowel or a silent
h, au and **à la** become **à l'**.
les spaghetti **à l'**ail et **à l'**huile d'olive   *spaghetti flavoured with garlic and olive oil*

E 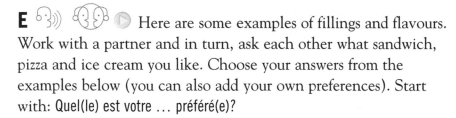 Here are some examples of fillings and flavours.
Work with a partner and in turn, ask each other what sandwich,
pizza and ice cream you like. Choose your answers from the
examples below (you can also add your own preferences). Start
with: Quel(le) est votre ... préféré(e)?

You'll find more practice
using à/de + articles on
www.accesslanguages.com

au	à la	aux
thon	crème fraîche	œufs
poulet	moutarde	fruits
jambon	vanille	cornichons
fromage	salade	fraises
chocolat	mayonnaise	champignons
café	banane	anchois

ACCESS **FRENCH**

✓

Check that you can...

- choose a restaurant from leaflets and brochures
- invite someone for a drink or a meal
- accept or refuse an invitation
- use **vouloir, pouvoir, devoir**
- understand menus and place an order
- express what you like or dislike.

5 Qu'est-ce que c'est 'shepherd's pie'?

A AC ▷ Voici une liste de mots et d'expressions qui se réfèrent à trois plats traditionnels britanniques. Can you work out what dish each description refers to?

steak and kidney pie   shepherd's pie   Ploughman's

cuit au four – en croûte – un plat froid – de l'agneau haché –
de la salade – du pain – des rognons – des pickles – des légumes –
du bœuf – de la purée de pommes de terre – du fromage

B  Répondez aux questions suivantes. Write your answers following the model (you can use the vocabulary in activity 5A):

– Qu'est-ce que c'est 'Lancashire hotpot'?

– **C'est** une spécialité du nord de l'Angleterre. **C'est** de l'agneau **avec** des carottes, du céleri, des poireaux **et** des pommes de terre cuits au four.

1 – Qu'est-ce que c'est 'steak and kidney pie'?

   – C'est une spécialité anglaise. C'est…

2 – Qu'est-ce que c'est 'Ploughman's'?

   – C'est un plat froid. C'est…

3 – Qu'est-ce que c'est 'shepherd's pie'?

   – C'est…

LEARNING TIP:
Dedans…

In a restaurant, to ask exactly what is in a dish, say:

Qu'est-ce qu'il y a dedans?
What's in it?

To check whether an ingredient is in a dish or not, say:

Il y a de la viande **dedans?**
Is there any meat in it?

6 Quelle soirée!

A  Ecoutez Blanca et Thierry. Ils sont dans un restaurant. Things don't seem to be going very well… In the summary below, choose the correct details according to what you hear.

Blanca is $\boxed{thirsty}$ / $\boxed{hungry.}$ They've been waiting for $\boxed{45 \ minutes}$ / $\boxed{one \ hour.}$ The waitress eventually brings a $\boxed{rare}$ / $\boxed{medium\text{-}rare \ steak}$ for Thierry and a $\boxed{sole}$ / $\boxed{trout}$ for Blanca. The waitress then puts some $\boxed{vegetables}$ / $\boxed{bread}$ on the table.

Blanca is suddenly horrified as she sees a $\boxed{hair}$ / $\boxed{fly}$ on her fish, and at the same time, Thierry notices that his steak is $\boxed{not \ cooked \ enough}$ / $\boxed{too \ cooked.}$ Thierry calls the waitress. She apologises and takes the plates $\boxed{to \ the \ kitchen}$ / $\boxed{to \ the \ head \ waiter.}$

UNIT **5**

85

B [A C] Regardez les phrases suivantes.

Can you match them with the right picture?

1 Il y a une mouche dans ma salade, c'est dégoutant!

2 Il y a du rouge à lèvres sur mon verre.

3 Ma fourchette est sale, donnez-m'en une autre s'il vous plaît.

4 Il y a du poulet dedans et je suis végétarien.

5 Il y a une erreur dans l'addition.

a

b

c

d

e

READY TO MOVE ON?

✓

Check that you can...

- explain or describe a dish
- ask for an explanation
- make a complaint in a restaurant.

Découverte de la FRANCOPHONIE

La France (suite)

A [AC] (((·))) ▷ Look at the article about 'Les Restos du cœur'. On a piece of paper, make two colums. In the first, list the words that you understand by context or because they look like English words; in the second, list the words that don't look like English words but that you understand nonetheless.

LE 26 SEPTEMBRE 1985

Sur l'antenne d'Europe 1, Coluche lance sa petite phrase sans se douter qu'elle allait devenir une grande aventure: c'est la naissance des Restos du Cœur.

«J'ai une petite idée, comme ça... s'il y a des gens qui sont intéressés pour sponsoriser une cantine gratuite qu'on commencerait par faire à Paris, et puis qu'on étalerait dans les grandes villes de France, nous on est prêts à aider une entreprise comme ça, qui ferait un resto qui aurait comme ambition de faire deux à trois mille repas par jour, gratuitement.»

A table! UNIT 5

Les colis alimentaires

C'est l'idée de départ de Coluche, et l'activité la plus connue des Restos.

Nos moyens ne suffisent pas à satisfaire tous les besoins. Priorité est donc donnée aux plus démunis et à la période de l'année la plus critique: nous apportons aux plus nécessiteux un «coup de pouce» pour passer l'hiver, de décembre à mars.

L'aide alimentaire est distribuée dans près de 2 000 centres de distribution en France, dans lesquels les bénéficiaires se rendent plusieurs fois par semaine. Ce sont des lieux d'accueil, de rencontre et d'échange, où l'on peut boire un café, passer un moment au chaud, établir des contacts.

[...] Ce qu'on appelle un colis alimentaire est un ensemble de denrées dont la quantité est calculée en fonction du nombre de personnes au foyer. Il comprend:

– une viande ou un poisson
– un légume, des pâtes ou du riz
– un fromage ou un yaourt
– du pain
– des produits d'hygiène

Des produits de base sont ajoutés chaque semaine, comme le lait, le beurre, l'huile, le sucre, la farine.

Les repas chauds

Les repas chauds, c'est toute l'année, préparés dans la plupart des grandes villes. Ils sont destinés à ceux qui n'ont pas de cuisine ou même pas de chez eux. Aucun justificatif n'est demandé.

Chaque ville gère de façon autonome cette forme d'assistance. Les repas sont servis à table dans des centres de distribution, généralement le midi ou par les Camions du Cœur qui distribuent, le soir sur le trottoir, une soupe, un plat chaud et un café.

A Paris ou à Nantes, la Maraude circule dans les rues la nuit pour aller à la rencontre de ceux qui n'ont même plus la force ou l'envie d'aller jusqu'aux Camions.

Lors de ces repas, on peut écouter, informer et soutenir.

Pour nous permettre de fournir un repas chaud quotidien:

pendant 15 jours, il faut 10,37 €
pendant 1 mois, il faut 21,34 €
pendant 2 mois, il faut 42,68 €
pendant tout l'hiver, il faut 68,68 €

A une maman seule et son enfant, pour tout l'hiver, il faut 137,20 €.

B 🅐🅒 ✏️ ▶️ Essayez de compléter le résumé suivant en anglais:

«Les Restos du Cœur» is a national association founded by the actor and comedian Coluche in 1985. The purpose of this association is to distribute free goods and meals to destitute people.

«Les colis alimentaires» (food hampers) were Coluche's initial idea to help people get through the ( ) months (from ( ) to ( )). The hampers are available in about 2000 centres in France. The content of a hamper depends on the number of people in the household. It includes ( ) or fish, ( ), pasta or rice, ( ) or yoghurt, ( ) and toiletries.

Every ( ), primary food such as milk, ( ), oil, sugar and ( ) is added to the hamper.

«Les repas chauds» (hot meals) are available throughout the year in ( ) ( ). They are prepared for those who don't have a ( ) or those who have no home. A meal consists of ( ), ( ) ( ) and coffee. In order to provide a daily «repas chaud» to someone for a fortnight, the association needs ( )€. For the whole winter, «Les Restos du Cœur» needs 68.68€, and for a single ( ) and her ( ), it needs 137.20€.

A table!

GLOSSARY

Nouns

addition (f)	bill
agneau (m)	lamb
ail (m)	garlic
besoin (m)	need
billet (m)	ticket
bœuf (m)	beef
cadre (m)	decor
champignon (m)	mushroom
chandelle (f)	candle
cheveu (m)	hair
chèvre (f)	goat
climatisation (f)	air conditioning
cornichon (m)	gherkin
costume (m)	suit
déjeuner (m)	lunch
dessert (m)	dessert
dîner (m)	dinner
entrée (f)	starter
épinard (m)	spinach
estragon (m)	tarragon
fermeture (f)	closing
four (m)	oven
fourchette (f)	fork
fromage (m)	cheese
genre (m)	kind/sort
hiver (m)	winter
huître (f)	oyster
menthe (f)	mint
mouche (f)	fly
moutarde (f)	mustard
naissance (f)	birth
noix (f)	walnut
ouverture (f)	opening
pain (m)	bread

pâtes (fpl)	pasta
plat (m)	dish
plat (m) **principal**	main course
poireau (m)	leek
poisson (m)	fish
pomme (f) **de terre**	potato
poulet (m)	chicken
régime (m)	diet
repas (m)	meal
riz (m)	rice
rognon (m)	kidney
rouge (m) **à lèvres**	lipstick
saumon (m)	salmon
tenue (f)	dress code
thon (m)	tuna
veau (m)	veal
verre (m)	glass
viande (f)	meat
ville (f)	town/city
yaourt (m)	yoghurt

Adjectives

chaud(e)	hot/warm
cuit(e)	cooked
décontracté(e)	relaxed
dernier/dernière	last
frais/fraîche	fresh
froid(e)	cold
fumé(e)	smoked
gentil(le)	kind
gratiné(e)	grilled
haché(e)	minced
pané(e)	battered
servi(e)	served
sympa	kind
végétarien(ne)	vegetarian

GLOSSARY

Verbs

adorer	to love
aimer	to like/to love
apprendre	to learn
boire	to drink
conseiller	to advise
déjeuner	to lunch
devenir	to become
devoir	to have to/must
dîner	to have dinner
donner	to give
écouter	to listen
emporter	to take away
pouvoir	to be able to/can
prendre l'apéritif	to have a pre-dinner drink
prendre le bus	to catch the bus
rester	to stay
savoir	to know
se douter	to suspect
se retrouver	to arrange to meet
soutenir	to support
vouloir	to want/will

Expressions

à point	medium rare (steak)
bien cuit	well done (steak)
bleu	very rare (steak)
saignant	rare (steak)
J'ai faim	I'm hungry
J'ai soif	I'm thirsty
C'est…	It's…
Qu'est-ce qu'il y a dedans?	What's in it?

LOOKING FORWARD

In **Unit 6**, we will be sightseeing in France, giving and understanding directions and talking about the weather.

To prepare, look at the sentences below and note those that apply to your town (use a dictionary if necessary):

Dans ma ville, il y a un magnifique château • Il y a le marché chaque semaine • La cathédrale est splendide • Il y a une banque sur la place • Il pleut souvent

UNIT 6
Ici et là

A table!

UNIT 5

UNIT **6**
Ici et là

1 Vous vous souvenez?

A Travaillez avec un partenaire. In turn, ask each other the following questions and try to answer, giving as many details as you can:

1 Quel est votre plat préféré?

2 Qu'est-ce que vous mangez en général au petit déjeuner?

3 Donnez une spécialité traditionnelle britannique. Qu'est-ce que c'est exactement?

4 Vous aimez faire la cuisine?

5 Quelle est votre spécialité?

B  Trouvez l'intrus! Have a look at these groups of words. Try to spot the odd one out in each line:

entrée   fourchette   plat principal   dessert

bleu   saignant   salé   bien cuit

saumon   thon   truite   chèvre

pommes   poireaux   épinards   champignons

cuillère   assiette   verre   mouche

2 Qu'est-ce qu'il y a à faire?

A Regardez la page d'accueil du site Internet de la ville de Douai dans le nord de la France. From the list of sights below, can you pick out those that don't appear on the home page?

> **castle – opera house – church – theatre – cathedral –
> peal of bells – canals – music academy – science museum – belfry**

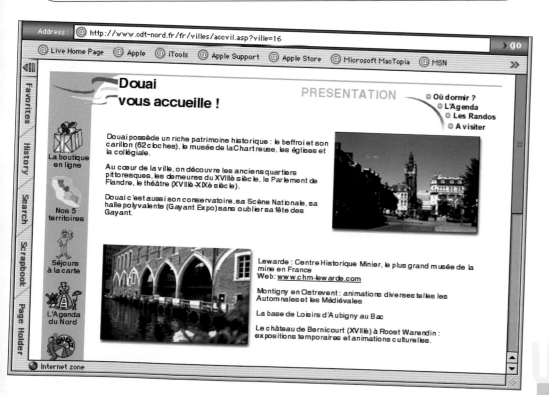

ACCESS **FRENCH**

LANGUAGE FOCUS

On peut…

To describe what you can do or see in your town, use the expression **On peut…**
(*We/People/One can…*) followed by a verb.

On peut aller au jardin botanique.   *We/People can go the the Botanical gardens.*
On peut visiter le château.   *We/People can visit the castle.*

French people use **on** quite a lot in conversational French. It usually
replaces **nous**, but is used in the singular form (like **il** or **elle**):

On va au marché.   *We're going to the market.*
On va au marché?   *Shall we go to the market?*
On y va?   *Shall we go?*

B 🎲 🔊 ▷ Regardez les colonnes ci-dessous. Try to
make up as many sentences as you can. Here is an example:
A Paris on peut visiter la Tour Eiffel.

à Paris	on peut visiter	Big Ben
à Londres	on peut voir	la Tour Eiffel
à Douai	on peut aller	le carillon
	on peut écouter	les maisons du XVIIIe siècle
	on peut faire	à la Cathédrale Notre-Dame
	il y a	au Palais de Buckingham
		le musée de la mine
		le tour de la ville dans un bus à impérial

Invite your French friend
out for the day in our
web-based activity.

C ✍ 🔊 ▷ Use the model in the previous activity to give
details of what you can do, see or visit in your nearest town or city.

3 Il y a un distributeur de billets près d'ici?

A (((•))) ▶ Ecoutez les quatre petites conversations et notez les mots que vous entendez.

> cinéma – à 10 minutes – banque – hôpital – à pied –
> en voiture – en face – là-bas – rue – le syndicat d'initiative
> – pharmacie – près d'ici – désolé – devant – derrière

B (((•))) ▶ Ecoutez encore une fois les dialogues. In what order do you hear the following places? Number each illustration from 1 to 8.

LEARNING TIP:
Savoir *and* Connaître

Savoir means *to know (a fact)*:
Je sais *I know* / Je ne sais pas
I don't know

Connaître means *to know (a person or a place)*:
Je connais Paris mais je ne connais pas Lyon.

Savoir + verb means *to know how to…* or *can…*

Je sais conduire. *I can drive (I know how to drive)*.

Je ne sais pas nager.
I can't swim.

UNIT **6**

95

ACCESS FRENCH

LANGUAGE FOCUS

Les prépositions

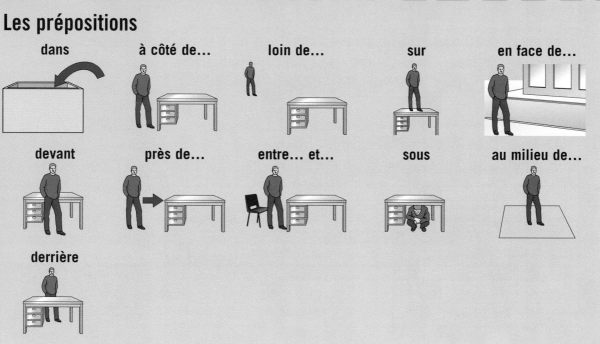

dans   à côté de...   loin de...   sur   en face de...

devant   près de...   entre... et...   sous   au milieu de...

derrière

C Listen to six statements and decide whether the following illustrations are correct or not.

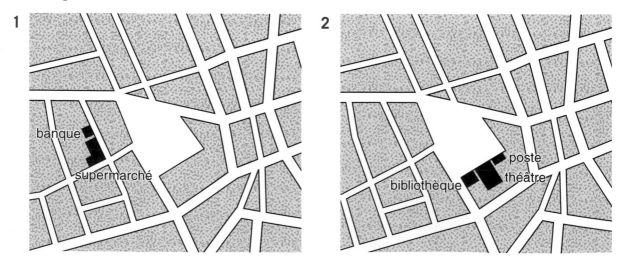

1   banque   supermarché

2   bibliothèque   poste   théâtre

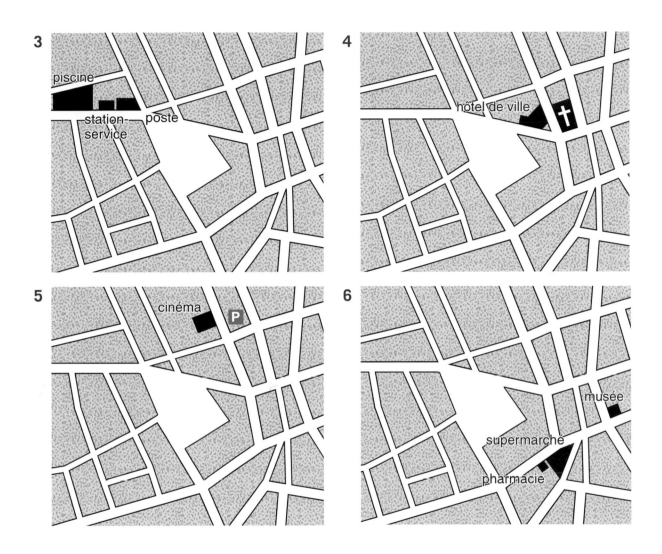

D 👂🎧 ▶ Travaillez à deux. Your teacher will give you a card with some details missing. In turn, find out where the missing places are located by asking your partner questions. Start with **Où est.../Où se trouve...?** (*Where is…?*)

Ici et là UNIT **6**

4 Pour aller au stade, s'il vous plaît?

LANGUAGE FOCUS

A droite et à gauche

The verb in the imperative form (used when giving orders or instructions to people) is made from the 'vous' part of the present tense but without the actual word 'vous':

~~Vous~~ **prenez** la première rue à droite.
Take the first street on the right.

Continuez/Allez tout droit.
Continue/Go straight on.

Tournez à gauche.
Turn left.

Traversez la place.
Cross the square.

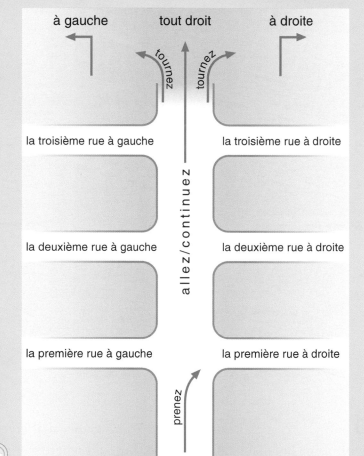

à gauche   tout droit   à droite

tournez   tournez

la troisième rue à gauche   la troisième rue à droite

allez/continuez

la deuxième rue à gauche   la deuxième rue à droite

la première rue à gauche   la première rue à droite

prenez

LEARNING TIP:
First, second, third...

le **premier**/la **première**   *the first*
le/la deux**ième**   *the second*
le/la trois**ième**   *the third*
le/la dix**ième**   *the tenth*
le/la vingt**ième**   *the twentieth*
le/la vingt-et-un**ième**   *the twenty-first*

etc.

A 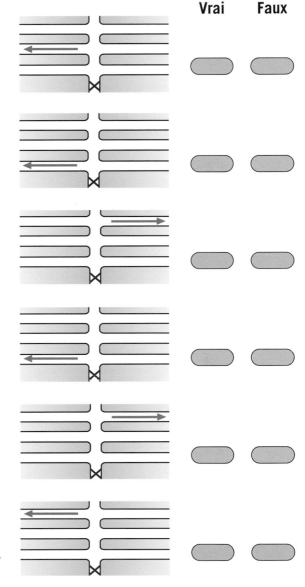 Regardez les pictogrammes ci-dessous. Start from the cross and decide whether the statements are true or false (vrai ou faux).

Vrai Faux

1 – Pour aller au musée, s'il vous plaît?

– Prenez la deuxième à gauche.

2 – Où est le marché, s'il vous plaît?

– C'est à droite.

3 – Il y a une banque près d'ici?

– Oui, prenez la troisième à gauche.

4 – Pour aller à l'hôtel Malvert, s'il vous plaît?

– C'est ici, juste à droite.

5 – Pour aller à la zone industrielle, s'il vous plaît?

– C'est très simple, c'est toujours tout droit.

6 – Pour aller à l'aéroport, s'il vous plaît?

– Prenez la troisième à gauche et c'est tout droit.

B  Regardez les pictogrammes et complétez les phrases ci-dessous:

1 – Pour aller à la plage, s'il vous plaît?

— Continuez tout ⬭.

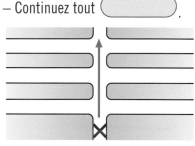

2 – Où est l'hôtel de ville?

— Prenez la ⬭ à ⬭.

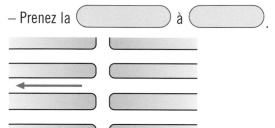

3 – Il y a une pharmacie près d'ici?

— Oui, ⬭.

4 – Pardon monsieur, où est la gare, s'il vous plaît?

— ⬭

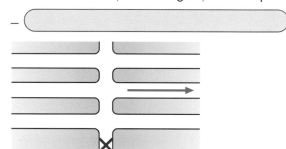

5 – Il y a une station de métro près d'ici?

— Oui, alors ⬭.

puis

6 – Pour aller à l'hôtel de ville, s'il vous plait?

— ⬭

puis

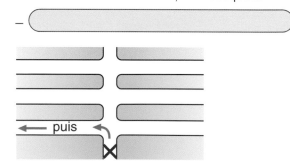

C 🎧 ▷ Ecoutez les instructions de quatre personnes. For each person, start from the arrow and identify the place they reach on the map below.

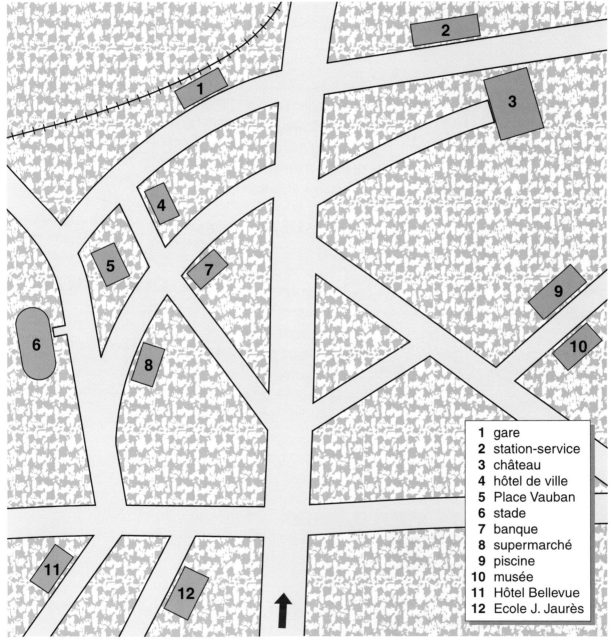

1 gare
2 station-service
3 château
4 hôtel de ville
5 Place Vauban
6 stade
7 banque
8 supermarché
9 piscine
10 musée
11 Hôtel Bellevue
12 Ecole J. Jaurès

Ici et là**UNIT 6**

D A C ✏ ▷ Vous êtes invité(e) à un mariage en France.
Your friends have sent you directions to the venue. Look
at the letter and complete the summary in English.

LEARNING TIP:
Linking words.

When giving instructions to
people, make your explanation
sound better by adding some
linking words between phrases.
Here are a few examples:

et	*and*
puis	*then*
ensuite	*then*
après	*after*
mais	*but*

Chers Vanessa et John,

Comme promis, voici l'itinéraire pour arriver jusqu'à
chez nous ici à Neuville:
Alors quand vous arrivez à Calais, prenez la direction
de Lille. Quand vous arrivez à Lille, vous suivez la
direction de Valenciennes. Prenez la sortie 9 et
tournez à droite vers Douchy-les-mines. Au carrefour,
tournez à droite et continuez jusqu'aux feux. Tournez
à gauche et continuez toujours tout droit pendant
environ 3 km. Juste après le pont, tournez à gauche
et continuez jusqu'au carrefour. Il y a le cimetière sur
votre droite; allez tout droit. Prenez la troisième à
gauche, c'est la rue Pasteur, et nous sommes au
numéro 26.
Nous espérons que vous trouverez facilement. Si vous
vous perdez, téléphonez-nous, vous avez notre numéro
de portable...
A la semaine prochaine et bonne route.
Grosses bises de nous deux.

Véro et Christian

When you arrive in Calais, ().

When you reach Lille, ().

(), and turn () towards Douchy-les-mines.

(), turn right and drive on to ().

Turn () and carry on straight on ().

Just (), turn left.

The cemetery is ().

Take the (), rue Pasteur, number 26.

E Travaillez avec un partenaire et utilisez la carte de l'activité 4C. Give your partner directions to follow on the map and ask where he or she ended up. Start from the arrow.

Link to French routefinders — we have some ideas on our website.

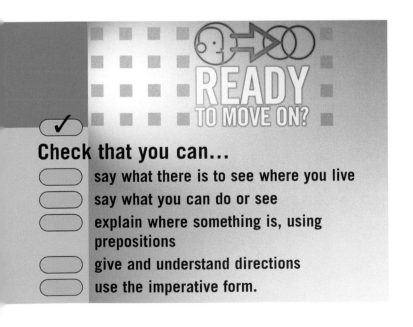

Check that you can...
- say what there is to see where you live
- say what you can do or see
- explain where something is, using prepositions
- give and understand directions
- use the imperative form.

5 Quel temps de chien! (What dreadful weather!)

A  Regardez la carte ci-dessous.
Read the statements and check whether
they are correct or not.

1 A Lyon, il fait du soleil.

2 A Paris, il fait chaud.

3 Dans le Nord, il fait 10°C.

4 Dans les Alpes, il fait de l'orage.

5 En Corse, il fait du vent.

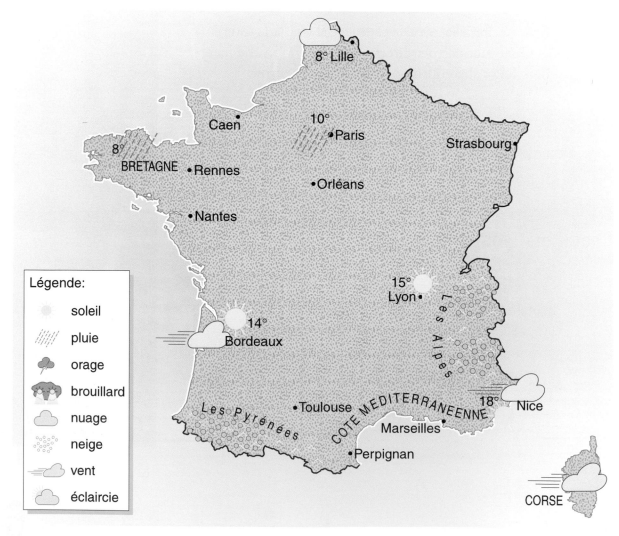

Légende:

soleil	
pluie	
orage	
brouillard	
nuage	
neige	
vent	
éclaircie	

8° Lille

Caen

10° Paris

Strasbourg

8° BRETAGNE •Rennes

•Orléans

•Nantes

15° Lyon• Les Alpes

14° Bordeaux

18° Nice

•Toulouse COTE MEDITERRANEENNE

Les Pyrénées

Marseilles

•Perpignan

CORSE

B Ecoutez le bulletin météorologique. Try to complete the map below. Note down little symbols or temperatures for each of the boxes.

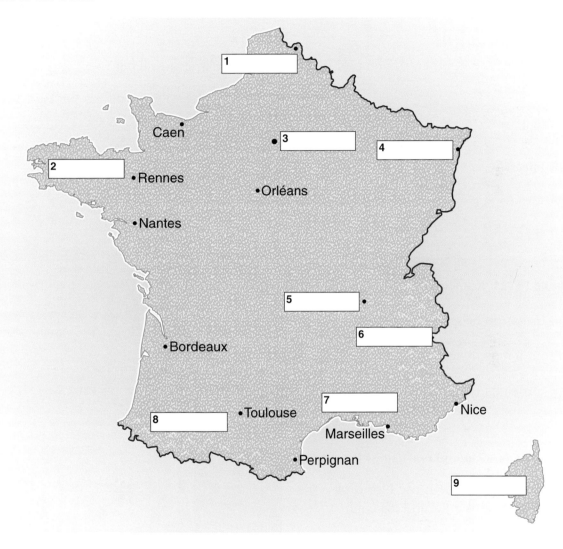

Ici et là

LANGUAGE FOCUS

Quel temps fait-il?

To talk about the weather, the French generally use the expression **Il fait...**

Il fait + adjective

Il fait beau

Il fait mauvais

Il fait chaud

Il fait froid

Il fait un temps + adjective

Il fait un temps couvert

Il fait un temps nuageux

Il fait un temps pluvieux

Il fait de + noun / **Il y a de** + noun

Il fait / Il y a du soleil

Il fait / Il y a du vent

Il fait / Il y a de l'orage

Il fait / Il y a du brouillard

Verbs

Il pleut

Il neige

Il gèle

C How would you say in French...

1 In winter (en hiver), in the North of France, it rains a lot and it's cold.

2 In spring (au printemps), in Brittany, it's not cold but it's very cloudy and windy.

3 In summer (en été), in the South, it's very hot and sunny.

4 In autumn (en automne), it snows in the Alps.

5 Today it's foggy here and it's only 11°C.

READY TO MOVE ON?

✓

Check that you can...

describe what the weather is like

understand the weather forecast.

La Belgique

A 🎲 ▶ Je clique où exactement? Regardez la page d'accueil du site Internet de la ville de Liège en Belgique. On the left side of the page is a list of links (**liens**). Read the following statements and decide which link you would click to find further information.

1 Vous voulez visiter des galeries d'art.

2 Vous voulez manger des plats belges.

3 Vous voulez des informations sur les trains et les bus.

4 Vous voulez des informations sur les écoles à Liège.

5 Vous voulez voir des photos de Liège.

B [A C] ▷ Découvrir Liège… Look at the following details about Liège and try to complete the quiz:

voyager • voyager • voyager • voyager

Liège, carrefour des connaissances...

Liège, cité épiscopale millénaire, métropole économique et culturelle de Wallonie s'est hissée, après dix ans de croissance, au rang de troisième port fluvial du continent, au cœur des réseaux TGV et autoroutiers trans-européens. Cette situation est confortée par des pôles d'excellence internationale pour le transport et la logistique, les bio-technologies, la recherche spatiale. Bien sûr, les pôles traditionnels, l'électricité et le métal, demeurent deux fleurons, aujourd'hui soutenus par les technologies de l'information appliquées à l'audiovisuel, les animations de synthèse, la 3D, les systèmes géographiques numériques…

Liège, agréable à vivre

Pourtant, loin de souffrir de la frénésie des grandes métropoles, Liège et ses habitants sont privilégiés par la nature, grâce au fleuve et aux vertes collines dont les douces ondulations équilibrent la vie. Dans le centre historique et commercial, à dimension humaine, les Liégeois cultivent un art de vivre où l'hospitalité spontanée n'est pas une formule creuse: on y flâne, de terrasse en magasin... Ardeur à l'ouvrage et créativité ne sont-elles pas favorisées par un bon cadre de vie et une attention soutenue aux relations sociales et interculturelles?

Liège, entreprenante... et épicurienne

En TGV Thalys ou par une des nombreuses autoroutes qui y convergent, vous rejoindrez Liège aisément pour affaires, congrès ou séminaires. Ensuite, vous pourrez goûter aux plaisirs de la gastronomie locale, française, italienne, asiatique, latino-américaine... puis choisir entre l'Opéra, l'Orchestre Philharmonique, le Théâtre, des cinémas parmi les plus high-tech d'Europe...

Liège, cultivée...

Visitez nos galeries d'art, admirez PICASSO, MONET, GAUGUIN, CHAGALL, ENSOR, RODIN, DELVAUX, MAGRITTE qui vous attendent dans nos musées, également dévolus à l'art religieux, verrier, au mobilier ou aux armes à feu.

Au-dehors, l'art urbain, conservation du patrimoine et rénovation urbaine, marient tradition séculaire et œuvres contemporaines.

QUIZ

First paragraph:

1   Can you give one detail about the port of Liège?

2   Can you give one detail about the situation/location of Liège?

3   Can you name three sectors for which Liège is renowned

Second paragraph:
What are the two natural attractions that make Liège a pleasant place to be?

Third paragraph:

1   What makes Liège easy to access?

    a   Its international airport.

    b   Its motorway network.

    c   Its underground.

    d   Its high-speed rail network.

2   Is Liège a suitable venue for business meetings? oui ⬭ non ⬭

3   Can you list three leisure attractions in Liège?

Fourth paragraph:
Apart from the art galleries, what are the other four museums in Liège?

1   Textile museum.

2   Religious art museum.

3   Glassworks museum.

4   Coal-mine museum.

5   Furniture museum.

6   Gun museum.

7   Motor museum.

8   Clock museum.

Ici et là UNIT **6**

C Pardon madame, où est la bibliothèque s'il vous plaît?
Work with a partner. In turn, ask each other the following
questions and try to explain how to get to the different places from
the 'Vous êtes ici' sign.

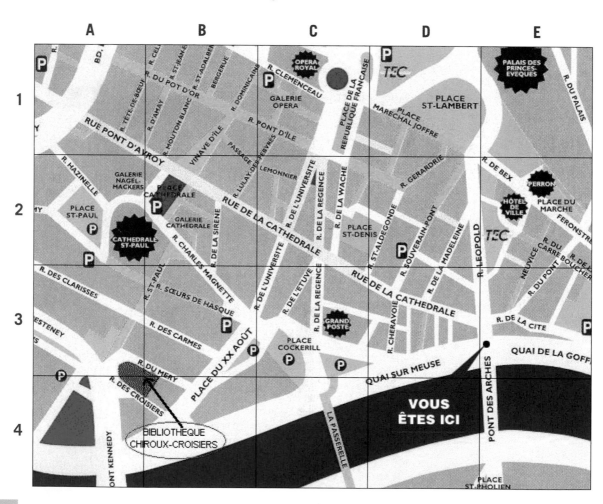

1 Où est le Palais des Princes-Evêques, s'il vous plaît? (E1)

2 Pardon, je cherche la cathédrale Saint-Paul, s'il vous plaît. (A2)

3 Où se trouve l'hotel de ville? (E2)

4 Il y a un parking près d'ici? (C3)

5 Où est la Bibliothèque Chiroux-Croisiers? (B4)

6 Je cherche la Place Saint-Denis, s'il vous plaît. (C2)

GLOSSARY

Nouns

arme (f) **à feu**	firearm
automne (m)	autumn
autoroute (f)	motorway
beffroi (m)	belfry
bibliothèque (f)	library
bise (f)	kiss
brouillard (m)	fog
carillon (m)	peal of bells
carrefour (m)	crossroad
château (m)	castle
colline (f)	hill
conservatoire (m)	music academy
distributeur (m) **de billets**	cashpoint
église (f)	church
été (m)	summer
feux (mpl)	traffic lights
fleuve (m)	river
gare (f)	railway station
hiver (m)	winter
hôtel de ville (m)	town hall
maison (f)	house
marché (m)	market
mobilier (m)	furniture
orage (m)	thunder storm
piscine (f)	swimming pool
place (f)	square
pont (m)	bridge
portable (m)	mobile phone
printemps (m)	spring
réseau (m)	network
route (f)	road
rue (f)	street
soleil (m)	sun
supermarché (m)	supermarket
syndicat (m) **d'initiative**	tourist office
temps (m)	time/weather
vent (m)	wind

Adjectives

beau/belle	beautiful/nice
chaud(e)	hot
couvert(e)	cloudy
désolé(e)	sorry
froid(e)	cold
mauvais(e)	bad
nuageux/euse	cloudy
numérique	digital
pluvieux/euse	rainy

Verbs

aller	to go
conduire	to drive
connaître	to know (a place/a person)
continuer	to continue
écouter	to listen
espérer	to hope
flâner	to walk around
geler	to freeze
nager	to swim
neiger	to snow
pleuvoir	to rain

Ici et là

GLOSSARY

prendre	to take	derrière	behind
savoir	to know (a fact)	devant	in front of/outside
se perdre	to get lost	en face de	opposite
se trouver	to be located	en voiture	by car
suivre	to follow	ensuite	then
traverser	to cross	entre… et…	between… and…
voir	to see	et	and
		ici	here
Expressions		jusqu'à	up to
à côté de	next to	là-bas	over there
à droite	to/on the right	loin de	far from
à gauche	to/on the left	mais	but
à pied	on foot	près d'ici	nearby
après	after	puis	then
au bout de	to/at the end of	sous	under
au cœur de	in the heart of	sur	on
au milieu de	in the middle of	tout droit	straight on
dans	in		

LOOKING FORWARD

In **Unit 7**, we will be talking about travelling and future plans.

To prepare, have a look at the following sentences and note those that apply to you:

UNIT 7
Voyages, voyages…

Je vais au travail en bus • **J'adore prendre le train** • **Pour aller en France, le ferry est plus économique** • **Je commence le travail à 9h00** • **Je préfère voyager en avion et ensuite louer une voiture**

UNIT 7
Voyages, voyages...

▶ **By the end of this unit you will be able to:**

- Talk about how you travel
- Use the pronoun 'y'
- Explain future plans
- Tell, understand and ask for the time
- Make a travel booking
- Hire a car

1 Vous vous souvenez?

A ▶ Regardez les pictogrammes ci-dessous. Choose the correct expression to describe each of them:

1

Il fait du vent.
Il fait du soleil.
Il fait froid.

2

Il y a des nuages.
Il pleut.
Il fait beau.

3

Le temps est splendide.
Il pleut.
Le vent est froid.

4

Il neige.
Il fait chaud.
Il y a des éclaircies.

5

Il gèle.
Il fait du brouillard.
Il fait de l'orage.

B 🗣️ 🎧 ▶️ Travaillez avec un partenaire. Regardez l'image ci-dessous. In turn, make up examples to describe places in the street using the following prepositions: **dans, devant, à côté de, entre…et…, sur, en face de, au milieu de.**

Example: La banque est **à côté** du cinéma.

2 On y va comment? (How shall we get there?)

A 🎲 ▶️ Regardez les expressions ci-dessous. Can you match them with the right pictures?

1 en bateau/ferry	4 en bus/car	7 en avion
2 à pied	5 en métro	8 en train
3 à moto	6 en voiture	9 à vélo

d

g

a

b

e

h

c

f

i

B Leila pose des questions à des gens sur leurs plans pour les vacances. Can you understand where these people are going and how they will be travelling? Fill in the grid:

	Destination(s)	Moyen(s) de transport
1		
2		
3		
4		
5		

LANGUAGE FOCUS

J'y vais en voiture

To avoid repeating the name of a place, you can replace it with the word **y** (*there*) placed just before the verb:

Je vais **en France** cet été. **J'y** vais en voiture.
I'm going to France this summer. I'm going (there) by car.

Vous allez **à Londres** pour combien de jours? – J'**y** vais pour une semaine.
How many days are you going to London for? – I'm going (there) for a week.

Tu vas **à la soirée** chez Jérome? – Non, je n'**y** vais pas, je vais rester chez moi.
Are you going to Jérome's party? – No, I'm not going (there), I'm staying in.

C Try to answer the following questions replacing the words in bold with **y** and using the clues in brackets:

1 Vous allez souvent **au pub?** (tous les jours)

2 Vous allez **au travail** en voiture? (en train ou en bus)

3 Est-ce que vous allez **à la piscine** régulièrement? (deux fois par semaine)

4 Est-ce qu'il travaille toujours **à la banque?** (plus depuis un mois)

5 Il va **en Chine** avec sa fiancée? (avec ses parents)

UNIT **7**

115

D Ecoutez encore une fois les cinq conversations de l'activité 2B.
Decide whether the following statements are true or false (**vrai ou faux**):

		Vrai	Faux
1	He's going on holiday with his daughter.		
	They're going for three weeks.		
2	She's flying to Canada and will then hire a bike over there.		
	She's going for two months.		
3	She's meeting relatives in Manchester.		
	She's staying in Edinburgh for a fortnight.		
4	He will spend his holiday motorcycling around Brittany.		
	He'll be away for about a week.		
5	They're going to Tunisia for a fortnight.		
	They'll hire a car over there.		

LANGUAGE FOCUS

Le futur

Expressing the future is quite straightforward in French as it follows the
same patterns as English.

- Using the present tense with a word or expression that refers to
  the future:

  Demain, **je commence** à 9h00.   *Tomorrow,* **I'm starting** *at 9.00 am.*
  Je prends l'avion ce soir à 19h00.   **I'm catching** *the plane tonight at 7.00.*

- Using the verb **aller** (*to go*) in the present tense followed by a verb in
  the infinitive form:

  Je vais acheter une nouvelle voiture.   **I'm going to buy** *a new car.*
  Nous allons réserver deux chambres.   **We're going to book** *two rooms.*

Voyages, voyages...

For more practice on
the future, go to
www.accesslanguages.com

E  ▷ Mettez les mots suivants dans l'ordre correct pour faire des phrases:

1 ce soir / reste / à la maison / je

2 va / vélo / louer / un / il

3 maison / l'année prochaine / notre / allons / nous / vendre

4 demain / banque / je / aller / à la / vais / matin

5 vas / semaine / à / prochaine / tu / Londres / la / ?

F ▷ Your teacher will give you cards with details of holiday plans. Work with a partner and try to find out what his or her plans are by asking each other questions. Here is an example:

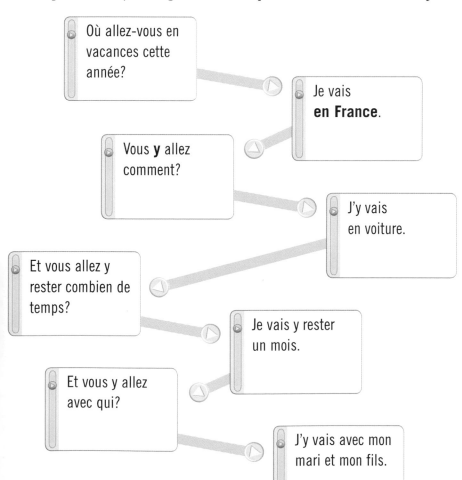

Où allez-vous en vacances cette année?

Je vais **en France**.

Vous **y** allez comment?

J'y vais en voiture.

Et vous allez y rester combien de temps?

Je vais y rester un mois.

Et vous y allez avec qui?

J'y vais avec mon mari et mon fils.

UNIT **7**

117

3 Je vais réserver le ferry par Internet

A Regardez la page Internet suivante. Try to spot the factual errors in the summary.

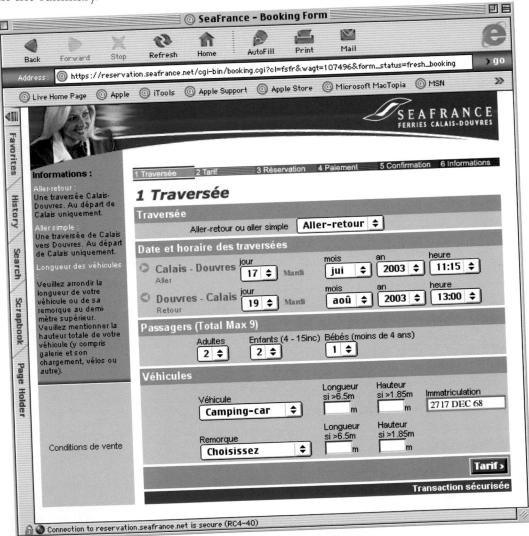

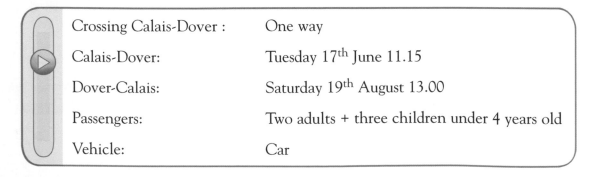

Crossing Calais-Dover :	One way
Calais-Dover:	Tuesday 17th June 11.15
Dover-Calais:	Saturday 19th August 13.00
Passengers:	Two adults + three children under 4 years old
Vehicle:	Car

B  You had a computer problem and the Internet booking didn't go through so the reservation had to be made by phone.

1 AC Look at the following dialogue. The answers given to the operator are jumbled. Can you put them in the right order?

Seafrance: Seafrance, bonjour!

Client: Non, en camping-car avec cinq passagers.

Seafrance: Oui, pour quelle traversée?

Client: 13h00.

Seafrance: Oui, pour quelle date?

Client: Pour le 17 juillet.

Seafrance: A quelle heure?

Client: Bonjour, j'ai un problème de connection Internet, et je voudrais faire une réservation.

Seafrance: D'accord, et le retour, pour quelle date?

Client: Non, deux adultes, deux enfants et un bébé.

Seafrance: A quelle heure?

Client: Le 19 août.

Seafrance: Oui d'accord, et vous voyagez en voiture?

Client: 11h15.

Seafrance: Cinq adultes?

Client: Calais–Douvres, aller-retour.

Seafrance: Très bien, ça fait 490€.

2 Read out the dialogue with a partner.

LEARNING TIP:
am and pm

For 'am', use the expression **du matin.**

For 'pm', use the expression **de l'après-midi** for the afternoon.

du soir for the evening.

LANGUAGE FOCUS

Quelle heure est-il?

A common way of expressing time in French is to use the 24-hour clock with the hours and the minutes separated by the word **heure(s)**.

11.15	onze **heures** quinze
13.30	treize **heures** trente
20.40	vingt **heures** quarante
01.25	une **heure** vingt-cinq

Alternatively, use the following model:

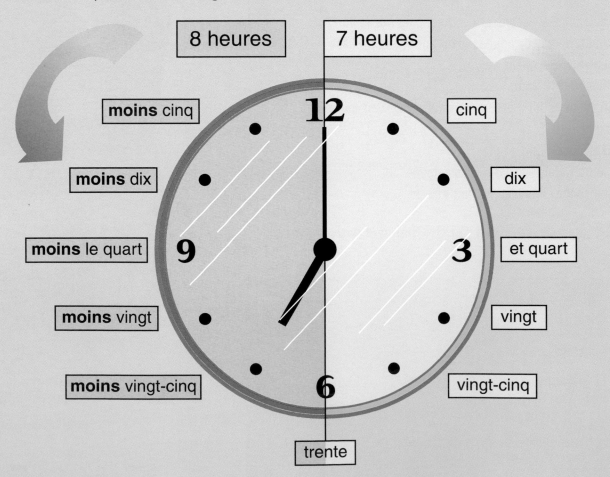

Remember always to start with the hours followed by the minutes.

www.accesslanguages.com has
more practice in telling the time.

C Ecoutez les heures suivantes. Number them in the
order you hear them.

17h30 ⬭	03h45 ⬭	05h30 ⬭	14h40 ⬭
13h45 ⬭	12h15 ⬭	23h55 ⬭	08h00 ⬭

D On a piece of paper, jot down five different times
using the 12-hour and 24-hour clock. Read them out in French to
your partner who will write them down. Check answers and swap roles.

READY TO MOVE ON?

✓

Check that you can...

- talk about how you travel
- use the pronoun **y**
- explain what you are doing later or what you are going to do
- tell, understand and ask the time.

4 A la gare (At the station)

A Isabelle réserve un billet de train pour Amsterdam. Have a look at
the following statements and choose the correct options:

1 Isabelle is going to Amsterdam next week / next month.

2 She wants to go on Monday / Tuesday.

3 She has to be in Amsterdam by 6.00 pm / 8.00 pm.

4 She's returning to Brussels on Thursday / Saturday.

5 She'll be travelling on her own / with her son.

6 She wants to pay cash / by credit card.

UNIT **7**

B 🎧 🎲 ▶ Ecoutez encore une fois Isabelle et complétez le formulaire de réservation suivant:

ALLER SIMPLE ☐   ALLER-RETOUR ☐

ALLER

ORIGINE:_____

DESTINATION:_____

DATE:_____

HEURE DE DÉPART:_____

HEURE D'ARRIVÉE:_____

PASSAGERS: ADULTE(S): ☐

ENFANT(S) −15ANS: ☐

BÉBÉ(S) −3ANS: ☐

RETOUR

ORIGINE:_____

DESTINATION:_____

DATE:_____

HEURE DE DÉPART:_____

HEURE D'ARRIVÉE:_____

PASSAGERS: ADULTE(S): ☐

ENFANT(S) −15ANS: ☐

BÉBÉ(S) −3ANS: ☐

PRIX TOTAL (EN EUROS): ☐

PAIEMENT: LIQUIDE ☐   CHÈQUE ☐   CARTE DE CRÉDIT ☐

NOM: *ISABELLE MOUTIER*

C 🎲 ▶ Pouvez-vous associer les questions suivantes et leurs réponses?

1   A quelle heure est le premier train pour Paris?

2   A quelle heure est le prochain vol pour Londres?

3   Le train pour Marseilles part de quel quai?

4   C'est combien l'aller-retour pour Valenciennes?

5   Je voudrais une place 'fumeur', s'il vous plaît.

6   Le vol Londres–Paris arrive à quel aéroport exactement?

a   Il part du quai numéro 14.

b   Je suis désolé, monsieur, tous nos services sont désormais non-fumeurs.

c   Roissy–Charles-de-Gaulle.

d   Il est à 15h40 du quai numéro 3.

e   26€.

f   Dans 45 minutes. L'embarquement commence dans 20 minutes, porte numéro 48.

D  Voici des réponses données aux voyageurs à l'aéroport. Can you work out what the questions were?

1   Le prochain vol pour Londres est à 9h50.

2   Le vol AF541? C'est porte 22.

3   L'embarquement commence à 14h20.

4   Il arrive à Edimbourg à 17h50.

5   Je suis désolé, mais tous nos vols sont non-fumeurs.

6   Oui, le personnel de bord est bilingue.

5 On peut louer une voiture…

A Patrick has just arrived at Valenciennes station and needs to hire a car. Look at the following words and expressions, listen to Patrick and pick out the words you hear:

permis de conduire

clé

grand

louer

vol

aujourd'hui

250.29€

location

sorte

formulaire

kilométrage limité

lundi

emplacement

UNIT **7**

B Ecoutez encore une fois Patrick et complétez les blancs dans le texte ci-dessous:

Claire: Bonjour monsieur, je peux vous ⬭ ?

Patrick: Oui, bonjour, je voudrais louer une ⬭ , s'il vous plaît.

Claire: Oui, pour ⬭ exactement?

Patrick: A partir d'aujourd'hui jusqu'à la ⬭ prochaine, au 23 exactement, jeudi 23.

Claire: (*typing in*)... du 16/09 au 23/09, d'accord... et quel ⬭ de véhicule désirez-vous?

Patrick: Le plus ⬭ modèle, je voyage seul.

Claire: Très bien, (*typing in*) catégorie A. Alors, le prix pour cette location est de ⬭ euros et il comprend la TVA, le kilométrage limité à ⬭ km et la garantie en cas de vol. Le véhicule est une Peugeot 206 verte.

Patrick: C'est bon, je la prends.

Claire: OK, vous avez votre permis de conduire, monsieur?

Patrick: Oui, bien sûr. Le voilà.

Claire: Merci. Alors voilà la liste des différentes options que vous pouvez choisir et qui ne sont pas ⬭ dans la location et un formulaire d'informations à remplir.

A moment later...

Claire: Merci monsieur. A quelle heure pensez-vous ramener la voiture jeudi prochain?

Patrick: Vers ⬭ .

Claire: Parfait, alors voici vos ⬭ et votre clé. Le véhicule se trouve sur le parking de la ⬭ , à l'emplacement 12.

Patrick: Je vous remercie, à bientôt mademoiselle.

Claire: Au revoir, monsieur.

C (A C) 🖋 ▶ Here is the list of additional items Claire gave Patrick. Some details are missing. Look at the French version then try to complete the English one beneath.

Europcar

CONDITIONS TARIFAIRES

Le conducteur doit être âgé au minimum de 21 ans. Votre tarif comprend:

- TVA comprise
- Participation aux frais d'immatriculation (PFI)
- Garantie contractuelle en cas de vol (TW)
- Garantie contractuelle en cas de dommages au véhicule (CDW).
  Hors Franchise Non Rachetable. Merci de vérifier au départ de votre location.

Options: vous devrez les valider au départ de votre location
(non incluses dans le tarif ci-dessus, TVA non incluse):

- Assurance jeune conducteur 16.72€ par jour
- Assurance effets personnels 1.67€ par jour
- Super Garantie contractuelle en cas de dommages au véhicule (CDW)
  et Garantie contractuelle en cas de vol (TW) 4.18€ par jour
- Super Garantie contractuelle en cas de dommages au véhicule (CDW)
  et Garantie contractuelle en cas de vol (TW) 3.34€ par jour
- Assurance Personnes Transportées 2.39€ par jour
- Conducteur Additionnel 2.09€ par jour

CONDITIONS

The driver should be _____ than 21 years of age.
Rental charges include:

- VAT _____
- Licences and fees
- _____ waiver
- _____ waiver. Unwaivable charges may apply: please check at pick-up time.

You may select additional items at your pick-up location
(not included in reservation price, VAT _____ _____):

- _____ driver cover 16.72€ per day
- Super Personal _____ Cover 1.67€ per day
- Super Collision Damage Waiver and Theft Waiver 4.18€ per day
- Super Collision Damage Waiver and Theft Waiver 3.34€ per day
- Personal Accident cover 2.39€ per day
- _____ _____ 2.09€ per day

Voyages, voyages UNIT 7

D Vous avez une bonne mémoire? Look at the picture below. Have a look at the words for about 90 seconds then close your book. How many of them can you remember?
Work with a partner and try to jot down as many as possible.

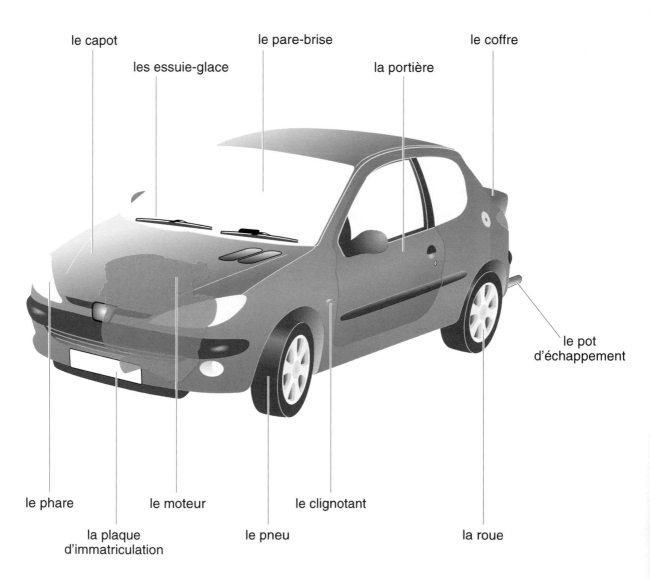

le capot

les essuie-glace

le pare-brise

la portière

le coffre

le pot d'échappement

le phare

le moteur

la plaque d'immatriculation

le pneu

le clignotant

la roue

E 🎲 ▶ Des problèmes et encore des problèmes! How would you explain the following problems? Try to match the expressions with the pictures.

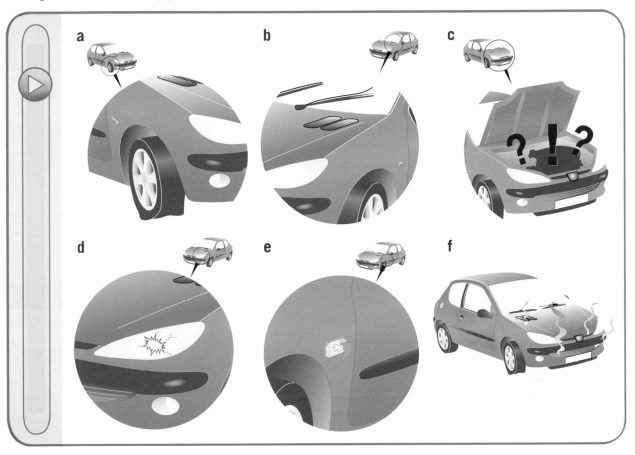

1 Le moteur fait un bruit bizarre.

2 J'ai un phare cassé.

3 J'ai un pneu crevé.

4 Ma voiture est en panne.

5 Mes essuie-glace ne marchent plus.

6 Le clignotant ne marche pas.

UNIT 7

Découverte de la FRANCOPHONIE

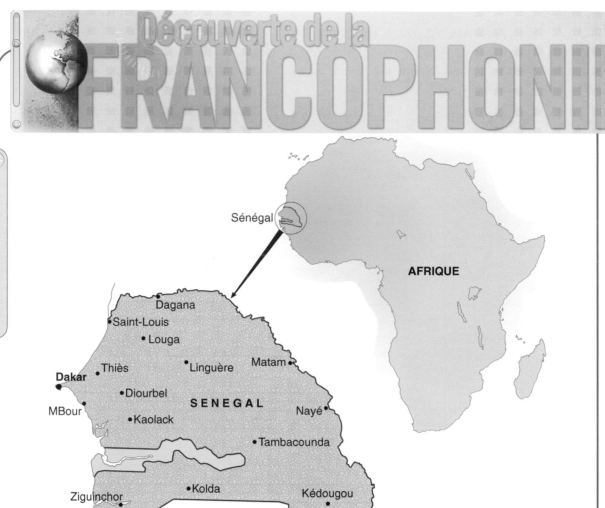

Sénégal

AFRIQUE

SENEGAL

Dagana
Saint-Louis
Louga
Thiès · Linguère · Matam
Dakar ·
Diourbel
MBour · Kaolack · Nayé
· Tambacounda
Ziguinchor · Kolda · Kédougou

Le Sénégal

A [AC] 🎧 ○ Lisez les informations sur le transport et les communications au Sénégal. Read the paragraph on page 129 then try to find the words in bold in the grid. They are hidden horizontally and vertically. **Bonne chance!**

Bienvenue
Ville de Dakar

F	M	A	R	I	T	I	M	E	T	M
E	R	V	O	W	U	R	T	L	U	Y
R	E	N	T	R	E	T	I	E	N	R
R	S	T	Y	A	R	O	B	M	V	O
O	E	A	S	L	O	L	I	M	A	U
V	A	A	Z	R	O	U	T	E	S	T
I	U	E	P	F	I	L	U	H	I	I
A	E	R	O	D	R	O	M	E	S	E
I	F	I	J	U	P	Y	E	N	L	R
R	A	E	B	E	S	N	E	B	L	I
E	T	N	E	P	A	Y	S	A	E	S

Transport et communications

A l'indépendance, le Sénégal disposait d'un **réseau** de transport terrestre d'assez bonne qualité. L'équipement du **pays** s'est poursuivi par l'extension du réseau **routier**. Celui-ci couvre pratiquement l'ensemble du territoire avec environ 14 000 km de routes, dont 27 % **bitumées**. Depuis 1980 s'est fait jour la volonté d'investir dans **l'entretien** du réseau existant plutôt que dans la poursuite de l'extension du réseau bitumé, ce qui a surtout permis la réfection **des routes** nationales, dont le rôle économique est déterminant. Le trafic fluvio-maritime se limite au port de Ziguinchor, ceux de Kaolack et de Saint-Louis attendant, sans grand espoir, une relance des activités économiques régionales. Le port **maritime** de Dakar, avec un trafic marchand de plus de 6 millions de tonnes, reste la seule structure fonctionnelle. Le trafic **aérien** est concentré sur l'aéroport international de Dakar, relié aux **aérodromes** de Ziguinchor et de Saint-Louis. Le réseau **ferroviaire**, surtout dynamique sur la ligne Dakar–Bamako et pour l'évacuation des phosphates de Thiès, n'est pas concurrentiel pour le trafic passager.

Voyages, voyages UNIT 7

B Voici quelques informations sur la ville de Dakar. Lisez-les et répondez aux questions.

Se déplacer à Dakar...

LES TAXIS

A partir de l'Aéroport L.S. Senghor pour rejoindre le centre ville: 2 500 FCFA* de 5h à minuit, 3 000 FCFA* à partir de minuit. De 500 à 1 500 FCFA* maximum pour se déplacer en ville.

Taxis Brousse: environ 1 000 FCFA* les 100 kms

GARE ROUTIERE: Avenue Malick Sy
– Dakar–Ziguinchor: 7h
– Dakar–St Louis: 3h
– Dakar–MBour: 1h30

LES TAXIS

Peints en bleu et jaune, les cars rapides circulent surtout en banlieue. Le prix du ticket est très abordable; il varie entre 50 et 150 FCFA.
Les bus verts de la Sotrac ont des tarifs qui varient entre 150 et 200 FCFA. Avec une fréquence de 10 à 15 minutes, ces bus offrent la possibilité de se déplacer dans tout Dakar et sa banlieue.

*Francs CFA (Communauté Financière Africaine)

1 How much would it cost to go from the airport to the city centre by taxi at 5.00 pm?

2 From what time will you have to pay 3000 FCFA for the same journey?

3 Where is the coach station located?

4 There are two sorts of fast buses. What colours are they?

5 Which fast bus would you use if you wanted to travel within the city centre?

6 How often does it run?

Voyages, voyages

GLOSSARY

Nouns

adulte (m)	adult
aérodrome (m)	airfield
aéroport (m)	airport
année (f)	year
après-midi (m/f)	afternoon
arrivée (f)	arrival
assurance (f)	insurance
avion (m)	aeroplane
banque (m)	bank
bateau (f)	boat
bébé (m)	baby
bruit (m)	noise
bus (m)	bus
camping-car (m)	camper-van
capot (m)	bonnet
car (m)	coach
carte (f) **de crédit**	credit card
chameau (m)	camel
chèque (m)	cheque
clé/clef (f)	key
clignotant (m)	indicator
coffre (m)	boot (car)
départ (m)	departure
dommages (mpl)	damage
embarquement (m)	boarding
emplacement (m)	space/place
enfant (m)	child
entretien (m)	maintenance
essuie-glace (m)	windscreen wiper
formulaire (m)	form
gare (f)	station
heure (f)	hour; time
kilométrage (m)	mileage
location (f)	hire/rental
métro (m)	underground
moteur (m)	engine
moto (f)	motorbike
moyen (m) **de transport**	means of transport
pare-brise (m)	windscreen
passager (m)	passenger
pays (m)	country
permis (m) **de conduire**	driving licence
phare (m)	headlight
piscine (f)	swimming pool
plaque (f) **d'immatriculation**	registration plate
pneu (m)	tyre
portière (f)	car door
pot (m) **d'échappement**	exhaust pipe
prix (m)	price
réseau (m)	network
roue (f)	wheel
route (f)	road
soirée (f)	evening
sorte (f)	sort
temps (m)	weather
travail (m)	work
train (m)	train
traversée (f)	crossing
TVA (f)	VAT
type (m)	type
vacances (fpl)	holidays
vélo (m)	bicycle
voiture (f)	car
vol (m)	flight; theft

Adjectives

abordable	affordable
aérien(ne)	air
bitumé(e)	asphalted
bleu(e)	blue
compris(e)	included
crevé(e)	flat (tyre)
ferroviaire	railway
grand(e)	big/tall
illimité(e)	unlimited
jaune	yellow
limité(e)	limited
petit(e)	small
prochain(e)	next
rapide	fast
seul(e)	alone
vert(e)	green

Verbs

aider	to help
arriver	to arrive
casser	to break
choisir	to choose
comprendre	to include; to understand
louer	to hire
marcher	to walk; to work (operate)
partir	to leave/to depart
peindre	to paint
ramener	to bring back
réserver	to book
vérifier	to check
voyager	to travel

Expressions

aller-retour	return (ticket)
aller simple	single (ticket)
aujourd'hui	today
combien de temps	how long
combien	how much/many
en cas de	in case of
en liquide	cash
en panne	broken down
là-bas	over there
quand	when
quinze jours	a fortnight
vers	about; towards
voilà	here it is/there you go
voyage organisé	package holiday

Voyages, voyages UNIT 7

🎧 LOOKING FORWARD

In **Unit 8**, we will be looking at hotel facilities, booking hotel rooms, writing formal letters and making complaints at the hotel.

To prepare, have a look at the following information. Can you work out what these facilities are? (Use a dictionary if you're not sure.)

Services de l'hôtel

En plein cœur du centre ville notre hôtel vous propose dans ses 60 chambres:

la climatisation • la salle de bain individuelle • les 6 chaînes françaises • les chaînes «Canal Satellite»

Les autres services:

journaux quotidiens • restauration rapide à toute heure • blanchisserie • parking privé et surveillé 24h/24

UNIT 8
Hôtel du Lion d'Or

By the end of this unit you will be able to:

- Explain what you require when booking accommodation
- Understand hotel facilities and talk about them
- Use adjectives to describe things or people
- Make complaints verbally and in writing
- Give your opinion

1 Vous vous souvenez?

A Quelle heure est-il?

1   2   3   4   5

18:30

B 🎧 ✍️ ▶ Vous entendez (hear) les annonces suivantes.
Pour chaque message, où vous trouvez-vous exactement?
A l'aéroport? Sur le ferry? A la gare?

1 ⬭ 2 ⬭ 3 ⬭

4 ⬭ 5 ⬭

C 🎧 ▶ **Vrai ou faux?** Ecoutez encore une fois les annonces
précédentes et dites si les affirmations suivantes sont vraies ou fausses:

		Vrai	Faux
1	All flights cancelled because of a strike.	⬭	⬭
2	Train to Paris arriving Platform 4.	⬭	⬭
3	Flight to London ready for boarding Gate 76.	⬭	⬭
4	The 6.12 train to Perpignan will be leaving from Platform 2.	⬭	⬭
5	Leaving Portsmouth, all car passengers to leave their vehicles and go to upper decks.	⬭	⬭

2 Tout d'abord, il faut chercher un hôtel

A 🎲 ▶ Regardez la page Internet en face (opposite). Pour chaque situation, choisissez les critères de sélection correspondants.

1 You are looking for a hotel near the airport and you want air conditioning.

2 You want a hotel by the sea with air conditioning. You are in a wheelchair.

3 You are taking your family and your little dog to the countryside.

4 You'd like to find a place in the city centre. Although you're taking your car, you'd rather leave it in the car park and use the underground.

5 You want a quiet hotel in the mountains where you can have all your meals.

B Ecoutez les trois messages laissés sur le répondeur de l'Office du Tourisme de la région Provence-Alpes-Côte d'Azur. Pour chaque message, essayez de compléter le formulaire ci-dessous en anglais.

Name:		Telephone:
Place/town requested:		
Requirements:		

LEARNING TIP:
Je voudrais…

When you talk about what you're looking for or what you require, try to vary your vocabulary by using expressions such as:

**Je cherche… /
Nous cherchons…**

**Je désire… /
Nous désirons…**

**J'aimerais… /
Nous aimerions…**

**Je voudrais… /
Nous voudrions…**

**Je préfère… /
Nous préférons…**

**J'ai besoin de… /
Nous avons besoin de…**

C Ecoutez encore une fois les trois messages précédents et essayez d'associer les phrases qui sont à gauche avec celles qui sont à droite:

1 mais pas à Nice même

2 un endroit avec beaucoup d'espace

3 nous cherchons un petit hôtel

4 nous avons besoin d'une chambre au rez-de-chaussée

5 je recherche un hôtel dans les montagnes

6 je voudrais aussi un bon restaurant

a pour que les enfants puissent jouer

b car ma femme est dans une chaise roulante

c car j'aimerais goûter les spécialités de la région

d car il y a trop de monde

e si possible près de la plage et des magasins

f je n'aime pas la mer

UNIT **8**

You'll find additional practice to help you with holiday accommodation on our website.

D Vous téléphonez à l'Office du Tourisme pour obtenir des renseignements (information) sur les hôtels. Malheureusement, le bureau est fermé et vous devez laisser un message sur le répondeur. Préparez votre message sur papier. Vous pouvez ensuite l'enregistrer (record) ou le lire à votre partenaire.

▶▶ Say hello and explain that you are looking for a hotel near Monaco, but not in Monaco itself. You would like a comfortable hotel with swimming pool and space so that the children can play. You would like to visit the region and therefore you need some information about the area. You prefer half-board because you'd like to go to different restaurants and try Provençal specialities. Ask them to call you. Give your name and telephone number.

3 Cet hôtel a l'air sympa!

A Vous avez trouvé (you've found) des informations sur un hôtel près de Saint-Omer. Regardez les mots (words) et les expressions en anglais et trouvez leurs équivalents en français dans le texte.

- pond
- conservatory
- 5km from St Omer
- four-poster bed
- to relax
- bedrooms
- business
- century
- accommodation
- family rooms

Château Tilques ★★★★ *Restaurant Le Vert Mesnil*

Château Tilques ★★★★
Restaurant Le Vert Mesnil

Le château, bâti en 1891 sur les ruines d'un manoir du 17ème siècle, offre le charme et le style d'une résidence luxueuse.

Ses 53 chambres, son restaurant gastronomique, ses élégantes salles de réception et de conférence forment un emplacement unique pour combiner les affaires et le plaisir, au cœur de la région Nord Pas-de-Calais.

Sur place, nous vous proposons notre tennis, notre putting-green 9 trous et notre boulodrome.

L'hôtel Château de Tilques vous émerveillera par son grand parc boisé, son étang poissonneux, ses oiseaux d'ornement et exotiques.

L'hôtel

53 chambres, dont la majorité se situent dans le château, offrent un compromis parfait entre l'ancien et le contemporain. Elles sont toutes équipées de TV couleur et téléphone à ligne directe.

Diverses solutions vous sont proposées:
- Baldaquin
- Chambres familiales avec terrasse ou balcon
- Suite

Plusieurs formules sont à votre disposition:
- Hébergement simple
- Séjour gastronomique
- Séminaires
- Soirées diverses

Vous apprécierez le cadre qui vous est offert, notamment pour vous détendre dans le calme de notre salon.

Le petit déjeuner buffet est servi dans le jardin d'hiver avec vue sur le parc.

B  Ali décide de téléphoner au Château de Tilques pour obtenir des informations sur les tarifs et offres spéciales. Ecoutez-le et notez les mots que vous entendez.

> juin – compris – prix – séjour – 149€ – lendemain –
> semaine – simple – nuit – treizième – gratuite

C Ecoutez le dialogue encore une fois et répondez aux questions suivantes en anglais.

1 How much is a luxury room?

2 Does the price include breakfast?

3 What does the séjour gastronomique consist of?

4 How much does the second night cost per person?

5 How much is the third night?

6 What does Ali have to do to confirm his booking?

D Comment dit-on en français? Les éléments de réponse sont mélangés. A vous de les remettre (put back) dans le bon ordre...

1 I'd like to book a double room   double / je / une / voudrais / réserver / chambre

2 How much is a single room?   combien / une / simple / c'est / chambre / ?

3 Is breakfast included?   le / compris / petit déjeuner / est / ?

4 Is there a swimming pool?   piscine / y / une / il / a / ?

5 The third night is free   la / gratuite / nuit / troisième / est

6 Can I confirm my reservation by fax?   peux / réservation / par fax / je / ma / confirmer / ?

Hôtel du Lion d'Or UNIT 8

There's more help
with adjectives on
www.accesslanguages.com

E Vous téléphonez au Château de Tilques pour faire une réservation. Travaillez avec votre partenaire et complétez la conversation ci-dessous:

Réceptionniste: Château de Tilques, bonjour.
You: *Greet the receptionist and say that you would like to book a room.*
Réceptionniste: Oui, pour quelle date, monsieur/madame?
You: *Say it's for Friday 27th June.*
Réceptionniste: D'accord. Pour combien de nuits?
You: *Say it's for two nights only.*
Réceptionniste: Pour une seule personne, monsieur/madame?
You: *Say no, it's for two people; you'd like a double room with an en-suite bathroom.*
Réceptionniste: Pas de problème. Alors la chambre fait 145€ et le petit déjeuner est à 12€ par personne.
You: *Say that's fine, you'll have breakfast both mornings.*
Réceptionniste: Parfait. Est-ce que je peux avoir votre nom et aussi le numéro de votre carte de crédit pour confirmer la réservation?
You: *Of course! [Then give your name and spell it…]*

4 Les adjectifs

A C'est votre tour! Tout d'abord, essayez (try) d'associer un nom et un adjectif. Attention au masculin, féminin, singulier ou pluriel.

le vin	verte
la plante	difficiles
les spécialités	confortable
des films	heureux
un hôtel	rouge
un poisson	blanc
des devoirs	italiennes
un homme	français

Un *petit* hôtel *confortable*… (Les adjectifs)

Adjectives are words used to describe things and people. Words like *tall*, *modern*, *practical*, *red*, etc. are adjectives. In French, adjectives change according to what they describe: they can be masculine, feminine, singular or plural. Here are some examples:

Adjectives	Masc. sing.	Fem. sing.	Masc. plur.	Fem. plur.
tall	grand.	grand**e**	grand**s**	grand**es**
big	gros	gros**se**	gros	gros**ses**
practical	pratique	pratique	pratique**s**	pratique**s**
delicious	délicieux	délicieu**se**	délicieux	délicieu**ses**
sporty	sportif	sporti**ve**	sportif**s**	sporti**ves**
proud	fier	fi**ère**	fier**s**	fi**ères**
white	blanc	blan**che**	blanc**s**	blan**ches**
new	nouveau	nou**velle**	nou**veaux**	nou**velles**

In French, most adjectives are placed *after* the word they describe:

Il a un accent **anglais**.	*He has an **English** accent.*
C'est une voiture **bleue**.	*It is a **blue** car.*
une femme **élégante** et **charmante**	*an **elegant** and **charming** woman*

There are some exceptions. Adjectives like **jeune** (*young*), **petit** (*small*), **nouveau** (*new*), **vieux** (*old*), **gros** (*big/fat*), **beau** (*beautiful/handsome*) are placed before the word they describe, just as in English:

Je voudrais une **grosse** glace.	*I'd like a **big** ice cream.*
C'est une **belle petite** maison.	*It's a **beautiful little** house.*

You can mix adjectives from the table and from the list above:

C'est une **belle** femme **riche**.	*She's a **beautiful, rich** woman.*
Il y a un **gros** chat **blanc** là-bas.	*There is a **big white** cat over there.*

B ✏ ▷ Maintenant, essayez de compléter les phrases suivantes en utilisant les adjectifs entre parenthèses (in brackets):

1 C'est un hotel (spacieux / confortable).

2 C'est une chambre (petite / moderne).

3 Il y a un parc (beau / fleuri).

4 Il y a un restaurant près d'ici? (chinois)

5 Je n'aime pas l'eau, je préfère l'eau (gazeuse / plate).

6 J'adore les maisons (vieilles / romaines).

UNIT **8**

141

C 🎲 ✏️ ▷ Voici la description d'une chambre Novotel. Pouvez-vous identifier et noter tous les adjectifs qui se trouvent dans ce texte?

Harmonie: chambre à coucher, chambre à vivre.

La chambre Novotel est un véritable studio de 25 m²: entrée penderie, grand lit, coin salon avec canapé lit, espace bureau avec ligne téléphonique directe, prise d'ordinateur, TV couleur, réveil automatique, mini-bar, climatisation.

Un espace de détente fait de matières chaleureuses aux couleurs gaies.

Ambiance: la douceur de vivre dans la salle de bains.

La salle de bains Novotel est un concentré d'innovation et de bien-être: lavabo et baignoire avec douche alliant confort et design, robinetterie-mitigeur, éclairage modulable, sèche-cheveux, grandes serviettes douceur.

D 🎲 ✏️ ▷ Maintenant, lisez la traduction anglaise. Essayez de compléter les blancs en utilisant les éléments du texte ci-dessus (above):

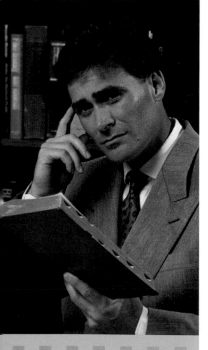

Harmony: a room to sleep in and a room to live in.

With its 25 m² area, a Novotel room is virtually a studio apartment, comprising an entrance with hanging space, double (   ), lounge area with (   ), office space with (   ), computer (   ), colour TV, automatic wake-up alarm, mini-bar and (   ).
It's a relaxing environment created with comfortable materials in cheerful colours.

Atmosphere: a life of luxury in the bathroom.
The Novotel bathroom is a focus for innovation and comfort: the (   ) and (   ) with (   ) combine comfort with good design: the (   ) are mixer units, the (   ) is adjustable and there's a (   ) and huge soft (   ) on offer.

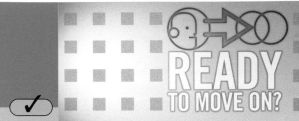

READY TO MOVE ON?

✓

Check that you can...

- find out information about hotels
- express your specific requirements about accommodation
- give simple explanations about what you would or wouldn't like
- use adjectives when describing things or people
- make a hotel booking.

LEARNING TIP:
Ça marche!

When something 'doesn't work' in English, the French use the verb *to walk*:

La télévision ne marche pas.
The TV doesn't work.

Mon balladeur ne marche plus.
My personal stereo doesn't work any more.

Ça ne marche jamais.
It never works.

5 Ça ne m'impressionne pas!

A A C ▷ Les choses vont mal! Associez les images ci-dessous avec la phrase correspondante en français:

1 L'ampoule de la chambre a grillé.

2 Il n'y a pas de serviette dans la salle de bains.

3 La chambre est trop petite.

4 Le lit n'est pas fait.

5 La télévision ne marche pas.

UNIT **8**

B Lisez la lettre ci-dessous et choisissez le résumé qui correspond au contenu de cette lettre:

a Nathalie Dhaussy is not very happy about her recent stay at the Victoria Hotel and is asking for compensation because of the serious shortcomings of the hotel.

b Nathalie Dhaussy is complaining to the manager of the Victoria Hotel. She is complaining about the shortcomings of the hotel and also the unhelpfulness of the staff. She is not asking for compensation but for a letter of apology from the Manager.

Aulnoye-Aymeries,
le 25 mars

Madame, Monsieur,

Suite à mon séjour dans votre hôtel la semaine dernière, je voudrais vous faire part de quelques commentaires sur la qualité des prestations offertes dans votre établissement.

Pour des raisons professionnelles, je voyage beaucoup en Europe et par conséquent, fréquente de nombreux hôtels. Les trois jours passés dans votre établissement n'ont été qu'une série d'erreurs et d'incidents dont voici quelques exemples:

La voiture que j'avais louée est tombée en panne sur l'autoroute. J'ai donc appelé votre hôtel de mon portable pour vous informer que j'arriverai après 21h00. La réceptionniste m'a dit qu'il n'y avait aucun problème, que ma chambre serait retenue. Quand je suis arrivée, à 21h15, ma chambre avait été louée à d'autres personnes. La seule chambre disponible était une petite chambre sans salle de bains, ni douche, ni toilettes.

Je suis ensuite descendue au restaurant et là, le Maître d'Hôtel m'a dit qu'il était trop tard pour un repas chaud. Votre réceptionniste m'avait pourtant promis qu'exceptionnellement, le chef me préparerait quelque chose. Votre Maître d'Hôtel n'a rien voulu savoir et était de toute évidence pressé de terminer son service et de partir. Je suis donc retournée dans ma chambre l'estomac vide.

Durant la nuit, il faisait tellement froid dans la chambre que j'ai dû utiliser la couverture qui était dans l'armoire. Le chauffage ne marchait pas…
Je pourrais continuer cette liste mais je pense que ces exemples sont déjà suffisants.

Je vous serais donc reconnaissante de bien vouloir me rembourser une partie de ma note qui s'élevait à 228€ au total.

Dans l'attente de vous lire prochainement, veuillez agréer, Madame, Monsieur, l'expression de mes sentiments distingués.

Nathalie Dhaussy

Practise complaining about your hotel problems on our website!

C AC ▶ Parmi les problèmes ci-dessous, quels sont ceux qui ne sont pas mentionnés dans la lettre?

1 The room was small.

2 The hotel is too noisy.

3 The food was awful.

4 There was no en-suite bathroom.

5 The room was stuffy.

6 The head waiter was unhelpful.

7 The room was given to somebody else.

D Comment expliqueriez-vous (would you explain) les situations suivantes au personnel de l'hôtel? Aidez-vous d'un dictionnaire et des mots-clés.

1   mot-clé: la douche

4   mot-clé: le bruit

2   mot-clé: fuir

5   mot-clé: coincée

3   mot-clé: le chauffage

E ✍ ▶ A votre tour! You are staying for two weeks at the Bellevue Hotel in Annecy. You are not very happy with the hotel. As you'll be away for a couple of days over the weekend, you decide to leave a note of your complaints at reception in the hope that they will find a solution to the problems before you return. Write the note in French.

- The room is too small.
- There is no view over the lake.
- The night club downstairs is far too noisy.
- The food is always cold.

LEARNING TIP:
La correspondance commerciale:

When writing to someone you don't know, start your letter with **Madame, Monsieur**. Do not use **Cher/chère...** (*Dear...*).

To end a commercial or business letter in French, use the expression **Veuillez agréer, Madame, Monsieur, l'expression de mes sentiments distingués** (*Yours faithfully/sincerely*).

Découverte de la FRANCOPHONIE

St-Denis
Ste-Suzanne
Le Port • La Possession
St-André
St-Paul
Salazie
St-Benoît
St-Gilles-les-Bains
LA RÉUNION
Cilaos
Ste-Rose
St-Leu
Entre-Deux
Etang-Salé • St-Louis • Le Tampon
St-Pierre
St-Joseph
St-Philippe

Hôtel du Lion d'Or

L'Ile de la Réunion

A Lisez les informations sur l'Ile de la Réunion ci-dessous. Pouvez-vous expliquer en anglais à quoi correspondent les chiffres et les mots suivants?

1 700 km   **2** 9 200 km   **3** la saison «fraîche»

4 3 000 000   **5** 30 km   **6** Africains, Malgaches, Chinois

www.accesslanguages.com has links to websites of tourist offices throughout the Francophone world.

Situation géographique

La Réunion est une île de l'océan indien. Parmi les îles voisines, on trouve Madagascar (700km à l'ouest), l'île Maurice (200km à l'Est) et les Seychelles (bien plus loin au Nord). Paris est à 9200km à vol d'oiseau. La Réunion est un département français d'outre mer. Le chef-lieu de l'île est Saint-Denis.

Climat

La Réunion connaît un climat tropical. On distingue deux saisons principales, la saison dite «fraîche», de mai à novembre et la saison dite «chaude», de novembre à avril. Pendant la saison fraîche les averses sont moins fréquentes et les températures moins lourdes. La saison chaude est la période où il fait le moins souvent beau, les sommets des massifs montagneux se couvrent très tôt d'un épais manteau nuageux et l'air ambiant est parfois très humide.

Géographie

La Réunion est une île volcanique. Elle a surgi des eaux il y a 3 millions d'années avec le Piton des Neiges (3070m). Au fil des siècles, l'activité volcanique a sculpté les paysages intérieurs. En s'affaissant, le Piton des Neiges a créé les cirques de Mafate, Cilaos et Salazie. L'île est constituée d'un second massif montagneux, le Piton de la Fournaise, qui est toujours actif. Les deux volcans sont séparés par la plaine des Cafres et la plaine des Palmistes.

La Réunion compte 207km de côte dont 30km de plage. Les plus belles se situent sur Saint-Gilles et ses environs: Boucan Canot, les Roches Noires, l'Hermitage et la Saline-les-Bains.

Population

La Réunion compte 710 000 habitants. L'une des grandes particularités de l'île est la diversité de sa population. Venus des quatre coins de l'océan indien, Africains, Blancs, Indiens, Tamouls, Malgaches, Comoriens et Chinois se sont retrouvés à la Réunion où ils continuent de faire vivre leurs traditions.

B  Voici le descriptif complet de l'appartement que vous avez loué sur l'Ile de la Réunion. Vous avez fait une liste d'objets à emporter (to take with you); parmi ces objets, certains (some of them) ne sont pas nécessaires car ils sont fournis avec l'appartement. Lesquels?

suncream	CD/cassette player	can opener
coat hangers	plastic cutlery and plates	hair dryer
bath towels	bottle opener	matches
tea towels	iron	

Vue de la terrasse

La salle de bains

Le salon

La chambre

Surface: 32 m^2

Terrasse Surface: 4,5 m^2

Prix: 800€ par semaine (7 nuits)

Equipement de cuisine: Réfrigérateur, four électrique, 2 plaques électriques, micro-ondes

Vaisselle pour 6 personnes: bols, tasses à café, verres, assiettes plates, assiettes creuses, assiettes à dessert, couverts

Ustensiles et batterie de cuisine: cuillère en bois, ouvre-boîtes, limonadier, pichet, saladier, poêle, casserole, passoire, bouilloire, dessous-de-plat, planche à découper, éponge, bassine

Literies: 2 banquettes lit 1 personne

Chambre: 2 lits simples, chaises

Salon: table basse, salle à manger (table + 4 chaises), cendrier, télévision 36 cm + télécommande décoration intérieure: miroir, cadres, vase, bouquet de fleurs

Terrasse: 1 table, 4 chaises

Rangements: placard, repose-valise, meuble cuisine, coffre-fort, cintres. Linge de lit et linge de bain fournis pour 7 jours, pour 2 personnes

Salle de bains:
- sèche-cheveux
- étendoir à linge
- WC séparés

Equipement d'entretien:
- Poubelles
- seau espagnol + serpillière
- balai
- pelle + balayette

UNIT **8**

149

C 🔊 👥 ▶ **A votre avis...** Voudriez-vous louer cet appartement pour vos vacances? Relisez le descriptif et les informations sur l'Ile de la Réunion. Qu'en pensez-vous? (*What do you think of it?*) Discutez avec votre partenaire.

Voici quelques expressions pour vous aider:

Je pense que...
Je trouve que...
C'est ... (+ adj.)
Ça a l'air... (+ adj.)
J'aime... / Je n'aime pas... / Je préfère...
Je suis d'accord / Je ne suis pas d'accord
A mon avis, ... / Selon moi, ...
Mais... / Cependant...
Au contraire,...

Check that you can...
- explain problems at the hotel
- make a formal complaint
- give your opinion of a place.

GLOSSARY 🎧

Nouns

ampoule (f)	bulb	**casserole** (f)	saucepan
armoire (f)	cupboard	**cendrier** (m)	ashtray
assiette (f)	plate	**chaise** (f) **roulante**	wheelchair
autoroute (f)	motorway	**chambre** (f)	bedroom
baignoire (f)	bath	**chauffage** (m)	heating
baldaquin (m)	four-poster (bed)	**cintre** (m)	coat hanger
banquette (f)	seat/bench	**climatisation** (f)	air conditioning
bouilloire (f)	kettle	**coffre-fort** (m)	safe
bruit (m) noise		**contenu** (m)	content
cadre (m)	frame	**couverts** (mpl)	cutlery
campagne (f)	countryside	**couverture** (f)	blanket
		douche (f)	shower

GLOSSARY

éclairage (m)	lighting	**séjour** (m)	stay
endroit (m)	place	**serviette** (f)	towel
étang (m)	pond	**siècle** (m)	century
étendoir (m) **à linge**	clothes dryer	**soirée** (f)	evening/party
hébergement (m)	accommodation	**tasse** (f)	cup
jardin (m) **d'hiver**	conservatory	**traduction** (f)	translation
lavabo (m)	washbasin		
lendemain (m)	following day		
limonadier (m)	bottle opener		
linge (m)	linen		
mer (f)	sea		

Adjectives

mer (f)	sea	**beau/belle**	handsome/beautiful
montagne (f)	mountain	**blanc(he)**	white
note (f)	bill (hotel)	**boisé(e)**	woody
mot-clé (m)	key word	**bruyant(e)**	noisy
nuit (f)	night	**chaque**	each, every
oiseau (m)	bird	**coincé(e)**	stuck
ordinateur (m)	computer	**disponible**	available
ouvre-boîtes (m)	can opener	**fier/fière**	proud
parenthèse (f)	bracket	**fleuri(e)**	in flower/flowery
passoire (f)	colander	**fourni(e)**	provided
penderie (f)	hall cupboard/wardrobe	**gazeux/gazeuse**	sparkling
petit déjeuner (m)	breakfast	**grand(e)**	tall/big
plage (f)	beach	**gratuit(e)**	free of charge
poêle (f)	frying pan	**gros(se)**	big/fat
portable (m)	mobile (phone)	**heureux/heureuse**	happy
poubelle (f)	bin	**jeune**	young
prise (f)	socket	**nombreux/nombreuse**	numerous
réfrigérateur (m)	fridge	**nouveau/nouvelle**	new
répondeur (m)	answerphone	**petit(e)**	small
rez-de-chaussée (f)	ground floor	**plat(e)**	flat/still (water)
salle à manger (f)	dining room	**proche**	near
seau (m)	bucket	**suivant(e)**	following
sèche-cheveux (m)	hair dryer	**vert(e)**	green
		vieux/vieille	old

UNIT **8**

GLOSSARY

Verbs

associer	to link/to match
chercher	to look for
choisir	to choose
cocher	to tick
désirer	to want
écouter	to listen
entendre	to hear
essayer	to try
être pressé(e)	to be in a hurry
fuir	to leak
griller	to grill/to fuse
marcher	to walk/to work (appliance)
mélanger	to mix
passer	to spend (time)
remettre	to put back
retourner	to go back
se détendre	to relax
trouver	to find

Expressions

à proximité	nearby
au bord de	by the side of
au cœur de	in the heart of
car	because
ci-dessous	below
ci-dessus	above
en demi-pension	half board
en pension complète	full board
il y a du monde	it's busy/crowded
parce que	because
parmi	among

LOOKING FORWARD

UNIT 9
A votre santé

In **Unit 9**, we will be talking about health, how to keep fit and how to explain minor health problems.

To prepare, have a look at the following list of symptoms and identify those that you would use to describe the flu (**la grippe**). Use a dictionary if you're not sure.

J'ai mal à l'estomac • J'ai mal à la tête • J'ai mal aux pieds • Je tousse • Je me sens fatigué(e) • J'ai le bras cassé • J'ai des courbatures • J'ai un coup de soleil

UNIT **9**
A votre santé

▷ **By the end of this unit you will be able to:**

- Talk about your health
- Say what you do to keep fit
- Say what you should do more (or less) of to keep fit
- Make an appointment by telephone
- Explain minor health problems
- Go to the chemist and buy medicines

1 Vous vous souvenez?

A  Complétez les phrases suivantes:

1 Je cherche un hôtel à la ⬭⬭⬭⬭⬭⬭⬭⬭⬭⬭, je n'aime pas la mer.

2 Je voudrais ⬭⬭⬭⬭⬭⬭⬭⬭⬭ une chambre double, s'il vous plaît.

3 Je suis dans une chaise roulante. Est-ce que vous avez des chambres pour ⬭⬭⬭⬭⬭⬭⬭⬭?

4 L'ampoule de la salle de bains a ⬭⬭⬭⬭⬭⬭⬭⬭.

5 Il fait froid dans la chambre, le chauffage ne ⬭⬭⬭⬭⬭⬭⬭⬭ pas.

6 Veuillez ⬭⬭⬭⬭⬭⬭⬭⬭, monsieur, l'expression de mes ⬭⬭⬭⬭⬭⬭⬭⬭ distingués.

B 🎧 ▷ Comment diriez-vous…? (*How would you say…?*)

1 He has a big black dog.

2 I have a small house in the countryside.

3 They have a modern and spacious kitchen.

4 It's a beautiful blue vase.

5 I prefer white bread.

2 A votre santé!

A 🎲 ▷ Lisez l'extrait du site canadien «Réseau canadien de la santé» et essayez de trouver à quoi se réfèrent les phrases suivantes:

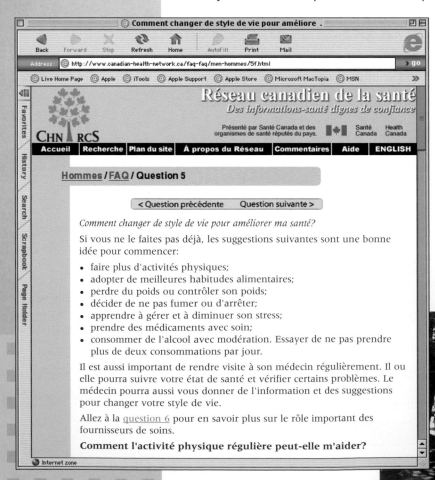

⊙ Comment changer de style de vie pour améliore .	

Back Forward Stop Refresh Home AutoFill Print Mail

Address: @ http://www.canadian-health-network.ca/faq-faq/men-hommes/5f.html › go

@ Live Home Page @ Apple @ iTools @ Apple Support @ Apple Store @ Microsoft MacTopia @ MSN

Réseau canadien de la santé
Des informations-santé dignes de confiance

CHN RCS

Présenté par Santé Canada et des organismes de santé réputés du pays.

Santé Canada   Health Canada

Accueil | **Recherche** | **Plan du site** | **À propos du Réseau** | **Commentaires** | **Aide** | **ENGLISH**

Hommes / FAQ / Question 5

‹ Question précédente   Question suivante ›

Comment changer de style de vie pour améliorer ma santé?

Si vous ne le faites pas déjà, les suggestions suivantes sont une bonne idée pour commencer:

- faire plus d'activités physiques;
- adopter de meilleures habitudes alimentaires;
- perdre du poids ou contrôler son poids;
- décider de ne pas fumer ou d'arrêter;
- apprendre à gérer et à diminuer son stress;
- prendre des médicaments avec soin;
- consommer de l'alcool avec modération. Essayer de ne pas prendre plus de deux consommations par jour.

Il est aussi important de rendre visite à son médecin régulièrement. Il ou elle pourra suivre votre état de santé et vérifier certains problèmes. Le médecin pourra aussi vous donner de l'information et des suggestions pour changer votre style de vie.

Allez à la <u>question 6</u> pour en savoir plus sur le rôle important des fournisseurs de soins.

Comment l'activité physique régulière peut-elle m'aider?

Internet zone

1 Do more of them.

2 Pay more attention to them.

3 Try to lose some.

4 Stop it.

5 Try to reduce it.

6 Take them with care.

7 Don't consume too much of it.

8 Do it regularly.

B  Didier interviewe Dr Smal sur les bienfaits du sport et des activités physiques. Ecoutez ce qu'ils disent et répondez aux questions suivantes:

1 Which of the following parts of the body are mentioned?

  a cœur   **d** muscles

  b visage   **e** os

  c poumons   **f** jambe

2 Which of the following activities are mentioned?

  a la marche   **d** des étirements

  b la natation   **e** la sieste

  c le football   **f** la musculation

C Voici un extrait de l'interview de Didier et du Dr Smal. Essayez de remplir (fill in) les blancs en choisissant les mots parmi la liste ci-dessous. Vérifiez ensuite vos réponses en réécoutant l'interview.

> **résistants – préserver – prévenir – remercie – monter – diminuer – perdre – faire – améliorer – porter**

Didier: Dr Smal, en quoi est-ce que l'activité physique, le sport peuvent-ils aider à (⎯⎯⎯⎯) ma santé?

Dr Smal: Et bien tout d'abord, une activité physique régulière peut vous aider à (⎯⎯⎯⎯) du poids. Elle peut aussi aider à (⎯⎯⎯⎯) votre humeur et (⎯⎯⎯⎯) l'anxiété. Le sport peut aussi (⎯⎯⎯⎯) les maladies du cœur, le diabète, sans oublier les douleurs du dos.

Didier: Mais quelles activités dois-je faire exactement?

Dr Smal: [...] il y a des activités de force, qui vont vous aider à garder les muscles et les os plus (⎯⎯⎯⎯), par exemple, (⎯⎯⎯⎯) et descendre les escaliers, (⎯⎯⎯⎯) des sacs plus ou moins lourds, (⎯⎯⎯⎯) de la musculation, etc.

Didier: Dr Smal, je vous (⎯⎯⎯⎯) pour tous ces conseils.

A votre santé

LANGUAGE FOCUS

Je vais faire plus d'exercices physiques

more:	**plus de** + noun	Je voudrais gagner **plus d'**argent. *I'd like to earn **more** money.*
	plus + adjective/adverb	L'anglais est **plus** difficile **que** le français. *English is **more** difficult **than** French.* Je devrais aller en France **plus** souvent. *I should go to France **more** often.*
less/fewer:	**moins de** + noun	J'ai **moins de** soucis maintenant. *I've got **fewer** worries now.*
	moins + adjective/adverb	C'est **moins** cher ici **qu'**à Paris. *It's **less** expensive here **than** in Paris.*
too much/ too many:	**trop de** + noun	Il y a **trop d'**insectes ici. *There are **too many** insects here.*
	trop + adjective/adverb	Cette voiture est **trop** chère. *This car is **too** expensive.*
not enough:	**pas assez de** + noun	Il n'y a **pas assez de** place. *There is **not enough** room.*
	pas assez + adjective/adverb	La cuisine n'est **pas assez** grande. *The kitchen is **not** big **enough**.*

D Vous avez décidé de prendre de bonnes résolutions. Avec l'aide des conseils (advice) donnés sur la page Internet et les éléments de réponses suivantes, choisissez 3 résolutions. Expliquez à votre partenaire ce que vous allez faire et pourquoi.

Exemple: Change eating habits / don't eat enough vegetables / too fat

Je vais changer mes habitudes alimentaires parce que je **ne** mange **pas assez de** légumes et je suis **trop** gros(se).

Do more exercise / too fat / want to lose weight

Lose weight / eat too much / never exercise

Stop smoking / smoke too much / too expensive

Reduce stress / work too much / want to go out with friends more often

Drink less / go out too much / shouldn't drink more than 2 units per day

Change eating habits / only cook pasta / need to eat more green vegetables

3 Un rendez-vous chez le dentiste

A  Annie téléphone au Centre Médical de Valenciennes. Ecoutez-la et choisissez la réponse correcte aux questions suivantes:

1 Annie can't get through to the dentist's surgery because:
   a the line is engaged   **b** Dr Démory is on holiday
   c the surgery is closed.

2 Annie decides to:
   a call back later   **b** wait for a little while
   c leave a message.

3 Annie initially wanted an appointment for:
   a next week   **b** tomorrow afternoon
   c tomorrow 12.00 noon.

4 Annie's appointment is on:
   a Thursday 10.00 am   **b** Thursday 2.00 pm
   c Wednesday 10.00 am.

5 Annie wants to see the dentist:
   a because she's got a gum infection
   b because she's got a bad toothache
   c just for a check-up.

A votre santé

B [A C] ⓘ La conversation entre Annie et la secrétaire du Dr Démory a été mélangée. Pouvez-vous la remettre dans le bon ordre? Réécoutez la conversation pour vérifier vos réponses.

Secrétaire: Cabinet dentaire, bonjour.
Annie: Merci, au revoir.
Secrétaire: Oui, pour quel jour, madame?
Secrétaire: Malheureusement, demain ça sera difficile... par contre jeudi matin, le docteur peut vous prendre à 10h00.
Annie: Demain après-midi?
Secrétaire: Votre nom, madame?
Annie: Oui, c'est bien, ce n'est pas urgent de toute façon, c'est juste pour un contrôle.
Annie: Mme Boutin, Annie.
Annie: Bonjour, je voudrais prendre rendez-vous avec le Dr Démory, s'il vous plaît.
Secrétaire: Donc, jeudi 10h00, madame.

C ✏️ 🗣️ 🎧 ⓘ Complétez le dialogue ci-dessous en français, puis lisez-le avec votre partenaire.

Secrétaire: Cabinet dentaire, bonjour!
Vous: *Greet her. You would like to make an appointment with Dr Philippe.*
Secrétaire: Oui, quel jour, monsieur/madame?
Vous: *Today if possible, you have a toothache* (avoir mal aux dents). *It's very painful* (douloureux).
Secrétaire: Je suis désolée, monsieur/madame, mais le carnet de rendez-vous du docteur est complet pour aujourd'hui.
Vous: *What about tomorrow morning?*
Secrétaire: Demain matin, 8h30, ça vous convient?
Vous: *Yes, perfect. Ask if you have to bring* (apporter) *your form E111 with you?*
Secrétaire: Oui, bien sûr. Quel est votre nom, monsieur/madame?
Vous: *Give an appropriate reply.*
Secrétaire: Très bien, alors demain 8h30.
Vous: *Thank you. See you tomorrow.*

D Annie doit retéléphoner au cabinet du Dr Démory à cause d'un imprévu (something unexpected). Ecoutez le dialogue et essayez de corriger les erreurs dans le résumé suivant:

Annie téléphone au dentiste car elle voudrait changer son rendez-vous. Elle voudrait en prendre un autre le mois prochain parce qu'elle part en vacances à Rome ce jeudi. Son nouveau rendez-vous avec Dr Démory est à 11h00.

E Faites correspondre les expressions en français avec leurs versions anglaises.

1	Ne quittez pas!	**a**	I'd like to cancel my appointment.
2	La ligne est occupée.	**b**	The line is busy.
3	Je vous passe sa secrétaire.	**c**	I'll call back later.
4	Je rappellerai plus tard.	**d**	Leave your details with me.
5	Voulez-vous laisser un message?	**e**	I'll put you through to his/her secretary.
6	Je voudrais annuler mon rendez-vous.	**f**	Do you want to leave a message?
7	Laissez-moi vos coordonnées.	**g**	Hold the line.

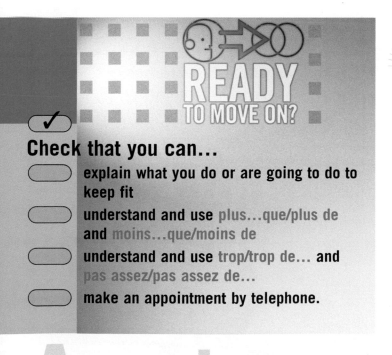

Look for links to health-related websites on www.accesslanguages.com

Check that you can...

- explain what you do or are going to do to keep fit
- understand and use plus...que/plus de and moins...que/moins de
- understand and use trop/trop de... and pas assez/pas assez de...
- make an appointment by telephone.

A votre santé UNIT 9

4 J'ai une fièvre de cheval

A Ecoutez la conversation deux fois, puis essayez d'associer les élements suivants:

1	J'ai mal…	**a**	…de fièvre?
2	Je me sens…	**b**	…fatiguée.
3	La gorge…	**c**	…votre tension.
4	Vous n'avez pas…	**d**	…un comprimé.
5	Je vais jeter un œil…	**e**	…à la tête et aux jambes.
6	Je vais vérifier…	**f**	… de repos.
7	Vous avez besoin…	**g**	…me fait un peu mal.
8	Je vais vous faire…	**h**	…à votre gorge.
9	Prenez…	**i**	…une ordonnance.

LANGUAGE FOCUS

J'ai mal partout!

To explain that a part of your body aches or is sore, the French use the expression:
J'ai mal à…

J'ai mal **à la** gorge. (*feminine*)	*I've got a sore throat.*
J'ai mal **au** genou. (*masculine*)	*I've got a bad knee.*
J'ai mal **aux** pieds. (*plural*)	*My feet hurt.*

Ça fait mal / Ça me fait mal.   *It hurts.*

To explain how you feel, use the verb **se sentir**:

Je me sens mal.	*I feel sick/ill.*
Je ne me sens pas bien.	*I'm not feeling well.*
Je me sens fatigué(e).	*I feel tired.*
Vous vous sentez bien?	*Are you feeling all right?*

To say to someone that he/she looks poorly, for example, use the expression **avoir l'air…**

Tu n'as pas l'air bien.	*You're not looking well/you look poorly.*
Vous avez l'air fatigué.	*You look tired.*
Tu as l'air en forme.	*You look on form / well.*

B  Ecoutez encore une fois Marie et le Dr Lemoine, et répondez aux questions suivantes en anglais:

1 What are Marie's symptoms?

2 What does the doctor say about Marie's blood pressure?

3 How many vitamin C tablets per day does Marie have to take?

4 When does she have to take the Efferalgan tablets?

5 How much is the doctor's consultation?

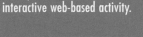

Treat your ailment with our interactive web-based activity.

C Associez les expressions aux images correspondantes:

a

b

c

d

e

f

1 Il a mal au dos.

2 Elle a de la fièvre.

3 Il a le mal de mer.

4 Ils ont mal aux dents.

5 Ils ont un coup de soleil.

6 Elle a mal à l'estomac.

7 Elles ont un rhume.

g

A votre santé **UNIT 9**

D  A la pharmacie. Les mots des phrases suivantes sont mélangés. Pouvez-vous les remettre dans l'ordre d'après (according to) les phrases en anglais?

1 I'm not feeling well   Je / bien / ne / pas / sens / me

2 I've got a bad stomach-ache.   J' / très / l'estomac / mal / ai / à

3 Do you have anything for a
      blocked nose?   Vous / quelque chose / le nez / pour / avez / bouché?

4 I'd like some syrup for a dry
      cough.   Je / sirop / toux / pour / voudrais / du / sèche / une

5 Do you have any cream for
      warts?   Vous / verrues / pour / une crème / les / avez / ?

5 Je me sens déjà mieux!

A  Vous êtes dans une pharmacie et entendez ce dont certains clients ont besoin. Pouvez-vous associer le type de médicament demandé avec ce dont ces personnes souffrent?

1

2

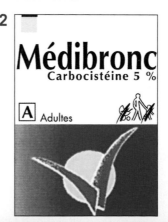

3

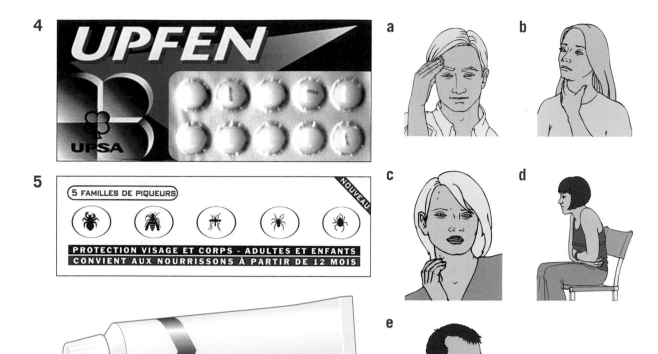

4 UPFEN B UPSA

5 5 FAMILLES DE PIQUEURS — NOUVEAU

PROTECTION VISAGE ET CORPS - ADULTES ET ENFANTS
CONVIENT AUX NOURRISSONS À PARTIR DE 12 MOIS

B **Vrai ou faux**. Ecoutez encore une fois les cinq dialogues.
Les affirmations suivantes sont-elles vraies ou fausses?

	Vrai	Faux
1 Syrup to be taken twice daily: one teaspoon in the morning and one in the evening.		
2 Do not exceed nine tablets per day.		
3 Take one lozenge every five hours. Do not exceed three per day.		
4 Take two capsules with lots of water.		
5 Apply cream twice a day.		

LEARNING TIP:
Cuill. à café...

For *tablespoon*, the French use
the word **cuillère à soupe**,
abbreviated to **cuill. à soupe**.

For *teaspoon*, the French use
the word **cuillère à café**,
abbreviated to **cuill. à café**.

C Ⓐ🅒 ⓑ Lisez «Le contenu de la boîte à pharmacie». Parmi les articles suivants, quels sont ceux qui n'apparaissent pas dans le descriptif?

tweezers	mouthwash	sleeping tablets	condoms	plasters
wasp	soap	lips	cotton buds	safety pins

Le contenu de la boîte à pharmacie:

- Les savons liquides antiseptiques;
- Des produits désinfectant;
- Les pansements: pansements, adhésifs, bandes de gaze;
- Les instruments: ciseaux à bout rond, pince à épiler, thermomètre digital, épingles de sûreté;
- Les antidouleurs et antifièvres: aspirine, paracétamol, antalgique;
- Les pommades, crèmes: arnica pour les coups, Biafine pour les brûlures, Homéoplasmine pour les plaies, pommade anti-inflammatoire pour les foulures;
- Les médicaments prescrits par ordonnances: cœur, diabète (avec les seringues), somnifères, calmants, tension.

Il est possible d'étoffer le contenu de sa pharmacie, en fonction de son lieu d'habitation ou de la saison.

- *En hiver:* stick pour les lèvres;
- *En été:* crème pour les coups de soleil, spray pour les piqûres d'insecte.

D Ⓐ🅒 ✎ ⓑ Relisez les informations sur la boîte à pharmacie et essayez de répondre aux questions suivantes en anglais:

1 What kind of scissors should be in the medicine chest?

2 What is Arnica used for?

3 What is Biafine used for?

4 What should you add to your medicine chest in the summer?

E 🎧 👥 ⓑ Et vous, pouvez-vous décrire le contenu de votre armoire à pharmacie à votre partenaire?

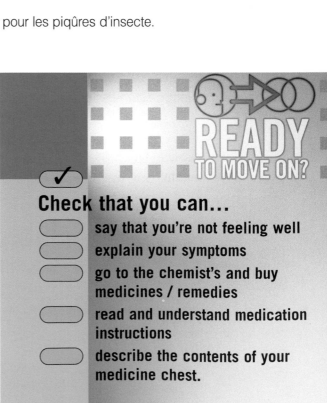

READY TO MOVE ON?

✓

Check that you can...

- say that you're not feeling well
- explain your symptoms
- go to the chemist's and buy medicines / remedies
- read and understand medication instructions
- describe the contents of your medicine chest.

Address: @ http://www.vanuatutourism.com/fr/index1.htm) go

- Recherchez...
- **English version**
- **Page d'accueil**
- **Office National du Tourisme**
- **Vanuatu**
- **Calendrier**
- **Carte**
- **Comment vous y rendre?**
- **Où séjourner?**
- **Activités**
- **Plongée**
- **Info pour les voyageurs**
- **Shopping**
- **Restauration**
- **Educative/ Enfants**
- **Bulletin**
- **Informations officielles**
- **Liens**
- **Brochure**
- **Destination - Vanuatu**

Bienvenue au *Vanuatu*

Le sourire du Pacifique

Si vous utilisez un navigateur qui ne peut pas lire les cadres, cliquez ici

Si vous ne pouvez pas voir le cadre du sommaire sur la gauche, cliquez ici.

Si vous voulez la version en Anglais de ce site, cliquez ici

Venez avec nous à la découverte des îles du Paradis....

Vous êtes dans le site officiel de l'Office National du Tourisme du Vanuatu.

Pour prévoir un voyage au Vanuatu, voici le meilleur point de départ.

Vous trouverez des pages sur toutes les îles principales de l'archipel et une liste complète de l'hébergement au Vanuatu - du quatre étoiles au simple bungalow sur la plage. Des circuits pour tous les goûts - de la petite excursion en bus, au trekking sur les volcans en passant par la plongée, la croisière à voile, la randonnée en forêt et des conseils pratiques pour les voyageurs que vous ne trouverez pas ailleurs. Et puis il y a des liens partout qui vous renvoient à d'autres pages pour plus de détails sur les excursions.

 Internet zone

Vanuatu

A Ecoutez les informations sur la géographie de l'archipel de Vanuatu. Parmi les chiffres ci-dessous, cochez (✔) ceux qui sont mentionnés dans ce passage. Pouvez-vous expliquer ce qu'ils représentent?

1 80
   90

2 120
   25

3 2 172
   2 162

4 5 750
   5 570

B Ecoutez le passage sur Vanuatu encore une fois et répondez aux questions suivantes en anglais:

1 How long does it take to fly from the archipelago of Vanuatu to Sydney?

2 How many volcanoes are still active in the archipelago?

3 What is Port Vila?

4 What are the three official languages in the archipelago of Vanuatu?

C Voici quelques renseignements et précautions à prendre avant de partir à Vanuatu. Lisez ces informations et essayez de répondre aux questions ci-dessous:

1 What do travel agencies recommend that travellers do?

2 Why should travellers use a sunblock?

3 There are three French health specialists in Port-Vila. What do they specialise in?

4 What happens if someone becomes seriously ill?

5 What is the archipelago officially free of?

@ National Tourism Office of Vanuatu

Back Forward Stop Refresh Home AutoFill Print Mail

Address: @ http://www.vanuatutourism.com/fr/index1.htm   › go

Favorites | History | Search | Scrapbook | Page Holder

Vanuatu

- Recherchez...
- **English version**
- **Page d'accueil**
- **Office National du Tourisme Vanuatu**
- **Calendrier**
- **Carte**
- **Comment vous y rendre?**
- **Où séjourner?**
- **Activités**
- **Plongée**
- **Info pour les voyageurs**
- **Shopping**
- **Restauration**
- **Educative/Enfants**
- **Bulletin**
- **Informations officielles**
- **Liens**
- **Brochure Destination - Vanuatu**

Santé

Le paludisme est endémique au Vanuatu, et les agences de voyage vous recommanderont de prendre un traitement préventif, surtout si vous devez vous rendre dans les autres îles de l'archipel. Attention, la plupart de ces médicaments sensibilisent davantage la peau au soleil! Prévoyez des crèmes solaires écran total (15+) même pendant l'hiver austral. L'hépatite B et la tuberculose existent aussi dans l'archipel mais le voyageur prenant les précautions normales ne devrait pas être concerné.

Il y a un hôpital central à Port-Vila et un autre à Luganville. Des petits dispensaires ou cliniques sont installés dans tout l'archipel. Un médecin, un dentiste et un kinésithérapeute français sont installés à Port-Vila: Docteur J. Bador, tél. 23065, Dentiste: H. Collard, tél. 22306, et Masseur/Kinésithérapeute G. Sariani, tél. 25777.

Malgré ces soins et moyens médicaux disponibles sur place, les personnes gravement malades ou accidentées seront évacuées sur la Nouvelle-Calédonie, la Nouvelle-Zélande ou l'Australie. Prenez une bonne assurance-voyage. Le pays semble être encore épargné par la pandémie du SIDA – tout du moins il n'y a pas de malades recensés officiellement. Prenez donc quand même toutes les précautions qui s'imposent.

paludisme (m)	*malaria*
se rendre	*to go*
davantage	*more*
peau (f)	*skin*
prévoir	*(here) to take*
dispensaire (m)	*surgery*
kinésithérapeute (m, f)	*physiotherapist*
malgré	*in spite of*
épargné(e)	*spared*

Internet zone

Nouns

archipel (m)	archipelago	**gélule** (f)	capsule
armoire (f)	cupboard	**genou** (m)	knee
bienfait (m)	benefit	**gorge** (f)	throat
brûlure (f)	burn	**humeur** (f)	mood
cabinet (m)	surgery/cabinet	**île** (f)	island
cachet (m)	tablet	**îlot** (m)	small island
chair (f)	flesh	**imprévu** (m)	something unexpected
chat (m)	cat	**jambe** (f)	leg
cheval (m)	horse	**kinésithérapeute** (m, f)	physiotherapist
chien (m)	dog	**langue** (f)	language/tongue
ciseaux (mpl)	scissors	**lèvre** (f)	lip
cœur (m)	heart	**maladie** (f)	illness
comprimé (m)	tablet	**marche** (f)	walk
conseil (m)	advice	**médicament** (m)	medicine, medication
contenu (m)	content	**moitié** (f)	half
contrôle (m)	check-up	**musculation** (f)	body-building
coordonnées (fpl)	one's details	**ordonnance** (f)	prescription
coup (m)	bruise	**os** (m)	bone
coup (m) **de soleil**	sunburn	**pansement** (m)	plaster
cuillère (f)	spoon	**pastille** (f)	lozenge
dent (f)	tooth	**peau** (f)	skin
dos (m)	back	**pied** (m)	foot
douleur (f)	pain	**pince** (f) **à épiler**	tweezers
épingle (f) **de sûreté**	safety pin	**piqûre** (f)	bite (insect)/ injection
escalier (m)	stairs	**plaie** (f)	wound
estomac (m)	stomach	**poids** (m)	weight
étirement (m)	stretching	**pomme** (f)	apple
fièvre (f)	temperature	**poule** (f)	hen
foulure (f)	sprain	**poumon** (m)	lung
		rendez-vous (m)	appointment
		repos (m)	rest

GLOSSARY

réunion (f)	meeting	**apprendre**	to learn
rhume (m)	cold	**arrêter**	to stop
santé (f)	health	**attendre**	to wait
savon (m)	soap	**corriger**	to correct
sieste (f)	nap	**démanger**	to itch
somnifère (m)	sleeping tablet	**dépasser**	to exceed/to overtake (driving)
superficie (f)	surface area	**descendre**	to go down
tension (f)	blood pressure	**diminuer**	to reduce
tête (f)	head	**donner**	to give
toux (f)	cough	**gérer**	to manage
verrue (f)	wart	**laisser**	to leave (something)
visage (m)	face	**monter**	to go up/to climb up
		patienter	to wait

Adjectives

		porter	to carry/to wear
alimentaire	food	**prendre**	to take
bouché(e)	blocked	**prescrire**	to prescribe
dentaire	dental	**préserver**	to preserve
douloureux (euse)	painful	**prévenir**	to prevent/to warn
fatigué(e)	tired	**prévoir**	to plan/to foresee
lourd(e)	heavy	**rappeler**	to call back/to remind
occupé(e)	busy/engaged (phone line)	**réduire**	to reduce
sous-marin(e)	submarine	**remercier**	to thank
		reporter	to postpone

Verbs

		se sentir	to feel
améliorer	to improve	**sembler**	to seem
annuler	to cancel	**sensibiliser**	to sensitise
appliquer	to apply	**sucer**	to suck
apporter	to bring	**vérifier**	to check

Expressions

Ça vous convient?	Is it convenient for you?	moins	less
de toute façon	anyway	par contre	on the other hand
jeter un œil	to have a look	partout	everywhere
		plus	more

Looking forward

In **Unit 10**, we will be talking about houses, homes and interiors. We will also shop for clothes and talk about past events.

To prepare, look at the following words for rooms in a house. For each of them, decide whether they are normally located on the ground floor or on the first floor.

	Rez-de-chaussée	*1er étage*
salon		
cuisine		
chambre		
cellier		
entrée		
W.C.		
bureau		
salle de bains		
salle à manger		

A votre santé

UNIT 10
Les goûts et les couleurs

By the end of this unit you will be able to:

- Describe your home
- Buy clothes
- Describe what people wear
- Talk about past events

1 Vous vous souvenez?

A Complétez le pictogramme ci-contre en français. N'oubliez pas les articles (**le**, **la**, **les**).

B  Travaillez avec un partenaire et suivez les instructions dans la conversation suivante. Changez les rôles lorsque vous avez fini.

A la pharmacie…

You: *Greet the pharmacist .*

Pharmacien: Bonjour, je peux vous aider?

You: *Say that you want something for a cold and a sore throat.*

Pharmacien: Oui, alors j'ai un très bon sirop pour calmer votre mal de gorge.

You: *Explain that you prefer something stronger, like tablets.*

Pharmacien: Est-ce que vous avez de la fièvre?

You: *Say no, but you're feeling cold.*

Pharmacien: Voici des comprimés pour les états grippaux.

You: *Ask how many tablets you should take.*

Pharmacien: Vous en prenez deux le matin et deux le soir.

You: *It's fine. Ask how much it is.*

Pharmacien: 2.38 euros.

2 A la maison

A Ecoutez deux ou trois fois le passage sur l'influence des couleurs dans la maison et répondez aux questions suivantes:

1 Which colours are not mentioned?

yellow	blue
brown	green
white	black
violet	orange
red	pink

2 Which parts of the house are not mentioned?

bedroom	bathroom	kitchen
entrance hall	corridor	lounge
dining room	study	

Les goûts et les couleurs UNIT 10

B Réécoutez ce passage et essayez de relier les éléments suivants en fonction des couleurs et de leurs influences dans les différentes pièces (rooms) de la maison. Exemple: orange – helps digestion – dining room.

Colours	*Effects*	*Rooms*

1

a stability

b warmth

2

c stimulates brain

3

d comfort

e helps digestion

4

f security

g space (two colours)

5

h calm

i good for meditation

6

j relaxation (two colours)

LEARNING TIP:
clair et foncé

When talking about colours, the word for *dark* is **foncé** and the word for *light* is **clair**.

bleu foncé   *dark blue*
gris clair   *light grey*

C  Regardez la page d'accueil du site «se loger» et complétez les phrases:

1 Vous désirez voir les détails des propriétés à vendre. Cliquez sur (   ).

2 Vous désirez décorer votre maison et refaire la salle de bains. Cliquez sur (   ).

3 Vous désirez louer un appartement. Cliquez sur (   ).

4 Vous désirez acheter un château ou une villa. Cliquez sur (   ).

5 Vous cherchez des conseils pour transporter vos meubles dans votre nouvelle maison.

Cliquez sur (   ).

Les goûts et les couleurs

D 🔡 ✏️ ▶ Vous avez sélectionné trois propriétés. Lisez les trois descriptifs et les résumés en anglais. Pouvez-vous relever les erreurs dans ces résumés?

1 Maison

Située à Lille Fives (59800)
Proximité: Métro et commerces

43 450 €

Chauffage central électrique, double vitrage, volet électrique, 2 chambres, petite dépendance et petite cour devant. Idéal jeune couple ou étudiant!
Téléphone: 03 20 34 07 07

2 Maison (90 m² environ)

Située à Douai (59500)

82 323 €

Maison de ville à conforter avec salon, séjour, cuisine, 2 chambres, grenier aménagé et jardin.

Téléphone: 03 27 71 51 41

3 Maison (194 m² environ)

Située à Tourtour (83690)

1 050 000 €

Sur un terrain arboré de 3 600 m² environ, très belle maison d'architecte, en pierres, composée: entrée, cuisine aménagée avec coin barbecue, salle à manger, très grand salon avec coin feu (baies vitrées donnant sur le panorama), WC indépendant, 2 chambres, salle de bains avec baignoire, douche, vasque, bidet et WC, salle d'eau avec WC. Nombreux placards. Étage. Au-dessus du coin feu, une petite chambre ronde. Piscine traditionnelle au sous-sol. Vue exceptionnelle.

Téléphone: 04 94 67 77 88

1 House in Lille close to railway station. Double glazing, shutters, large yard at the back of the house. Two bedrooms.

2 House in Douai with lounge, kitchen, two bedrooms, utility room and garden. Needs decorating.

3 House in Tourtour. Wooded area. Stone house with fitted kitchen, lounge, fireplace in dining room, three toilets, bathroom. Two bedrooms upstairs. Outdoor swimming pool.

E A C ▷ Voici les plans de votre nouvelle maison. Regardez-les et complétez la description suivante. Choisissez vos réponses parmi les mots ci-dessous:

> salle de bains – campagne – dehors – bureau – étage – terrasse – cabinet de toilette – équipée – salle à manger – chambre à coucher – rez-de-chaussée

Nous avons acheté une grande maison à la ⬭⬭⬭⬭⬭⬭⬭: elle est magnifique.

Au ⬭⬭⬭⬭⬭⬭⬭, il y a une grande salle de séjour et une ⬭⬭⬭⬭⬭⬭⬭.

Il y a une belle cuisine ⬭⬭⬭⬭⬭⬭⬭ et mon ⬭⬭⬭⬭⬭⬭⬭ est très spacieux aussi.
Nous avons une ⬭⬭⬭⬭⬭⬭⬭ au rez-de-chaussée avec un petit ⬭⬭⬭⬭⬭⬭⬭.

Au premier ⬭⬭⬭⬭⬭⬭⬭, il y a une autre chambre et une grande ⬭⬭⬭⬭⬭⬭⬭.

Nous avons aussi une mezzanine pour la table de billard.

⬭⬭⬭⬭⬭⬭⬭, il y a une grande ⬭⬭⬭⬭⬭⬭⬭ dont une partie est couverte.

C'est vraiment la maison de nos rêves…

F ▷ Et vous, comment est votre maison? Ecrivez un paragraphe similaire à l'activité précédente décrivant votre maison ou votre appartement.

G ▷ Travaillez avec un partenaire. Sans regarder l'activité E, décrivez maintenant votre maison oralement. Posez des questions supplémentaires pour obtenir plus de détails.

> Practise describing accommodation on www.accesslanguages.com

Les goûts et les couleurs UNIT **10**

3 J'ai besoin d'un nouveau jean

A [AC] ▶ Regardez les photos ci-dessous et essayez d'associer les descriptions correspondantes.

a

d

b

e

c

f

1 – Le gilet Spectrum de QUIKSILVER

Maille côtes 1/1 bien lourde et très douce 50 % coton, 50 % acrylique.

Manches longues contrastantes avec empiècement rayures reliefées.

Col montant en côtes. Etiquette poitrine. Finition droite base et bas de manches.

Longueur 70 cm environ. Tour de poitrine en cm.

2 – La veste rayée Comptoir des Cotonniers

Tailleur stretch rayé 60% polyester, 21% laine, 17% viscose, 2% élasthanne lycra®.

La veste rayée: Superbe coupe tailleur, c'est la plus féminine des vestes... inspirée des costumes masculins!

Une rayure discrète, un boutonnage 2 boutons, une très belle longueur, un tissu stretch... elle apporte à toutes vos tenues une note 100% actuelle.

A tester sur un jean ou un pantalon ville avec le même succès. 2 poches à rabat. Doublée 100 % polyester. Long. 68 cm.

60% polyester, 21% laine, 17% viscose, 2% élasthanne lycra®.
Coloris fond: gris, anthracite.

3 – La chemise SOFT GREY

Très tendance, la maille imprimée 50% coton, 50% modal.

Col à pointes libres. Empiècement dos. Pans arrondis. Boutons façon nacre.

Encolures en cm.

4 – La robe fines bretelles BLUELITA

Sexy, mais pas trop, je la porte le jour comme le soir.

En maille résille flockée. Découpe sous poitrine. Bas légèrement évasé. Long. 90 cm env.

Dessus 100% polyamide, doublé maille polyamide parme.

Coloris: noir/parme.

5 – Le top buste galbé en dentelle stretch

A porter avec les jupons de saison ou à mélanger avec les jeans usés, ce top noir ou écru, fait dans la dentelle et cumule les effets.

Buste galbé, mancherons et col roulé.

Empiècement devant et dos transparent.

Finition point bourdon. Long. 55 cm env.

En dentelle stretch 75 % polyamide, 14 % viscose, 11 % élasthanne.

Buste doublé maille 100 % polyester.

6 – Le pardessus SOFT GREY

Coupé dans un très beau drap de laine (80 % laine, 20 % polyamide). Fermé par 3 boutons. 2 poches à rabat passepoilées, 2 poches intérieures passepoilées. Entièrement doublé. Fente dos.

Longueur 100 cm.

Valeur sûre, garantie 6 mois. Tailles 46 au 56. Coloris: fauve, noir.

Les goûts et les couleurs UNITÉ **10**

LEARNING TIP:
En soie et à carreaux

To explain what something is made of, use the preposition **en** followed by the material:

une cravate en soie
a silk tie

des chaussures en cuir
leather shoes

une chemise en coton
a cotton shirt

une bague en or
a gold ring

une montre en plastique
a plastic watch

To describe patterns, use the preposition **à** followed by the pattern:

une cravate à rayures
a stripy tie

une robe à carreaux
a checked dress

une chemise à pois
a polka-dot shirt

un papier peint à fleurs
a flowery wallpaper

une veste unie
a plain jacket

B [A C] ▶ Lisez les descriptions, de l'activité A encore une fois et essayez de trouver les mots correspondants en français.

1 long sleeves   collar   chest (measurement).

2 stripy   pocket   jacket.

3 very trendy   buttons   shirt.

4 dress   colours.

5 lace   skirt.

6 wool   length.

C ▶ Aurélie et Julien sont dans un magasin de prêt-à-porter. Ecoutez-les et essayez de compléter la conversation suivante avec les mots ci-dessous:

> **celui-là – taille – kaki – caisse – au fond – chemise – cabines d'essayage – essayer – serré**

Julien: Aurélie, regarde ces jeans. Ils sont sympas, non?
Aurélie: Ah oui, regarde le noir, il est bien aussi. Tu fais quelle (⬚)?
Julien: Normalement, du 44.
Aurélie: Et bien, essaie un noir et un bleu, ils sont chouettes tous les deux.
Julien: Tu as raison. Attends, où sont les (⬚)?
Aurélie: Là-bas (⬚) du magasin, à gauche.
Julien: OK, j'arrive…

A moment later…

Julien: Ecoute, c'est marrant, le noir est trop (⬚), par contre le bleu me va bien; pourtant c'est la même taille… bizarre, non?
Aurélie: Tu prends le bleu alors?
Julien: Oui, et puis j'ai besoin d'une (⬚) ou d'un T-shirt aussi. Tiens, (⬚) est sympa.
Aurélie: Oh non, pas encore un rouge, regarde celui-ci, vert (⬚), c'est à la mode. Essaie-le… tu fais L ou M?
Julien: L. Je vais l' (⬚)…

A moment later…

Aurélie: Super! Il te va bien. Ah ouais, moi, j'aime bien!
Julien: OK, je prends le T-shirt et le jean. Où est la (⬚)?

LANGUAGE FOCUS

Lequel? – Celui-là...

	this/that *these/those*	*which one(s)?*	*this one/that one* *these/those*
Masc.	ce (pantalon) cet (arbre)	lequel?	celui-ci/celui-là
Fem.	cette (chemise)	laquelle?	celle-ci/celle-là
Masc. plural	ces (T-shirts)	lesquels?	ceux-ci/ceux-là
Fem. plural	ces (chaussures)	lesquelles?	celles-ci/celles-là

D Regardez les pictogrammes à la page 180 et complétez l'exercice selon le modèle suivant:

— J'aime bien **ces** chemises.

— **Laquelle** préférez-vous?

— Je préfère **celle-ci**.

You will find more practice on our website.

Les goûts et les couleurs UNIT 10

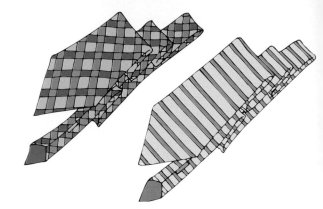

1 – J'aime bien ⬭ costumes.

– ⬭ préférez-vous?

– Je préfère ⬭.

2 – J'aime beaucoup ⬭ cravate.

– Oh non, moi, je préfère ⬭.

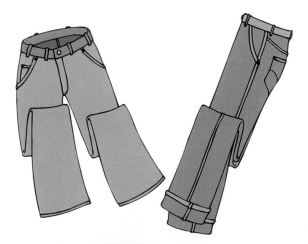

3 – J'aime bien ⬭ chaussures.

– ⬭ préférez-vous?

– Je préfère ⬭.

4 – Regarde ⬭ jean, il est génial!

– Il n'est pas mal, mais je préfère ⬭.

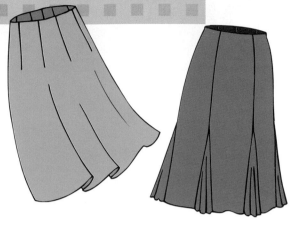

5 – ⬚ jupe est très jolie, non?

– Bof, je préfère ⬚.

6 – Oh, regardez ⬚ chapeaux!

– ⬚ préférez-vous?

– J'adore ⬚.

E 🗣️ 👥 ▶️ **Discussion**. Travaillez avec un partenaire. Vos amis Nathalie et Jean-Luc vous demandent quelques conseils sur ce qu'ils doivent porter lors d'un entretien d'embauche (job interview). Aidez-les en leur donnant des exemples de ce qu'ils doivent ou ne doivent pas porter, les couleurs à éviter, etc.

Check that you can...

- ⬚ describe your house
- ⬚ understand adverts
- ⬚ describe what you are wearing
- ⬚ talk about colours and patterns
- ⬚ use the expressions 'this one, that one, these'.

UNIT 10

4 J'ai passé un excellent week-end

A [A C] ▶ Lisez les phrases suivantes et essayez de les associer aux pictogrammes correspondants:

1 Nous avons mangé au restaurant.

2 J'ai dormi jusqu'à midi.

3 J'ai acheté une robe.

4 J'ai peint le salon.

5 Je suis allée chez le dentiste.

6 Nous avons regardé la télévision.

a

d

b

e

c
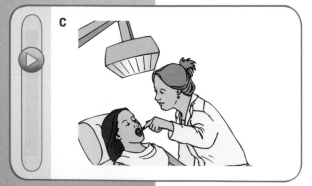

f

Le passé composé

Have another look at activity 4A. All the statements refer to an event that happened in the past (ie last weekend).

To construct the past tense in French (*I did, I bought, I ate*), you need **two** elements. For most verbs, the past tense is formed as follows:

avoir (*to have*) followed by the **past participle** of the verb.

J'ai **mangé**	*I ate (literally: I have eaten)*
Nous **avons acheté**	*We bought (literally: We have bought)*
Avez-vous **fini** l'exercice?	*Did you finish the exercise? (literally: Have you finished the exercise?)*
Ils n'**ont** pas **entendu** le signal.	*They did not hear the signal (literally: They have not heard the signal.)*

Here are some more examples:

passer	J'ai **passé** le week-end à la mer.	*I spent the weekend by the sea.*
oublier	Tu as **oublié** l'anniversaire de Martine.	*You forgot Martine's birthday.*
mentir	Il a **menti** à son meilleur ami.	*He lied to his best friend.*
finir	Elle **a fini** à 15h00.	*She finished at 3.00pm.*
perdre	Nous avons **perdu** les billets.	*We lost the tickets.*
vendre	Vous avez **vendu** votre maison.	*You sold your house.*

Making the past participle can sometimes be a bit tricky as there are lots of irregular verbs. The best thing to do is to learn them as you come across them. Here are some examples:

boire	Ils ont **bu** toute la nuit.	*They drank all night.*
faire	Elles ont **fait** du shopping.	*They did some shopping.*
mettre	J'ai **mis** les clés sur la table.	*I put the keys on the table.*
prendre	Il a **pris** le bus ce matin.	*He took the bus this morning.*
avoir	J'ai **eu** la grippe.	*I had the flu.*
être	Nous avons **été** surpris.	*We were surprised.*

Some verbs in French do not work with **avoir** but with **être**. This time the past participle agrees with the subject. Look at the examples on page 183.

Les goûts et les couleurs UNIT **10**

ACCESS FRENCH

You'll find more practice on the past tense on our website.

LANGUAGE FOCUS

Je **suis** all**é** au cinéma.   *I went to the cinema. (masculine)*

Je **suis** all**ée** au cinéma.   *I went to the cinema. (feminine)*

Nous **sommes** rest**és** 3 jours.   *We stayed for 3 days. (masc. plural)*

Nous **sommes** rest**ées** 3 jours.   *We stayed for 3 days. (fem. plural)*

Vous **êtes** ven**us** en voiture?   *Did you come by car? (mixed genders: masc. plur.)*

Look at the following examples of verbs that also use **être** in the past:

venir	Je suis venu(e) avec mon ami(e).	*I came with my friend.*
naître	Tu es né(e) en quelle année?	*Which year were you born?*
tomber	Elle est tombée de la chaise.	*She fell off the chair.*
partir	Le train est parti à 8h00.	*The train left at 8.00 am.*
sortir	Nous sommes sortis vers 17h00.	*We came out at about 5.00 pm.*
arriver	Vous êtes arrivé(e)s à quelle heure?	*What time did you arrive?*
mourir	Mes poissons rouges sont morts.	*My goldfish died.*

Finally, note that all reflexive verbs also work with **être**:

Je **me suis levé(e)** à 7h00.	*I got up at 7.00 am.*
Nous **nous sommes réveillé(e)s** tôt.	*We woke up early.*

B Choisissez un élément de chaque colonne pour faire une phrase cohérente:

Je / J'	ai	né(e)	le journal
Nous	suis	commencé	au théâtre
Vous	sommes	allés	malade
	avons	fait	le ménage
	êtes	pris	rendez-vous chez le dentiste
	avez	lu	le 27 décembre
		eu	un problème avec ma voiture
		été	à 9h00

C Lundi matin, au bureau, Annie explique à Yasmin ce qu'elle a fait pendant le week-end. Ecoutez-les et mettez les dessins ci-dessous dans l'ordre correct.

1

4

2

5

3

6

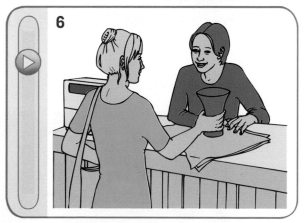

Les goûts et les couleurs UNIT**10**

D Regardez le résumé ci-dessous et mettez les verbes entre parenthèses au passé. Les verbes avec (*) utilisent **être**.

Annie (**passer**) un bon week-end. Son mari et elle (**aller***) chez des amis pour un barbecue. Ils (**manger**), ils (**boire**) et ils (**danser**). Le lendemain, ils (**avoir**) mal à la tête. Samedi après-midi, elle (**faire**) du shopping, Daniel (**ranger**) la chambre des enfants. Le soir, toute la famille (**rester***) à la maison. Dimanche, Annie, Daniel et les enfants (**aller***) à la plage. Ils (**jouer**) au football et au badminton. Annie (**prendre**) un coup de soleil.

E Et vous, qu'avez-vous fait le week-end dernier? Travaillez avec un partenaire et racontez-lui ce que vous avez fait. N'hésitez pas à poser des questions pour obtenir plus d'informations.

READY
TO MOVE ON?

✓

Check that you can...

- talk about past events
- construct the past tense with avoir
- construct the past tense with être
- explain what you did recently.

Découverte de la FRANCOPHONIE

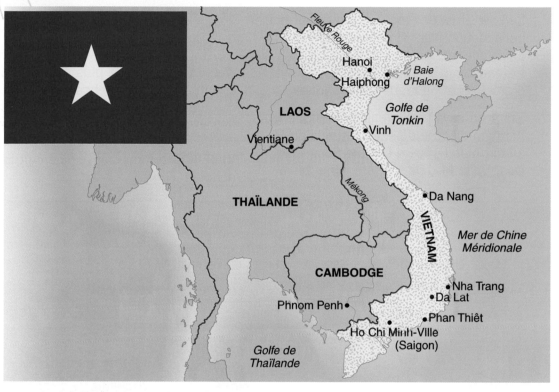

La République Socialiste du Vietnam

A 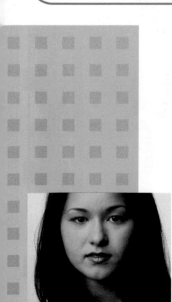 Lisez les informations à la page suivante sur le Vietnam et répondez aux questions ci-dessous en anglais:

1 What features make Vietnam an ideal destination for tourists?

2 What is special about HaLong Bay?

3 What can tourists see at Da Lat?

4 What regional products can be found at Da Lat?

5 What happened in 1995?

Grâce aux bonnes conditions naturelles, historiques et culturelles, le Vietnam dispose d'un potentiel touristique très riche: forêts, mer, montagnes, grottes, anciens vestiges, festivals, etc. font de ce pays une destination touristique de premier choix.

La baie d'HaLong est non seulement une belle station balnéaire, mais elle est aussi une merveille naturelle. Elle s'étend sur 1 500 km^2 avec des milliers de rochers et de grottes magnifiques.

Etant un pays tropical, il semble que le Vietnam dispose de sites naturels au climat plus tempéré comme Sapa, Tam Dao, Bach Ma, Da Lat, etc. Une fois à Da Lat, les visiteurs peuvent découvrir un ensemble naturel de chutes d'eau, de beaux lacs, des vallées de fleurs et des pâturages. Ils pourront notamment goûter des produits locaux renommés comme les kakis, prunes, pommes, poires, pêches, etc. et entendre des instruments de musique originaux comme le T'rung ainsi que les gongs à l'occasion des fêtes et des festivals.

Avec une histoire de plus de 4 000 ans, le Vietnam conserve encore des vestiges historiques de grande valeur. En 1995, l'ensemble des vestiges de l'ancienne capitale Hué a été reconnu par l'UNESCO comme patrimoine culturel mondial.

B Lisez les informations sur les costumes du Vietnam. Notez les noms de vêtements que vous reconnaissez dans le texte.

Les costumes traditionnels

Tunique *(ao dai)*

La tunique de la femme vietnamienne change et se perfectionne. Les deux pans descendent jusqu'au mollet, laissant transparaître un pantalon de fine soie. Les manches sont assez amples et légèrement évasées et ne couvrent que les trois quarts de l'avant-bras. Récemment, les modes étrangères sont introduites au Vietnam mais ce costume traditionnel est toujours prisé des Vietnamiennes.

Dans l'ensemble, les costumes vietnamiens sont variés. Presque toutes les ethnies ont leur propre costume traditionnel. Les fêtes sont pour elles l'occasion de porter leurs vêtements préférés. Au fil des années, les costumes des ethnies changent mais gardent toujours leur originalité, leur caractéristique.

Chapeau conique au poème *(non bai tho)*

De pair avec la tunique, les femmes portent de charmants chapeaux coniques en feuille de latanier. Ces chapeaux sont portés à des fins de protection contre le soleil et la pluie.

Costume des groupes ethniques

Le costume des groupes ethniques du Vietnam est très varié; chaque costume a ses propres caractéristiques régionales. Dans la région montagneuse basse, les ethnies qui habitent dans les maisons sur pilotis portent des pantalons et jupes décorés des motifs imitant les fleurs et animaux de la forêt. Les bijoux (bracelets, boucles d'oreilles, colliers en cuivre ou en argent) sont des objets indispensables quand on parle de leur costume.

station (f) balnéaire	*seaside resort*
mollet (m)	*calf (leg)*
manche (f)	*sleeve*
évasé(e)	*(here) flared*
avant-bras (m)	*forearm*
étranger/ère	*foreign*
mode (f)	*fashion*
prisé(e)	*appreciated*

C Relisez le texte sur les costumes et dites si les affirmations suivantes sont vraies ou fausses:

		Vrai	Faux
1	The trousers that the women wear are made of cotton.		
2	Traditional costumes are becoming less and less popular because of the influence of international fashion.		
3	Traditional costumes vary according to people's origins.		
4	The hat is a protection against sun and rain.		
5	In the mountain regions, costumes are generally plain.		
6	Women don't normally wear jewellery.		

GLOSSARY

Nouns

bague (f)	ring
baignoire (f)	bath
bijou (m)	piece of jewellery
bois (m)	wood
boucle (f) **d'oreille**	earring
bouton (m)	button
bureau (m)	office/study
cabine (f) **d'essayage**	fitting room
ceinture (f)	belt
cerveau (m)	brain
chambre (f)	bedroom
chapeau (m)	hat
chauffage (m)	heating
chaussure (f)	shoe
chemise (f)	shirt
coin (m)	corner
col (m)	collar
collier (m)	necklace
conseil (m)	advice
costume (m)	suit
coton (m)	cotton
couloir (m)	corridor
cour (f)	yard
cravate (f)	tie
cuisine (f)	kitchen
cuisse (f)	thigh
dentelle (f)	lace
dessin (m)	drawing
double vitrage (m)	double glazing

GLOSSARY

douceur (f)	softness
grenier (m)	attic
grotte (f)	cave
jardin (m)	garden
lendemain (m)	following/next day
longueur (f)	length
maison (f)	house
manche (f)	sleeve
mollet (m)	calf
montre (f)	watch
papier (m) **peint**	wallpaper
pardessus (m)	overcoat
pierre (f)	stone
placard (m)	cupboard
poche (f)	pocket
pointure (f)	shoe size
poitrine (f)	chest
rayure (f)	stripe
rez-de-chaussée (m)	ground floor
robe (f)	dress
salle (f) **à manger**	dining room
salon (m)	sitting room, lounge
séjour (m)	living room, lounge
soie (f)	silk
sous-sol (m)	basement
station (f) **balnéaire**	seaside resort
taille (f)	size
veste (f)	jacket
vêtement (m)	clothes/piece of clothing
volet (m)	shutters

Adjectives

blanc(he)	white
bleu(e)	blue
jaune	yellow
joyeux(euse)	happy
marron	brown
noir(e)	black
orange	orange
rose	pink
rouge	red
vert(e)	green
vif/vive	bright
violet(te)	purple, violet

Verbs

acheter	to buy
boire	to drink
dormir	to sleep
essayer	to try
louer	to rent
mentir	to lie
mourir	to die
naître	to be born
oublier	to forget
passer	to spend (time)
peindre	to paint
prendre	to take
savoir	to know
tomber	to fall
vendre	to sell

Les goûts et les couleurs UNIT 10

LANGUAGE SUMMARY

Nouns

French has two genders. Nouns are either masculine or feminine:

masculine
croissant (*croissant*)
père (*father*)

feminine
bouteille (*bottle*)
mère (*mother*)

To form the plural many nouns add an **-s**, but there are exceptions. For example, nouns ending with **-eau**, **-au** and **-eu** in the singular usually take an **-x** in the plural. Adjectives that describe a noun also change according to the gender and whether they are singular or plural (see **Adjectives** below).

Articles

Definite article (*the*)

Masc.	**le, l'**
Fem.	**la, l'**
Plur.	**les**

le poulet (*the chicken*)
la moutarde (*the mustard*)
les pois (*the peas*)

le and **la** change to **l'** when the following noun begins with a vowel or a silent **h**:
l'eau (*the water*), **l'**huile (*the oil*)

Indefinite article (*a/an*)

Masc.	un
Fem.	une
Plur.	des

un croissant (*a croissant*)
une bouteille (*a bottle*)
des frites (*chips*)

Note that **des** is often not translated in English.

some/any

Masc.	**du, de l'**
Fem.	**de la, de l'**
Plur.	**des**

Du, de la, des are used to translate the English *some* and *any*. **Du** and **de la** become **de l'** in front of a vowel or a silent **h**.
de la moutarde (*feminine*)
du vin (*masculine*)
des frites (*plural*)
de l'eau (*feminine*)
de l'argent (*masculine*)

Adjectives

Adjectives are words used to describe things and people. In French, adjectives change according to what they describe: they can be masculine, feminine, singular or plural.

Here are some examples:

Adjectives	Masculine singular	Feminine singular	Masculine plural	Feminine plural
tall	grand	grande	grands	grandes
big	gros	grosse	gros	grosses
practical	pratique	pratique	pratiques	pratiques
delicious	délicieux	délicieuse	délicieux	délicieuses
sporty	sportif	sportive	sportifs	sportives
proud	fier	fière	fiers	fières
white	blanc	blanche	blancs	blanches
new	nouveau	nouvelle	nouveaux	nouvelles

Most adjectives are placed **after** the word they describe:

Il a un accent **anglais**.	He has an **English** accent.
C'est une voiture **bleue**.	It is a **blue** car.
Une femme **élégante** et **charmante**.	An **elegant** and **charming** woman.

There are some exceptions: **jeune** (*young*), **petit** (*small*), **nouveau** (*new*), **vieux** (*old*), **gros** (*big/fat*), **beau** (*beautiful/handsome*) are placed before the word they describe, as in English:

| Je voudrais une **grosse** glace. | I'd like a **big** ice cream. |
| C'est une **belle petite** maison. | It's a **beautiful little** house. |

Demonstratives

	this/that these/those	which one(s)?	this one/that one these ones/those ones
masculine	**ce** pantalon	**lequel?**	**celui-ci/celui-là**
			cet arbre
feminine	**cette** chemise	**laquelle?**	**celle-ci/celle-là**
masc. plural	**ces** T-shirts	**lesquels?**	**ceux-ci/ceux-là**
fem. plural	**ces** chaussures	**lesquelles?**	**celles-ci/celles-là**

LANGUAGE SUMMARY

Personal pronouns

je	*I*
tu	*you (familiar singular)*
il	*he/it (masc.)*
elle	*she/it (fem.)*
on	*one (you/we)*
nous	*we*
vous	*you (plural & formal singular)*
ils	*they (masc.)*
elles	*they (fem.)*

Note that if the following word starts with a vowel or the letter **h**, **je** becomes **j'**:

j'ai   *I have*
j'habite   *I live*

Possessive pronouns

Possessive pronouns (*my, your, his, her, its, our* and *their*) agree in French with the noun that follows and change according to the gender and the number of this word.

the father	**le** père	(masculine)
my father	**mon** père	

the mother	**la** mère	(feminine)
my mother	**ma** mère	

the parents	**les** parents	(plural)
my parents	**mes** parents	

	père *(masc.)*	**mère** *(fem.)*	**enfants** *(plur.)*
my	mon	ma	mes
your	ton	ta	tes
his/her/its	son	sa	ses
our	notre	notre	nos
your	votre	votre	vos
their	leur	leur	leurs

Prepositions

à	*to/towards (see opposite)*
de	*of/from (see opposite)*
dans	*in*
devant	*in front of/outside*
derrière	*behind*
à côté de	*next to*
près de	*near*
loin de	*far from*
entre... et...	*between ... and...*
sur	*on*
sous	*under*
en face de	*opposite*
au milieu de	*in the middle of*

à + le = au
à + la = à la
à + les = aux

Je vais **au** cinéma.	*I go to the cinema.*
Je vais **à la** piscine.	*I go to the swimming pool.*
Je joue **aux** cartes.	*I play cards.*

If the word starts with a vowel or a silent **h**, **au** and **à la** become **à l'**:

les spaghetti **à l'**ail	*spaghetti flavoured with garlic*

de + le = du
de + la = de la
de + les = des

à côté **du** cinéma	*next to the cinema*
près **de la** piscine	*near the swimming pool*
loin **des** magasins	*far from the shops*

If the word starts with a vowel or a silent **h**, **du** and **de la** become **de l'**:

près **de l'**hôtel	*near the hotel*

Comparison

more

plus de + noun
Je voudrais gagner **plus d'**argent.   *I'd like to earn **more** money.*
plus + adjective/adverb
L'anglais est **plus** difficile **que** le français.   *English is **more** difficult **than** French.*
Je devrais aller en France **plus** souvent.   *I should go to France **more** often.*

less/fewer

moins de + noun
J'ai **moins de** soucis maintenant.   *I've got **fewer** worries now.*
moins + adjective/adverb
C'est **moins** cher ici **qu'**à Paris.   *It's **less** expensive here **than** in Paris.*

too much/ too many

trop de + noun
Il y a **trop d'**insectes ici.   *There are **too many** insects here.*
trop + adjective/adverb
Cette voiture est **trop** chère.   *This car is **too** expensive.*

not enough

pas assez de + noun
Il n'y a **pas assez de** place.   *There is **not enough** room.*
pas assez + adjective/adverb
La cuisine **n'**est **pas assez** grande.   *The kitchen is **not** big **enough**.*

Verbs: present tense

Regular verbs

travailler *to work*	**finir** *to finish*	**vendre** *to sell*
je travaill**e**	je fin**is**	je vend**s**
tu travaill**es**	tu fin**is**	tu vend**s**
il/elle/on travaill**e**	il/elle/on fin**it**	il/elle/on vend
nous travaill**ons**	nous fin**issons**	nous vend**ons**
vous travaill**ez**	vous fin**issez**	vous vend**ez**
ils/elles travaill**ent**	ils/elles fin**issent**	ils/elles vend**ent**

Irregular verbs

être *to be*
je suis
tu es
il/elle/on est
nous sommes
vous êtes
ils/elles sont

avoir *to have*
j'ai
tu as
il/elle/on a
nous avons
vous avez
ils/elles ont

aller *to go*
je vais
tu vas
il/elle/on va
nous allons
vous allez
ils/elles vont

faire *to do/to make*
je fais
tu fais
il/elle/on fait
nous faisons
vous faites
ils/elles font

vouloir *to want/to wish*
je veux
tu veux
il/elle/on veut
nous voulons
vous voulez
ils/elles veulent

pouvoir *can/to be able to*
je peux
tu peux
il/elle/on peut
nous pouvons
vous pouvez
ils/elles peuvent

devoir *must/to have to*
je dois
tu dois
il/elle/on doit
nous devons
vous devez
ils/elles doivent

Reflexive verbs

Reflexive verbs can be recognised by the word **se** at the front.

se laver *to have a wash*
je **me** lav**e**
tu **te** lav**es**
il/elle/on **se** lav**e**
nous **nous** lav**ons**
vous **vous** lav**ez**
ils/elles **se** lav**ent**

Imperative

The imperative form (used when you give orders or instructions to people)
is made from the present tense **vous** form without the actual word **vous**:

Prenez la première rue à droite.   *Take the first street on the right.*
Continuez/allez tout droit.   *Go straight on.*
Tournez à gauche.   *Turn left.*
Traversez la place.   *Cross the square.*

Verbs: the future

1 Present tense + word/expression referring to the future:
Demain, **je commence** à 9h00.   *Tomorrow, **I'm starting** at 9.00 am.*
Je prends l'avion ce soir à 19h00.   ***I'm catching** the plane tonight at 7.00.*

2 **aller** (*to go*) in the present tense + verb in the infinitive form:
Je vais acheter une nouvelle voiture.   ***I'm going to buy** a new car.*
Nous allons réserver deux chambres.   ***We're going to book** two rooms.*

Verbs: the past tense (le passé composé)

The past is generally formed by using **avoir** + **past participle**:

j'**ai mangé**	*I ate*
nous **avons acheté**	*we bought*
ils **ont entendu**	*they heard*

Here are some more examples:

passer	J'ai **passé** le week-end à la mer.	*I spent the weekend by the sea.*
oublier	Tu as **oublié** l'anniversaire de Martine.	*You forgot Martine's birthday.*
mentir	Il a **menti** à son meilleur ami.	*He lied to his best friend.*
finir	Elle a **fini** à 15h00.	*She finished at 3.00 pm.*
perdre	Nous avons **perdu** les billets.	*We lost the tickets.*
vendre	Vous avez **vendu** votre maison.	*You sold your house.*

However, there are a large number of irregular verbs and past participles should be learnt as you come across them:

avoir	J'ai **eu** la grippe.	*I had the flu.*
boire	Ils ont **bu** toute la nuit.	*They drank all night.*
être	Nous avons **été** surpris.	*We were surprised.*
faire	Elles ont **fait** du shopping.	*They did some shopping.*
mettre	J'ai **mis** les clés sur la table.	*I put the keys on the table.*
prendre	Il a **pris** le bus ce matin.	*He took the bus this morning.*

Some verbs work with **être**, not **avoir**. Important verbs that use **être** in the past are:

aller *to go*	**allé**
arriver *to arrive*	**arrivé**
descendre *to go down*	**descendu**
monter *to go up*	**monté**
mourir *to die*	**mort**
naître *to be born*	**né**
partir *to leave*	**parti**
rester *to stay*	**resté**
sortir *to go out*	**sorti**
tomber *to fall*	**tombé**
venir *to come*	**venu**

In this case, the past participle agrees with the subject :

Je suis allé au cinéma.	*I went to the cinema. (masculine)*
Je suis all**é**e au cinéma.	*I went to the cinema. (feminine)*
Ils sont resté**s** trois jours.	*They stayed for three days. (masculine plural)*
Elles sont resté**es** trois jours.	*They stayed for three days. (feminine plural)*
Elle est tombé**e** de la chaise.	*She fell off the chair.*
Nous sommes sort**is** vers 17h00.	*We came out at about 5.00 pm.*

Note that all reflexive verbs also work with **être**:

Je me suis **levé(e)** à 7h00.	*I got up at 7.00 am.*
Nous nous sommes **réveillé(e)s** tôt.	*We woke up early.*

LANGUAGE SUMMARY

Questions

Forming questions

There are three main ways of forming a question:

1 Using the sentence form with a rising, questioning intonation:
Nous allons au cinéma?   *We're going to the cinema?*
                          Are we going to the cinema?

2 Using **est-ce que:**
Est-ce que Bernard habite à Londres?   *Does Bernard live in London?*

3 Inverting the pronoun and verb:
Avez-vous fini l'exercice?   *Did you finish the exercise?*

Question words

where?	**où?**
why?	**pourquoi?**
how?	**comment?**
when?	**quand?**
who?	**qui?**
what?	**quel(le)/qu'est-ce que?**

Quel(le) is used to refer to a noun, **qu'est-ce que** to refer to an verb:
Quel est votre nom?   *What's your name?*
Qu'est-ce que vous faites lundi soir?   *What are you doing Monday night?*

Negatives

To make a sentence negative in French, you need to use **ne ... pas**.
Je travaille à Nice.   Je **ne** travaille **pas** à Nice.
Je vais à la banque.   Je **ne** vais **pas** à la banque.

ne becomes **n'** before a word beginning with a vowel:
J'ai faim.   Je **n'**ai **pas** faim.

ne and **pas** are placed round the auxiliary verb **avoir** or **être** in the past:
Ils ont joué au tennis.   Ils **n'**ont **pas** joué au tennis.
Je suis allé au cinéma.   Je **ne** suis **pas** allé au cinéma.

When using the negative form, **du, de la, des** and **de l'** are replaced by **de** or **d':**
Je n'ai pas **de** vin, **de** pain, **de** soupe, **de** frites.

y + verb

To avoid repeating the name of a place, the word **y** (*there*) can be placed just before the verb:
Je vais **en France** cet été; j'**y** vais en voiture.
I'm going to France this summer; I'm going (there) by car.

Vous allez **à Londres** pour combien de jours ? – J'**y** vais pour une semaine.
How many days are you going to London for? – I'm going (there) for a week.

Numbers

1 un/une	2 deux	3 trois	4 quatre	5 cinq
6 six	7 sept	8 huit	9 neuf	10 dix
11 onze	12 douze	13 treize	14 quatorze	15 quinze
16 seize	17 dix-sept	18 dix-huit	19 dix-neuf	

20 vingt	21 vingt-**et**-un	22 vingt-deux	25 vingt-cinq
30 trente	31 trente-**et**-un	32 trente-deux	36 trente-six
40 quarante	41 quarante-**et**-un	42 quarante-deux	47 quarante-sept
50 cinquante	51 cinquante-**et**-un	52 cinquante-deux	58 cinquante-huit
60 soixante	61 soixante-**et**-un	62 soixante-deux	69 soixante-neuf
70 soixante-dix	71 soixante-**et**-onze	72 soixante-douze	
80 quatre-vingts	81 quatre-vingt-un	88 quatre-vingt-huit	
90 quatre-vingt-dix	91 quatre-vingt-onze	96 quatre-vingt-seize	

100 cent	101 cent un	110 cent dix	199 cent quatre-vingt-dix-neuf
200 deux cents	232 deux cent trente-deux		
300 trois cents	362 trois cent soixante-deux		
500 cinq cents	900 neuf cents		
1000 mille	1001 mille un	2010 deux mille dix	
1 000 000 un million			

le premier/la première	*the first*
le/la deuxième	*the second*
le/la troisième	*the third*
le/la dixième	*the tenth*
le/la vingtième	*the twentieth*
le/la vingt-et-unième	*the twenty-first*

Days and months

Monday	lundi
Tuesday	mardi
Wednesday	mercredi
Thursday	jeudi
Friday	vendredi
Saturday	samedi
Sunday	dimanche

January	janvier
February	février
March	mars
April	avril
May	mai
June	juin
July	juillet
August	août
September	septembre
October	octobre
November	novembre
December	décembre

LANGUAGE SUMMARY

Monday 15th February	lundi 15 février
Thursday 19th September	jeudi 19 septembre
Friday 2nd June	vendredi 2 juin
Sunday 1st August	dimanche 1er (premier) août

Monday 15th February — lundi 15 février
Thursday 19th September — jeudi 19 septembre
Friday 2nd June — vendredi 2 juin
Sunday 1st August — dimanche 1er (premier) août

Days and months do not have capital letters in French.

To say **on** *Monday*, **on** *Wednesday*, just say **lundi**, **mercredi**.
To say **on** *Monday 5th June*, say **le lundi 5 juin**.
To say *Mondays*, say **le lundi** or **les lundis**.
To say **on the** *5th October*, say **le 5 octobre**.

Time

24-hour clock

A common way of expressing time in French is to use the 24-hour clock with the hours and the minutes separated by the word **heure(s)**.

11.15	onze **heures** quinze
13.30	treize **heures** trente
20.40	vingt **heures** quarante
01.25	une **heure** vingt-cinq

12-hour clock

… cinq	*five past …*
… dix	*ten past …*
… et quart	*quarter past …*
… vingt	*twenty past …*
… vingt-cinq	*twenty-five past …*
… et demie	*half past …*
… moins vingt-cinq	*twenty-five to …*
… moins vingt	*twenty to …*
… moins le quart	*quarter to …*
… moins dix	*ten to …*
… moins cinq	*five to …*

Remember always to start with the hours followed by the minutes.

deux heures cinq	*five past two*
six heures moins vingt-cinq	*twenty-five to six*

am = **du matin**
pm = **de l'après-midi** for the afternoon; **du soir** for the evening.

FRENCH-ENGLISH WORDLIST

These wordlists give the French words and phrases appearing in the course in alphabetical order (French–English and English–French), together with the unit number(s) in which they are presented.

A

à côté de	next to	6
à droite	to/on the right	6
à gauche	to/on the left	6
à mi-temps	part time	2
à pied	on foot	6
à plein-temps	full time	2
à point	medium-rare	5
à proximité	nearby	8
à quelle heure…?	(at) what time…?	2
abordable	affordable	7
accompagner	accompany, to	2
acheter	buy, to	2, 10
addition (f)	bill	5
adorer	love, to	2, 5
adulte (m)	adult	7
aérien(ne)	air	7
aérodrome (m)	airfield	7
aéroport (m)	airport	7
agneau (m)	lamb	5
aider	help, to	4, 7
ail (m)	garlic	5
aimer	like/ love, to	4, 5
aire (f) de jeu	playground	4
alimentaire	food (adj.)	9
alimentation (f)	food and drink	4
allemand(e)	German	2
aller	go, to	2, 6
aller-retour	return (ticket)	7

aller-simple	single (ticket)	7
améliorer	improve, to	9
américain(e)	American	2
ami/amie	friend	2
ampoule (f)	bulb	8
an (m)	year	1
ananas (m)	pineapple	3
anglais(e)	English	1, 2
Angleterre (f)	England	2
année (f)	year	7
anniversaire (m)	birthday/ anniversary	4
annuler	cancel, to	9
août	August	4
appliquer	apply, to	9
apporter	bring, to	9
apprendre	learn, to	5, 9
après	after	6
après-midi (m/f)	afternoon	7
archipel (m)	archipelago	9
argent (m)	money; silver	4
arme (f) à feu	firearm	6
armoire (f)	cupboard	8, 9
arrêter	stop, to	9
arrivée (f)	arrival	7
arriver	arrive, to	7
aspirateur (m)	vaccum cleaner	4
assiette (f)	plate	8
assurance (f)	insurance	7
attendre	wait, to	9

au bord de	by the side of	8
au bout de	to/at the end of	6
au cœur de	in the heart of	6, 8
au milieu de	in the middle of	6
au revoir	goodbye	1
aujourd'hui	today	7
automne (m)	autumn	6
autoroute (f)	motorway	6, 8
avion (m)	aeroplane	7
aviron (m)	rowing	4
avocat (m)	Avocado	3
avocat (m)	lawyer/solicitor	3
avoir	to have	1
avril	April	4

B

bague (f)	ring	10
baignoire (f)	bath	8, 10
balade (f)	walk	4
baldaquin (m)	four-poster (bed)	8
balladeur (m)	personal stereo	8
banquette (f)	seat/bench	8
bateau (m)	boat	7
bâtiment (m)	building	4
batterie (f)	drum	4
beau/belle	beautiful/nice/ handsome	6, 8
beaucoup	a lot	2
bébé (m)	baby	7
beffroi (m)	belfry	6

coordonnées *(fpl)*	details (personal)	9	désolé(e)	sorry	6	en pension complète
cornichon *(m)*	gherkin	5	dessert *(m)*	dessert	5	
corriger	correct, to	9	détester	hate, to	4	
costume *(m)*	suit	5, 10	devant	in front of/outside	6	
côte *(f)*	coast	4	devenir	become, to	5	
coton *(m)*	cotton	10	devoir	have to/must	5	
couloir *(m)*	corridor	10	devoirs *(mpl)*	homework	4	
coup *(m)*	bruise	9	dimanche *(m)*	Sunday	2, 4	
coup *(m)* de soleil	sunburn	9	diminuer	reduce, to	9	
cour *(f)*	yard	10	dîner	have dinner, to	5	
cours *(m)*	course	3	dîner *(m)*	dinner	4, 5	
courses *(fpl)*	shopping	4	directeur/directrice	manager	2	
coûter	cost, to	3	disponible	available	8	
couvert	cloudy	6	distributeur *(m)*			
couverts *(mpl)*	cutlery	8	automatique	vending machine	3	
couverture *(f)*	blanket	8	distributeur *(m)* de			
cravate *(f)*	tie	10	billets	cashpoint	6	
crème *(f)*	cream; milky coffee	3	divorcé(e)	divorced	1	
crevé(e)	flat (tyre)	7	dommages *(mpl)*	damage	7	
cuillère *(f)*	spoon	3, 9	donc	so, consequently	2	
cuisine *(f)*	kitchen/cooking	4, 10	donner	give, to	5, 9	
cuisinier/cuisinière	chef/cook	2	dormir	sleep, to	10	
cuisse *(f)*	thigh	10	dos *(m)*	back	9	
cuit(e)	cooked	5	double vitrage *(m)*	double-glazing	10	
			douceur *(f)*	softness	10	

en pension complète — full board — 8
en voiture — by car — 6
enchanté(e) — pleased to meet you — 1
endroit *(m)* — place — 8
enfant *(m/f)* — child — 1, 7
enregistrer — keep records of, to — 2
ensemble — together — 4
ensuite — then — 6
entendre — hear, to — 8
entre… et… — between… and… — 6
entrée *(f)* — starter — 5
entretien *(m)* — maintenance — 4, 7
épeler — spell, to — 1
épice *(f)* — spice — 3
épinard *(m)* — spinach — 5
épingle *(f)* de sûreté — safety pin — 9
escalade *(f)* — rock climbing — 4
escalier *(m)* — stairs — 9
espèces *(fpl)* — cash — 2
espérer — hope, to — 6
essayer — try, to — 8, 10
essuie-glace *(m)* — windscreen wiper — 7
estomac *(m)* — stomach — 9
estragon *(m)* — tarragon — 5
et — and — 6
étang *(m)* — pond — 8
été *(m)* — summer — 6
étendoir *(m)* à linge — dryer (clothes) — 8
étirement *(m)* — stretching — 9
étranger/étrangère — foreign — 2
être — be, to — 1
être pressé(e) — be in a hurry, to — 8
étudiant/étudiante — student — 1, 2
étudier — study, to — 2
Europe *(f)* — Europe — 2

D

dans	in	6	douche *(f)*	shower	8
de …	from …	1	douleur *(f)*	pain	9
de toute façon	anyway	9	douloureux/euse	painful	9
décembre	December	4	droit(e)	straight	4
décontracté(e)	relaxed	5			

E

défendre	defend, to	3	éclairage *(m)*	lighting	4, 8
déjeuner	lunch, to	5	écossais(e)	Scottish	2
déjeuner *(m)*	lunch	4, 5	Ecosse *(f)*	Scotland	2
démanger	itch, to	9	écouter	listen, to	5, 6, 8
dent *(f)*	tooth	9	église *(f)*	church	6
dentaire	dental	9	embarquement *(m)*	boarding	7
dentelle *(f)*	lace	10	emplacement *(m)*	space; place	7
dentifrice *(m)*	toothpaste	3	employer	employ, to	2
départ *(m)*	departure	7	emporter	take away, to	5
dépasser	exceed/overtake, to (driving)	9	en cas de	in case of	7
			en demi-pension	half board	8
dernier/dernière	last	5	en face de	opposite	6
derrière	behind	6	en liquide	cash (payment method)	7
descendre	go down, to	2, 9			
désirer	want, to	8	en panne	broken down	7

F

faire — do/make, to — 2, 4
famille *(f)* — family — 1, 4
fatigué(e) — tired — 9
femme *(f)* — wife/woman — 4
femme *(f)* d'affaires — businesswoman — 4

fermé(e)	closed	4
ferme *(f)*	farm	4
fermeture *(f)*	closing	5
ferroviaire	railway (adj.)	7
feux *(mpl)*	traffic lights	6
février	February	4
fier/fière	proud	8
fièvre *(f)*	temperature	9
fille *(f)*	daughter/girl	4
fils *(m)*	son	4
finir	finish, to	2
flâner	walk around, to	6
fleuri(e)	in flower/flowery	8
fleuve *(m)*	river	6
fois *(f)*	time	4
formulaire *(m)*	form	7
foulure *(f)*	sprain	9
four *(m)*	oven	5
fourchette *(f)*	fork	5
frais/fraîche	fresh	5
framboise *(f)*	raspberry	3
français(e)	French	1, 2
frère *(m)*	brother	4
frigo *(m)*	fridge	3
frites *(fpl)*	chips	3
froid(e)	cold	5, 6
fromage *(m)*	cheese	3, 5
fuir	leak, to	8
fumé(e)	smoked	5
fumer	smoke, to	2

G

gagner	earn/win, to	4
gallois(e)	Welsh	2
garçon *(m)*	boy	4
garderie *(f)*	creche	3
gare *(f)*	(railway) station	6, 7
garer	park, to	4
gazeux/euse	sparkling	8
geler	freeze, to	6
gélule *(f)*	capsule	9
genou *(m)*	knee	9
genre *(m)*	kind/sort	5
gentil(le)	kind (adj)	5
gérer	manage, to	9
glaçon *(m)*	ice cube	3
gorge *(f)*	throat	9
grand(e)	big/tall	2, 4, 7, 8
grandir	grow up, to	2

gratiné(e)	grilled	5
gratuit(e)	free of charge	4, 8
grenier *(m)*	attic	10
griller	grill/fuse, to	8
gros(se)	big/fat	8
grotte *(f)*	cave	10

H

habillement *(m)*	clothing	4
habiter	live, to	1
haché(e)	minced	5
haricot *(m)*	bean	3
haut(e)	high	4
hébergement *(m)*	accommodation	8
heure *(f)*	hour, time	7
heureusement	fortunately	4
heureux/euse	happy	8
hiver *(m)*	winter	5, 6
hollandais(e)	Dutch	2
hôte/hôtesse de caisse	cashier	2
hôtel *(m)* de ville	town hall	6
huile *(f)*	oil	3
huître *(f)*	oyster	5
humeur *(f)*	mood	9
hypermarché *(m)*	hypermarket	2

I

ici	here	6
il me faut…	I need…	3
il n'y a pas de…	there isn't/ aren't any…	4
il y a	there is/there are	4
il y a du monde	it's busy/crowded	8
île *(f)*	island	9
illimité(e)	unlimited	7
îlot *(m)*	small island	9
imprévu *(m)*	something unexpected	9
infirmier/infirmière	nurse	2
informaticien/ informaticienne	IT consultant	2
infusion *(f)*	herbal tea	3
irlandais(e)	Irish	2
Irlande *(f)*	Ireland	2

J

j'ai faim	I'm hungry	5
j'ai soif	I'm thirsty	5

j'ai besoin de…	I need…	3
j'aimerais bien!	I wish!	4
jamais	never	4
jambe *(f)*	leg	9
jambon *(m)*	ham	3
janvier	January	4
jardin *(m)*	garden	4, 10
jardin *(m)* d'hiver	conservatory	8
jardinier/jardinière	gardener	2
jaune	yellow	7, 10
je m'appelle…	my name is…	1
je prends…	I'll have, I'm having…	3
je suis né(e)…	I was born…	1
je voudrais…	I would like…	3
jeter un œil	have a look, to	9
jeu *(m)*	game	4
jeudi *(m)*	Thursday	2, 4
jeune	young	8
jouer	play, to	4
jour *(m)*	day	4
journée *(f)*	day(time)	4
joyeux/euse	happy	10
juillet	July	4
juin	June	4
jus *(m)* de fruit	fruit juice	3
jusqu'à	up to	6

K

kilométrage *(m)*	mileage	7
kinésithérapeute *(m,f)*	physiotherapist	9

L

là-bas	over there	6, 7
l'addition!	the bill!	3
laisser	leave (something), to	9
lait *(m)*	milk	3
langue *(f)*	language/tongue	1,2,9
lavabo *(m)*	washbasin	8
lendemain *(m)*	the following day	4, 8, 10
lessive *(f)*	washing	4
lèvre *(f)*	lip	9
lieu *(m)*	place	2
limité(e)	limited	7
limonadier *(m)*	bottle opener	8
linge *(m)*	linen	8

liquide (m)		
vaisselle	washing-up liquid	3
location (f)	hire/rental	4, 7
logement (m)	accommodation/	
	housing	4
loin de	far from	6
longueur (f)	length	10
louer	hire/rent, to	7, 10
lourd(e)	heavy	9
lundi (m)	Monday	2, 4

M

madame	madam/Mrs	1
mademoiselle	miss	1
magasin (m)	shop	2
mai	May	4
maintenant	now	2
mais	but	2, 6
maïs (m)	corn	3
maison (f)	house	4, 6, 10
mal	badly	2
maladie (f)	illness	9
manche (f)	sleeve	10
marbre (m)	marble	3
marchandises (fpl)	goods	2
marche (f)	walking/walks	4, 9
marché (m)	market	6
marcher	walk, to; work	
	(operate), to	7, 8
mardi (m)	Tuesday	2, 4
mari (m)	husband	4
marié(e)	married	1
marron	brown	10
mars	March	4
matin (m)	morning	2
mauvais(e)	bad	6
médicament (m)	medicine	9
ménage (m)	housework	4
menthe (f)	mint	5
mentir	lie, to	10
mer (f)	sea	8
merci	thank you	1
mercredi (m)	Wednesday	2, 4
mère (f)	mother	4
métro (m)	Underground	7
mettre	put, to	2

mobilier (m)	furniture	6
moins	less, fewer	9
mois (m)	month	4
moitié (f)	half	9
mollet (m)	calf	10
monde (m)	world	2
monsieur	sir/Mr	1
montagne (f)	mountain	4, 8
monter	go up/ climb up, to	9
montre (f)	watch	10
morceau (m)	piece	3
moteur (m)	engine	7
moto (f)	motorbike	7
mots (mpl) croisés	crossword(s)	4
mouche (f)	fly	5
mourir	die, to	10
moutarde (f)	mustard	3, 5
moyen (m) de		
transport	means of transport	7
moyen(ne)	medium	2
mur (m)	wall	4
muscade (f)	nutmeg	3
musculation (f)	body building	4, 9

N

nager	swim, to	6
naissance (f)	birth	5
naître	be born, to	1, 10
natation (f)	swimming	4
neiger	snow, to	6
neveu (m)	nephew	4
nièce (f)	niece	4
noir(e)	black	10
noix (f)	walnut	5
nom (m)	name	1
nombre (m)	number	2
nombreux/euse	numerous	4, 8
non	no	1
note (f)	bill (hotel)	8
nouveau/nouvelle	new	8
novembre	November	4
nuageux	cloudy	6
nuit (f)	night	8
numérique	digital	6
numéro (m)	number	1

O

occupé(é)	busy/engaged	
	(phone)	2, 9
octobre	October	4
oiseau (m)	bird	8
oncle (m)	uncle	4
or (m)	gold	3
orage (m)	thunderstorm	6
orange	orange	10
ordinateur (m)	computer	8
ordonnance (f)	prescription	9
os (m)	bone	9
oublier	forget, to	10
oui	yes	1
ouvert(e)	open	4
ouverture (f)	opening	5
ouvre-boîtes (m)	can opener	8

P

paiement (m)	payment	2
pain (m)	bread	3, 5
pamplemousse (m)	grapefruit	3
pané(e)	battered	5
pansement (m)	plaster	9
papier (m) peint	wallpaper	10
par contre	on the other hand	9
par exemple	for example	2
parapente (f)	paragliding	4
parce que	because	2, 8
pardessus (m)	overcoat	10
pare-brise (m)	windscreen	7
parenthèse (f)	bracket	8
parler	speak, to	2
partir	leave/to depart, to	7
partout	everywhere	9
passager (m)	passenger	7
passe-moi…	pass me…	
	(informal)	3
passer	spend (time), to	8, 10
passer l'aspirateur	vaccum, to	4
passez-moi…	pass me… (formal)	3
passoire (f)	colander	8
pastille (f)	lozenge	9
pâtes (fpl)	pasta	3, 5
patienter	wait, to	9

samedi (m)	Saturday	2, 4	sous-sol (m)	basement	10
santé (f)	health	4, 9	soutenir	support, to	5
s'appeler	be called, to	1	souvent	often	4
saumon (m)	salmon	5	station (f)		
savoir	know, to	4, 5, 6, 10	balnéaire	seaside resort	10
savon (m)	soap	9	station-service (f)	petrol station	3
se détendre	relax, to	8	sucer	suck, to	9
se douter	suspect, to	5	sucre (m)	sugar	3
se perdre	get lost, to	6	suivre	follow, to	6
se retrouver	arrange to meet, to	5	supermarché (m)	supermarket	2, 6
se sentir	feel, to	9	sur	on	6
se trouver	be located, to	6	sympa	kind	5
seau (m)	bucket	8	syndicat (m)		
sèche-cheveux (m)	hair dryer	8	d'initiative	tourist office	6

U

usine (f)	factory	2

V

vacances (fpl)	holidays	7
vaisselle (f)	washing-up	4
veau (m)	veal	5
végétarien(ne)	vegetarian	5
vélo (m)	bicycle	7
vendre	sell, to	2, 10
vendredi (m)	Friday	2, 4
vent (m)	wind	6
vérifier	check, to	3, 7
verre (m)	glass	3, 5
verrue (f)	wart	9
vers	about; towards	7
vert(e)	green	7, 8, 10
veste (f)	jacket	10
vêtement (m)	piece of clothing	10
veuf/veuve	widowed	2
viande (f)	meat	3, 5
vie (f)	life	2
vieux/vieille	old	8
vif/vive	bright	10
ville (f)	town/city	1, 2, 5
vin (m)	wine	3
violet(te)	violet	10
visage (m)	face	9
voici	here is/are	2
voilà	here it is/ there you go	7
voir	see, to	6
voiture (f)	car	4, 7
vol (m)	flight; theft	7
volet (m)	shutter	10
vouloir	want/wish, to	5
vous pouvez répéter, s'il vous plaît?	can you repeat please?	1
voyage (m) organisé	package holiday	7
voyager	travel, to	7
yaourt (m)	yoghurt	5

secrétaire (m,f)	secretary	2
séjour (m)	stay; lounge (room)	8, 10
sel (m)	salt	3
semaine (f)	week	3
sembler	seem, to	9
s'énerver	get annoyed, to	4
sensibiliser	sensitise, to	9
sentier (m)	path	4
septembre	September	4
serveur/serveuse	waiter/waitress	2
servi(e)	served	5
serviette (f)	towel	8
seul(e)	alone/lonely	4, 7
seulement	only	2
shampooing (m)	shampoo	3
siècle (m)	century	8
sieste (f)	nap	9
s'il te plaît	please (informal)	3
s'il vous plaît	please (formal)	1, 3
sirop (m)	syrup	3
s'occuper de	look after/deal with, to	2, 4
sœur (f)	sister	4
soie (f)	silk	10
soir (m)	evening	2
soirée (f)	evening; party	7, 8
soleil (m)	sun	6
somnifère (m)	sleeping tablet	9
sorte (f)	sort	7
sous	under	6
sous-marin(e)	submarine	9

T

tabac (m)	tobacco	4
tâche (f)	task	3
taille (f)	size	10
tante (f)	aunt	4
tasse (f)	cup	8
temps (m)	time; weather	6
tension (f)	blood pressure	9
tenue (f)	dress code	5
terrain (m)	ground/pitch	4
tête (f)	head	9
thé (m)	tea	3
thon (m)	tuna	3, 5
tir (m) à l'arc	archery	4
tomate (f)	tomato	3
tomber	fall, to	10
toujours	always	2, 4
tournoi (m)	tournament	4
tout droit	straight on	6
tout(e)	all	2
toux (f)	cough	9
train (m)	train	7
tranche (f)	slice	3
travail (m)	work	2
travailler	work, to	2
traversée (f)	crossing	7
traverser	cross, to	6
très	very	2
trouver	find, to	8
TVA (f)	VAT	7
type (m)	type	7

ENGLISH-FRENCH WORDLIST

A

a lot	beaucoup	2
about	vers	7
above	ci-dessus	8
accommodation	hébergement *(m)*	8
accompany, to	accompagner	2
accountant	comptable *(m/f)*	2
adult	adulte *(m)*	7
advice	conseil *(m)*	9, 10
advise, to	conseiller	5
aeroplane	avion *(m)*	7
affordable	abordable	7
after	après	6
afternoon	après-midi *(m/f)*	7
air *(adj.)*	aérien(ne)	7
air conditioning	climatisation *(f)*	5, 8
airfield	aérodrome *(m)*	7
airport	aéroport *(m)*	7
all	tout(e)	2
alone	seul(e)	4, 7
all right?	ça va?	2
always	toujours	2, 4
American	américain(e)	2
and	et	6
anniversary	anniversaire *(m)*	4
annoyed, to get	s'énerver	4
anyway	de toute façon	9
apple	pomme *(f)*	3, 9
apply, to	appliquer	9
appointment	rendez-vous *(m)*	9
April	avril	4

archery	tir *(m)* à l'arc	4
archipelago	archipel *(m)*	9
arrange to meet, to	se retrouver	5
arrival	arrivée *(f)*	7
arrive, to	arriver	7
as, like	comme	2, 4
ashtray	cendrier *(m)*	8
asphalted	bitumé(e)	7
at what time…?	à quelle heure…?	2
attic	grenier *(m)*	10
August	août	4
aunt	tante *(f)*	4
autumn	automne *(m)*	6
available	disponible	8
Avocado	avocat *(m)*	3

B

baby	bébé *(m)*	7
back	dos *(m)*	9
bad	mauvais(e)	6
badly	mal	2
bag	sac *(m)*	2
baker	boulanger/boulangère	2
basement	sous-sol *(m)*	10
bath	baignoire *(f)*	8, 10
battered	pané(e)	5
battery	pile *(f)*	3
be, to	être	1
be born, to	naître	1, 10
be called, to	s'appeler	1
be in a hurry, to	être pressé(e)	8

be located, to	se trouver	6
beach	plage *(f)*	4, 8
bean	haricot *(m)*	3
beautiful/nice	beau/belle	6, 8
because	parce que, car	2, 8
become, to	devenir	5
bedroom	chambre *(f)*	8, 10
beef	bœuf *(m)*	5
behind	derrière	6
belfry	beffroi *(m)*	6
below	ci-dessous	8
belt	ceinture *(f)*	10
bench	banquette *(f)*	8
benefit	bienfait *(m)*	9
between… and…	entre… et…	6
bicycle	vélo *(m)*	7
big (fat)	gros(se)	8
big (tall)	grand(e)	2, 4, 7, 8
bill	addition *(f)*	5
bill (hotel)	note *(f)*	8
bin	poubelle *(f)*	8
bird	oiseau *(m)*	8
birth	naissance *(f)*	5
birthday	anniversaire *(m)*	4
bite (insect)	piqûre *(f)*	9
black	noir(e)	10
blackcurrant	cassis *(m)*	3
blanket	couverture *(f)*	8
blocked	bouché(e)	9
blood pressure	tension *(f)*	9
blue	bleu(e)	7, 10

boarding	embarquement *(m)*	7		can you tell me…?		coach	car *(m)*	7
boat	bateau *(m)*	7			pouvez-vous me	coast	côte *(f)*	4
body building	musculation *(f)*	4, 9			dire…?	4	coat hanger	cintre *(m)*	8
bone	os *(m)*	9		can/be able		cocoa	cacao *(m)*	3
bonnet	capot *(m)*	7		to, to	pouvoir	1, 5	coffee	café *(m)*	3
book, to	réserver	7		cancel, to	annuler	9	colander	passoire *(f)*	8
boot (car)	coffre *(m)*	7		candle	chandelle *(f)*	5	cold *(adj.)*	froid(e)	5, 6
born…, I was	je suis né(e)…	1		canned food	conserves *(fpl)*	3	cold (illness)	rhume *(m)*	9
bottle	bouteille *(f)*	3		capsule	gélule *(f)*	9	collar	col *(m)*	10
bottle opener	limonadier *(m)*	8		car	voiture *(f)*	4, 7	computer	ordinateur *(m)*	8
boy	garçon *(m)*	4		car, by	en voiture	6	conservatory	jardin *(m)* d'hiver	8
bracket	parenthèse *(f)*	8		car door	portière *(f)*	7	consist of, to	consister à	2
brain	cerveau *(m)*	10		carry, to	porter	9	content(s)	contenu *(m)*	8, 9
bread	pain *(m)*	3, 5		cash	espèces *(fpl)*;		continue, to	continuer	6
break, to	casser	7			en liquide	2, 7	convenient?,		
breakfast	petit déjeuner *(m)*	4, 8		cashier	hôte/hôtesse de caisse	2	is it	ça vous convient?	9
bridge	pont *(m)*	4, 6		cashpoint	distributeur *(m)*		cooked	cuit(e)	5
bright	vif/vive	10			de billets	6	cooking	cuisine *(f)*	4, 10
bring, to	apporter	9		castle	château *(m)*	6	corn	maïs *(m)*	3
bring back, to	ramener	7		cat	chat *(m)*	9	corner	coin *(m)*	10
broken down	en panne	7		catch the bus,			correct, to	corriger	9
brother	frère *(m)*	4		to	prendre le bus	5	corridor	couloir *(m)*	10
brown	marron	10		cave	grotte *(f)*	10	cost, to	coûter	3
bruise	coup *(m)*	9		century	siècle *(m)*	8	cotton	coton *(m)*	10
bucket	seau *(m)*	8		check, to	vérifier	3, 7	cough	toux *(f)*	9
building	bâtiment *(m)*	4		check-up	contrôle *(m)*	9	country	pays *(m)*	1, 2, 7
bulb	ampoule *(f)*	8		cheese	fromage *(m)*	3, 5	countryside	campagne *(f)*	8
burn	brûlure *(f)*	9		chef/cook	cuisinier/cuisinière	2	course	cours *(m)*	3
bus	bus *(m)*	7		cheque	chèque *(m)*	2, 7	cream	crème *(f)*	3
businesswoman	femme *(f)* d'affaires	4		chest	poitrine *(f)*	10	creche	garderie *(f)*	3
busy	occupé(e)	2, 9		chicken	poulet *(m)*	3, 5	credit card	carte *(f)* de crédit	2, 7
but	mais	2, 6		child	enfant *(m/f)*	1, 7	crisps	chips *(mpl)*	3
button	bouton *(m)*	10		chips	frites *(fpl)*	3	cross, to	traverser	6
buy, to	acheter	2, 10		chives	ciboulette *(f)*	3	crossing	traversée *(f)*	7
bye!	salut!	1		choose, to	choisir	2, 7, 8	crossroad	carrefour *(m)*	6
				church	église *(f)*	6	crossword(s)	mots *(mpl)* croisés	4
C				cinnamon	cannelle *(f)*	3	cup	tasse *(f)*	8
				city	ville *(f)*	1, 2, 5	cupboard	placard *(m)*	3, 10
cabinet	cabinet *(m)*	9		climb up, to	monter	9	(wardrobe)	armoire *(f)*	8, 9
calf (leg)	mollet *(m)*	10		closed	fermé(e)	4	cutlery	couverts *(mpl)*	8
camel	chameau *(m)*	7		closing	fermeture *(f)*	5			
camper-van	camping-car *(m)*	7		clothing	habillement *(m)*	4	**D**		
can opener	ouvre-boîtes *(m)*	8		clothing					
can you repeat				(piece of)	vêtement *(m)*	10	damage	dommages *(mpl)*	7
please?	vous pouvez			cloudy	couvert(e);		daughter	fille *(f)*	4
	répéter, s'il vous plaît?	1			nuageux(euse)	6	day	jour *(m)*	4
							day(time)	journée *(f)*	4

ham	jambon (m)	3	how much does it come to?	ça fait combien?	3	kettle	bouilloire (f)	8

English	French	Unit
ham	jambon (m)	3
hand, on the other	par contre	9
handsome	beau	8
happy	heureux(euse); joyeux(euse)	8, 10
hat	chapeau (m)	10
hate, to	détester	4
have, to	avoir	1
have, I'll / having…, I'm	je prends…	3
have a look, to	jeter un œil	9
have a pre-dinner drink	prendre l'apéritif	5
have dinner, to	dîner	5
have to, to	devoir	5
head	tête (f)	9
headlight	phare (m)	7
health	santé (f)	4, 9
hear, to	entendre	8
heart	cœur (m)	4, 9
heating	chauffage (m)	4, 8, 10
heavy	lourd(e)	9
help, to	aider	4, 7
hen	poule (f)	9
herbal tea	infusion (f)	3
here	ici	6
here is/are…	voici…	2
here it is	voilà	7
hi!	salut!	1
high	haut(e)	4
hiking	randonnée (f)	4
hill	colline (f)	6
hire, to	louer	7, 10
hire/hiring	location (f)	4, 7
holidays	vacances (fpl)	7
homework	devoirs (mpl)	4
hope, to	espérer	6
horse	cheval (m)	4, 9
hot	chaud(e)	5, 6
hour	heure (f)	7
house	maison (f)	4, 6, 10
housework	ménage (m)	4
housing	logement (m)	4
how are you?	comment allez-vous?	2
how is it going?	comment ça va?	2
how long	combien de temps	7

English	French	Unit
how much does it come to?	ça fait combien?	3
how much is it?	c'est combien?	3
how much/many	combien	7
hungry, I'm	j'ai faim	5
husband	mari (m)	4
hypermarket	hypermarché (m)	2

I

English	French	Unit
ice cube	glaçon (m)	3
ice rink	patinoire (f)	4
illness	maladie (f)	9
improve, to	améliorer	9
in	dans	6
in case of	en cas de	7
in front of	devant	6
in the heart of	au cœur de	6, 8
in the middle of	au milieu de	6
include, to	comprendre	4
included	compris(e)	7
indicator	clignotant (m)	7
injection	piqûre (f)	9
insurance	assurance (f)	7
Ireland	Irlande (f)	2
Irish	irlandais(e)	2
ironing	repassage (m)	4
island	île (f)	9
island, small	îlot (m)	9
IT consultant	informaticien/ informaticienne	2
it's …	c'est …	5
it's busy/crowded	il y a du monde	8
itch, to	démanger	9

J

English	French	Unit
jacket	veste (f)	10
jam	confiture (f)	3
January	janvier	4
jewellery (piece of)	bijou (m)	10
July	juillet	4
June	juin	4

K

English	French	Unit
keep records of, to	enregistrer	2

English	French	Unit
kettle	bouilloire (f)	8
key	clé/clef (f)	7
kidney	rognon (m)	5
kind (adj.)	gentil(le), sympa	5
kind (sort)	genre (m)	5
kiss	bise (f)	6
kitchen	cuisine (f)	4, 10
knee	genou (m)	9
know, to (a thing)	savoir	4, 5, 6, 10
know, to (a place/person)	connaître	6

L

English	French	Unit
lace	dentelle (f)	10
lamb	agneau (m)	5
language	langue (f)	1, 2, 9
last	dernier/dernière	5
lawyer	avocat (m)	3
leak, to	fuir	8
learn, to	apprendre	5, 9
leave (thing), to	laisser	9
leave, to	partir	7
leek	poireau (m)	5
left, to/on the	à gauche	6
leg	jambe (f)	9
lemon	citron (m)	3
length	longueur (f)	10
less	moins	9
letter box	boîte (f) aux lettres	3
library	bibliothèque (f)	4, 6
lie, to	mentir	10
life	vie (f)	2
lighting	éclairage (m)	4, 8
like, to	aimer	4, 5
like…, I would	je voudrais…	3
lime	citron (m) vert	3
limited	limité(e)	7
linen	linge (m)	8
lip	lèvre (f)	9
lipstick	rouge (m) à lèvres	5
listen, to	écouter	5, 6, 8
live, to	habiter	1
living room	séjour (m)	10
lonely	seul(e)	4
look after, to	s'occuper de	2, 4

English	French	Unit
look for, to	chercher	8
lorry driver	routier (m)	4
lost, to get	se perdre	6
lounge	salon (m)/ séjour (m)	10
love, to	aimer	4, 5
love (adore), to	adorer	2, 5
lozenge	pastille (f)	9
luck	chance (f)	4
lunch	déjeuner (m)	4, 5
lunch, to	déjeuner	5
lung	poumon (m)	9

M

English	French	Unit
madam/Mrs	madame	1
main course	plat (m) principal	5
maintenance	entretien (m)	4, 7
make, to	faire	2, 4
manage, to	gérer	9
manager	chef (m/f); directeur/directrice	2
marble	marbre (m)	3
March	mars	4
market	marché (m)	6
married	marié(e)	1
May	mai	4
meal	repas (m)	5
means of transport	moyen (m) de transport	7
meat	viande (f)	3, 5
medicine	médicament (m)	9
medium	moyen(ne)	2
medium-rare (steak)	à point	5
meeting (encounter)	rencontre (f)	4
meeting (gathering)	réunion (f)	9
mileage	kilométrage (m)	7
milk	lait (m)	3
minced	haché(e)	5
mint	menthe (f)	5
miss	mademoiselle	1
mobile (phone)	portable (m)	6, 8
Monday	lundi (m)	2, 4
money	argent (m)	4
month	mois (m)	4
mood	humeur (f)	9
more	plus	9
morning	matin (m)	2

English	French	Unit
mother	mère (f)	4
motorbike	moto (f)	7
motorway	autoroute (f)	6, 8
mountain	montagne (f)	4, 8
Mr	monsieur	1
mushroom	champignon (m)	5
music academy	conservatoire (m)	6
must/have to, to	devoir	5
mustard	moutarde (f)	3, 5

N

English	French	Unit
name	nom (m)	1
name is…, my	je m'appelle…	1
nap	sieste (f)	9
near	proche; à proximité	8
nearby	près d'ici	6
necklace	collier (m)	10
need	besoin (m)	5
need…, I	il me faut…/ j'ai besoin de…	3
nephew	neveu (m)	4
Netherlands	Pays-Bas (mpl)	2
network	réseau (m)	6, 7
never	jamais	4
new	nouveau/nouvelle	8
next	prochain(e)	7
next to	à côté de	6
niece	nièce (f)	4
night	nuit (f)	8
no	non	1
noise	bruit (m)	7, 8
noisy	bruyant(e)	8
November	novembre	4
now	maintenant	2
number	nombre (m)	2
number	numéro (m)	1
numerous	nombreux(euse)	4, 8
nurse	infirmier/infirmière	2
nutmeg	muscade (f)	3

O

English	French	Unit
October	octobre	4
office/study	bureau (m)	2, 10
often	souvent	4
oil	huile (f)	3
old	vieux/vieille	8
on	sur	6
only	seulement	2
open	ouvert(e)	4

English	French	Unit
opening	ouverture (f)	5
opposite	en face de	6
orange	orange	10
outside	devant	6
oven	four (m)	5
over there	là-bas	6, 7
overcoat	pardessus (m)	10
overtake, to (driving)	dépasser	9
oyster	huître (f)	5

P

English	French	Unit
package holiday	voyage (m) organisé	7
paid for, to be/ not free	payant	4
pain	douleur (f)	9
painful	douloureux(euse)	9
paint, to	peindre	7, 10
paint/painting	peinture (f)	4
paragliding	parapente (f)	4
park, to	garer	4
parsley	persil (m)	3
part time	à mi-temps	2
pass me… (formal)	passez-moi…	3
pass me… (informal)	passe-moi…	3
passenger	passager (m)	7
pasta	pâtes (fpl)	3, 5
path	sentier (m)	4
payment	paiement (m)	2
peal of bells	carillon (m)	6
peanut	cacahuète (f)	3
pepper	poivre (m)	3
petrol station	station-service (f)	3
physiotherapist	kinésithérapeute (m/f)	9
piece	morceau (m)	3
pineapple	ananas (m)	3
pink	rose	10
pitch	terrain (m)	4
place	lieu (m) /endroit (m)	2, 8
place (space)	emplacement (m)	7
plan (foresee), to	prévoir	9
plaster	pansement (m)	9
plate	assiette (f)	8
play, to	jouer	4
playground	aire (f) de jeu	4
please (formal)	s'il vous plaît	1, 3
please		

(informal)	s'il te plaît	3	road	route (f)	6, 7	small	petit(e)	2, 7, 8

English	French	Ref
(informal)	s'il te plaît	3
pleased to meet you	enchanté(e)	1
pocket	poche (f)	10
Poland	Pologne (f)	2
Polish	polonais(e)	2
pond	étang (m)	8
postpone, to	reporter	9
potato	pomme (f) de terre	3, 5
prescribe, to	prescrire	9
prescription	ordonnance (f)	9
preserve, to	préserver	9
prevent, to	prévenir	9
price	prix (m)	7
proud	fier/fière	8
put, to	mettre	2
put back, to	remettre	8

R

English	French	Ref
railway station	gare (f)	6
railway (adj.)	ferroviaire	7
rain, to	pleuvoir	6
rainy	pluvieux(euse)	6
rare (steak)	saignant	5
rare, very (steak)	bleu	5
rarely	rarement	4
raspberry	framboise (f)	3
rather	plutôt	4
receive, to	recevoir	2
red	rouge	10
reduce, to	diminuer/ réduire	9
registration plate	plaque (f) d'immatriculation	7
relax, to	se détendre	8
relaxed	décontracté(e)	5
remind, to	rappeler	9
rent, to	louer	7, 10
rental/renting	location (f)	4, 7
reply, to	répondre	3
rest	repos (m)	9
return (ticket)	aller-retour	7
rice	riz (m)	3, 5
right, to/on the	à droite	6
ring	bague (f)	10
river	fleuve (m)	6

English	French	Ref
road	route (f)	6, 7
rock climbing	escalade (f)	4
rowing	aviron (m)	4

S

English	French	Ref
safe	coffre-fort (m)	8
safety pin	épingle (f) de sûreté	9
salmon	saumon (m)	5
salt	sel (m)	3
Saturday	samedi (m)	2, 4
saucepan	casserole (f)	8
scissors	ciseaux (mpl)	9
Scotland	Ecosse (f)	2
Scottish	écossais(e)	2
sea	mer (f)	8
seaside resort	station (f) balnéaire	10
seat	banquette (f)	8
secretary	secrétaire (m/f)	2
see, to	voir	6
seem, to	sembler	9
sell, to	vendre	2, 10
sensitise, to	sensibiliser	9
September	septembre	4
served	servi(e)	5
shampoo	shampooing (m)	3
shirt	chemise (f)	10
shoe	chaussure (f)	10
shoe size	pointure (f)	10
shop	magasin (m)	2
shopping	courses (fpl)	4
shower	douche (f)	8
shutter	volet (m)	10
side of, by the	au bord de	8
silk	soie (f)	10
silver	argent (m)	4
single	célibataire	1
single (ticket)	aller-simple	7
sir	monsieur	1
sister	sœur (f)	4
size	taille (f)	10
skate	patin (m)	4
skin	peau (f)	9
sleep, to	dormir	10
sleeping tablet	somnifère (m)	9
sleeve	manche (f)	10
slice	tranche (f)	3

English	French	Ref
small	petit(e)	2, 7, 8
smoke, to	fumer	2
smoked	fumé(e)	5
snow, to	neiger	6
so, consequently	donc	2
so, so! (formal)	comme ci, comme ça!	2
so, so! (informal)	bof!	2
soap	savon (m)	9
socket	prise (f)	8
softness	douceur (f)	10
solicitor	avocat (m)	3
sometimes	quelquefois	4
son	fils (m)	4
sorry	désolé(e)	6
sort	genre (m); sorte (f)	5, 7
space	emplacement (m)	7
sparkling	gazeux/gazeuse	8
speak, to	parler	2
spell, to	épeler	1
spend (time), to	passer	8, 10
spice	épice (f)	3
spinach	épinard (m)	5
spoon	cuillère (f)	3, 9
sprain	foulure (f)	9
spring(time)	printemps (m)	6
square	place (f)	6
stairs	escalier (m)	9
start, to	commencer	2
starter	entrée (f)	5
station	gare (f)	7
stay	séjour (m)	8
stay, to	rester	5
still (water)	plat(e)	8
stomach	estomac (m)	9
stone	pierre (f)	10
stop, to	arrêter	9
straight	droit	4
straight on	tout droit	6
street	rue (f)	6
stretching	étirement (m)	9
stripe	rayure (f)	10
stuck	coincé(e)	8
student	étudiant/étudiante	1, 2
study, to	étudier	2
submarine	sous-marin(e)	9

windscreen wiper	essuie-glace *(m)*	7
windsurfing board	planche *(f)* à voile	4
wine	vin *(m)*	3
winter	hiver *(m)*	5, 6
wish!, I	j'aimerais bien!	4
woman	femme *(f)*	4
wood	bois *(m)*	10
woody	boisé(e)	8
work	travail *(m)*	2
work, to	travailler	2
work (operate), to	marcher	7, 8
world	monde *(m)*	2
wound	plaie *(f)*	9

Y

yard	cour *(f)*	10
year	an *(m)*; année *(f)*	1, 7
yellow	jaune	7, 10
yes	oui	1
yoghurt	yaourt *(m)*	5
young	jeune	8

SOLUTIONS TO EXERCISES

UNIT 1

1 On Commence

A ✔ Profession ✔ Name
✔ Address Marital Status
Telephone number

B QUEL EST VOTRE NOM?
QUELLE EST VOTRE ADRESSE?
QUELLE EST VOTRE PROFESSION?

D **A** Bonsoir, je m'**appelle** Pierre Jacques. Mon **nom** est Jacques et mon **prénom** est Pierre.
B **Je** m'appelle Laure Boisin.
A **Enchanté.**
B Enchantée.

3 Qui suis-je?

A 1 I am a maths teacher. 2 I have two children. 3 I am married. 4 I live in Brussels. 5 I was born in Montreal. 6 I am Swiss. 7 I am twenty.

B 1 **b** Paul; 2 **d** Justine; 3 **a** Jamal;
4 **c** Nathalie.

C 1 Je **suis** garagiste. 2 J'**ai** quatre enfants. 3 Je **suis** célibataire. 4 J'**habite** en France. 5 Je **m'appelle** Jamal. 6 Je **suis** de Londres. 7 Je **suis** anglais. 8 J'**ai** 32 ans.

D 1 Il **s'appelle** Michel Bourgeois. 2 Je **suis** de Lille. 3 Brigitte **habite** à Birmingham. 4 Elle **est** française. 5 Christian **est** marié. 6 Il **a** deux enfants. 7 Vous **avez** un téléphone portable? 8 J'**ai** 55 ans.

E 1 Il est garagiste. 2 Il a quatre enfants. 3 Il est célibataire. 4 Elle habite en France. 5 Il s'appelle Jamal. 6 Il est de Londres. 7 Il est anglais. 8 Elle a 32 ans.

F a – 18 ✔ f – 41 ✔ k – 40 ✔
b – 24 g – 50 ✔ l – 68 ✔
c – 66 ✔ h – 50 m – 13 ✔
d – 40 i – 12 ✔ n – 31
e – 13 j – 16 o – 36

4 Et vous?

B Vous êtes marié(e)? Vous avez des enfants? Vous habitez Liverpool? Vous êtes de Bruxelles? Quelle est votre adresse? Vous êtes français(e)? Quelle est votre nationalité? Quel est votre prénom?

C **Lambert:** Philippe / divorcé / décorateur
Julien: Ablond / Calais / 2 / 33 / technicien
Dupont: Amandine / Nice / célibataire / 0 / 18 / étudiante

La Francophonie

A Group of countries or communities where French is the mother tongue, or used as the official or business language.

B a – le Canada ✔ f – le Royaume-Uni
b – la Belgique ✔ g – l'Egypte ✔
c – le Portugal h – l'Inde
d – la Suisse ✔ i – le Vietnam ✔
e – le Sénégal ✔ j – le Maroc ✔

UNIT 2

1 Vous vous souvenez?

A 1 **e**, 2 **d**, 3 **b**, 4 **a**, 5 **c**.

B Bonjour Julien. Voici Mary. Elle a 28 ans, elle est née à Cardiff et elle habite à Londres.

2 Quoi de neuf?

A 1 **f**, 2 **a**, 3 **c**, 4 **g**, 5 **d**, 6 **b**, 7 **e**.

B Marianne est mariée. Marianne travaille pour une petite entreprise. Yves travaille pour une compagnie hollandaise. Yves est chef de production.

ACCESS FRENCH

3 Les genres

A 2 Britney est américaine. 4 Véronique est mariée. 6 Marie est petite.

B 1 anglais – anglaise. 2 gallois – galloise. 3 écossais – écossaise. 4 irlandais – irlandaise.

4 Quelle est votre profession?

A 1 Cashier – **a** Justine. 2 Retired – **c** Thérèse. 3 Guide – **b** Mark.

B 1 Faux. 2 Vrai. 3 Vrai. 4 Vrai. 5 Vrai. 6 Vrai.

5 Le présent

A 1 J'étudie … 2 Nous emballons … 3 Vous accompagnez … 4 Elle choisit … 5 Les enfants grandissent … 6 Ils rendent … 7 Je descends … 8 je me réveille … 9 Nous nous promenons …

B 1 I study French and Italian at university. 2 We pack the customers' shopping. 3 Do you accompany the tourists to the hotel? 4 She's choosing a souvenir from Paris. 5 Children grow up quickly. 6 They visit Chantal regularly. 7 I'm going down the stairs. 8 I normally wake up at 7 o'clock. 9 We walk in the park every Sunday.

6 Compagnie internationale

A compagnie, Directeur Général, supermarchés, hypermarchés, Europe, employez, personnes.

B 1 supermarkets and hypermarkets; 2 25; 3 France, Germany, Belgium, Spain, Portugal, Czech Republic, and Poland.

C bureau, je sais, occupé, magasins, plein temps, c'est difficile, ça dépend.

7 Des nombres

A 1 **c**, 2 **d**, 3 **h**, 4 **b**, 5 **g**, 6 **a**, 7 **f**, 8 **e**.

C Québec-City: 89 employees. Boston: 72 employees. Valenciennes: 94 employees. Rouen: 75 employees.

8 Encore des questions?

A 1 **a** Je m'appelle Patrick Nadler. **b** N-A-D-L-E-R. **c** Je suis chiropracteur-ostéopathe. **d** Je travaille à Papeete, à Tahiti. **e** Quarante-deux, vingt-trois, trente. 2 **a** Ma compagnie s'appelle Buro online. **b** Mon prénom est Laurent. **c** Je suis Webmaster. **d** Oui, je travaille à Lognes. **e** Laurent 'point' greber 'arrobas' buronline 'point' com.

B *Dialogue 1:* étudiant, qu'est-ce que, tous les jours, mercredi. *Dialogue 2:* infirmière, à quelle heure, vers, le soir, quelquefois, jeudi, ménage.

C 1 Je ne fume pas. 2 Je ne parle pas italien. 3 Je ne suis pas marié(e).

La Francophonie

A **a** capital city, **b** number of inhabitants of Ottawa, **c** population of Canada, **d** people of French origin, **e** people of Dutch origin, **f** people of German origin, **g** second official language, **h** proportion of Jewish people, **i** subdivision of Canadian dollar.

B March, Charlemagne (Quebec); married, agent; eyes; self-determination, professionalism, discipline; drinks alcohol, drugs, smoke; white, red; shoes; singers.

Looking forward

cheese, tea, orange juice, bread, butter, oil, ham, jam.

UNIT 3
1 Vous vous souvenez

B 1 **c** étudiante, 2 **d** secrétaire, 3 **a** réceptionniste, 4 **b** avocate, 5 **e** dentiste.

2 Avant tout

A *Dans le placard:* le café, le thé, le sucre, les pâtes. *Dans le réfrigérateur:* la bière, le lait, la crème fraîche, les fruits, la limonade, le pâté, le vin blanc.

B 1 la salade, 2 l'eau, 3 l'huile et le vinaigre, 4 la sauce, 5 le sucre, 6 les légumes, 7 la limonade.

3 En route pour le shopping

A 1 Vrai (24h/24). 2 Vrai (garderie). 3 Faux (Monday to Saturday). 4 Faux (only clothes and batteries). 5 Vrai (presse).

B 1 Boucherie, 2 Epicerie salée, 3 Conserves, 4 Fruits, Légumes, 5 Produits Laitiers, 6 Boulangerie, 7 Produits Laitiers, 8 Vins, Alcools, 9 Soin, Hygiène, 10 Maison, 11 Boisson.

C 1 du poulet, 2 du fromage, 3 du vin rouge, 4 du liquide vaisselle, 5 de la confiture.

D 1 **roast beef**, oil, ham, carrots, beer 2 **beer**, bread, **3 kg of apples**, **1 cucumber**, shampoo 3 **coffee**, frozen chips, **margarine**, **lemon tart**, roast chicken, **paper napkins**.

E 1 du jambon, 2 la salade, 3 des chips, 4 le shampooing, 5 de la viande, 6 l'huile.

4 On prend un verre?

B Diabolo menthe, (café-)crème, jus de tomate, bière, vin rouge.

C désirez, soif, avec, prends, jus, voudrais, verre, addition, combien.

5 Les quantités

A 1 **e**, 2 **f**, 3 **g**, 4 **h**, 5 **i**, 6 **c**, 7 **j**, 8 **d**, 9 **a**, 10 **b**.

B 250 grammes de beurre, un kilo de pommes de terre, 750 grammes d'oranges, un litre d'huile d'olive, un paquet de biscuits, une tranche de jambon, un morceau de gâteau, un pot de confiture, une plaque de chocolat, un peu de sauce.

C 240 g de farine, 120 g de sucre, 120 g de beurre, 4 jaunes d'œufs, 80 g de sucre glace, 300 g de confiture de framboises, une pincée de sel.

La Francophonie

A 1 Catholic, Protestant and voodoo. 2 Creole. 3 Tropical climate. 4 Port-au-Prince. 5 Its culture, painting, music and for making visitors welcome. 6 Coffee beans, corn, rice, beans, bananas, cocoa beans, sugar cane, mangoes, pineapples, pawpaws, mandarins. 7 Marble.

B 2 avocados, 1 tin of crabmeat, chives, 1 shallot, red chillies, 1 lime, oil, salt, pepper, white wine, 2 kg tuna, 2 tomatoes, 1 onion, 2 lemons, thyme, parsley, 1l milk, cocoa powder, eggs, sugar, cinnamon stick, nutmeg, cornflour, vanilla, roasted peanuts or split almonds.

Looking forward

playing the piano, swimming, washing up, ironing, playing badminton, collecting stamps.

UNIT 4

1 Vous vous souvenez

A 1 du café, une tasse de café; 2 des pommes, un kilo de pommes; 3 de la quiche, un morceau de quiche; 4 du saucisson, une tranche de saucisson; 5 de l'eau, une bouteille d'eau.

2 On y va …

A crazy golf, bowls, swimming, archery.

B volley-ball, swimming pool, ice skating.

3 Mon temps libre

A 1 Quand je ne travaille pas… **b** et bien, je m'occupe de la maison. 2 Et le week-end, et bien, … **h** nous allons à la piscine le samedi matin. 3 Nous allons quelquefois…

g au cinéma et ensuite, nous allons au MacDo. 4 Je suis plutôt sportif: **e** je fais du football, de la musculation. 5 Le curling?… **c** C'est comme la pétanque, mais sur glace. 6 J'ai deux enfants… **f** et j'aime rester avec eux. 7 Nous regardons la télévision… **d** mais j'aide aussi ma femme dans les tâches ménagères. 8 Je suis aussi musicien… **a** et je joue de la guitare et de la batterie.

B *Interview 1*

… je m'occupe **de la maison** car j'ai **trois** enfants et croyez-moi, il y a du travail… Alors, je fais le ménage, et **j'ai horreur de** faire le ménage…

Interview 2

Homme: Et bien, je suis plutôt sportif: je fais du football, de la **musculation** et depuis quelques **mois**, je fais du curling.

Juliette: Du curling ? Qu'est-ce que c'est ?

Homme: Le curling? C'est comme la pétanque, mais sur glace. Je vais à la **patinoire** une fois par semaine, le samedi matin et **j'aime beaucoup** ce sport.

Interview 3

Je suis aussi **musicien** et je joue **de la guitare** et de la batterie. Ma femme **n'aime pas** quand je m'exerce à la batterie, je ne sais pas pourquoi…

C Je fais du basket. Je joue au ping-pong. Nous faisons les mots croisés. Je fais de la plongée sous-marine. Elle joue au hockey. Il joue du violon. Vous faites du sport? Tu joues aux jeux électroniques? Il fait de la peinture?

4 A la maison

A 1 **f** washing up, 2 **e** vacuuming, 3 **d** shopping, 4 **c** ironing, 5 **a** cooking, 6 **b** making the bed.

B **Juliette:** Excusez-moi, monsieur, vous êtes marié?

Homme: Oui, ma femme est là-bas, elle gare la **voiture**.

Juliette: Alors pouvez-vous me dire qui fait le ménage à la maison?

Homme: C'est moi! Je fais la cuisine et je

fais la vaisselle tous les soirs. Et puis dans la **journée**, je fais le lit, je fais la **lessive**, je passe l'aspirateur une fois par semaine et je fais le repassage aussi.

Juliette: Mais votre femme a beaucoup de **chance**. Tiens, la voilà! Bonjour madame, mais quelle chance d'avoir un mari qui vous **aide** dans les tâches ménagères!

Femme: Comment? Un mari qui m'aide? J'aimerais bien! Il ne fait **rien** à la maison! Moi, je travaille, et quand je rentre, je fais la cuisine, la lessive, le repassage, je fais les **poussières** et je fais aussi les courses. Un mari qui m'aide?

Homme: Mais ma puce, ne t'énerve pas, je fais la vaisselle **quelquefois**.

Femme: Quelquefois? Une **fois** par an, pour mon anniversaire! Allez, on rentre à la **maison** et je ne suis pas ta puce!

C toujours, souvent, quelquefois, occasionnellement, rarement, jamais.

D 1 Je fais rarement la vaisselle. 2 Je fais toujours le lit. 3 Vous allez quelquefois en boîte? 4 Je regarde toujours les feuilletons. 5 Je vais occasionnellement à la gym.

E 1 **a**, 2 **k**, 3 **e**, 4 **h**, 5 **d**, 6 **i**, 7 **f**, 8 **c**, 9 **g**, 10 **j**, 11 **b**.

F C'est le vingt-six décembre. C'est le vingt-trois avril. C'est le trente novembre. C'est le premier mars. C'est le dix mars. C'est le seize juin. C'est le quatorze février.

5 Ma famille

A grands-parents, grand-père, grand-mère, parents, oncle, frère, père, mère, tante, sœur, cousin(s), fils, nièce, neveu.

B 1 Nelly – **c**; 2 Pascale – **b**; 3 Thierry – **d**; 4 Aïsha – **a**.

C 1 Le père de **ma** mère est **mon** grand-père. 2 La sœur de **votre** mère est **votre** tante. 3 Les enfants de **notre** oncle sont **nos** cousins. 4 La fille de **votre** mère est **votre** sœur. 5 **Sa** maison et **son** jardin sont magnifiques. 6 **Son** chien est tellement mignon. 7 **Son** petit-ami est anglais, il habite à Londres. 8 Julien est de Paris, mais **sa** sœur est née à Nice.

6 Et pour finir …

A 1 Faux (18 months old). 2 Vrai. 3 Faux (she does some cleaning for elderly people). 4 Faux (her mother and sister-in-law help her). 5 Vrai. 6 Vrai.

B 1 Je suis le père de trois enfants. 2 Ma femme est femme d'affaires / dans les affaires. 3 Elle voyage partout en France et en Grande-Bretagne. 4 Je me rends compte que travailler pour 6,70 euros de l'heure n'en vaut pas la peine. 5 Ma belle-mère m'aide beaucoup. 6 Je dois préparer le dîner et faire la vaisselle.

La Francophonie

A **a** coastline, **b** largest beach in Europe, **c** highest mountain in France, **d** number of vegetable/plant species, **e** types of cheese.

B

6 Number work

Horizontal: metropole, départements, santé, logement, loisirs, alimentation, salaire

Vertical: territoires, transports, biens, chauffage, tabac

UNIT 5

1 Vous vous souvenez?

A mère, tante, femme, sœur, nièce.

B *Examples of answers:* Josiane, la mère de Bernard, tricote. Roger, le père de Nathalie, regarde la télévision. Bernard, le mari de Marie, fait des mots croisés. Marie, la belle-fille de Roger, fait de la peinture. Nathalie, la femme de Joussef, fait des courses. Joussef, l'oncle de Lucas, fait du repassage. Lucas, le fils de Marie, joue de la guitare. Lucie, la sœur de Lucas, fait du cheval/fait de l'équitation. Nathan, le cousin de Lucie, joue aux jeux électroniques.

2 On va au resto?

A 1 Le Tutti Frutti/La Petite Faim. 2 Mi Ranchito. 3 Le Tutti Frutti/La Petite Faim/A Cloche-Pied/Mi Ranchito/La Grande Brasserie. 4 Le Tutti Frutti/Mi Ranchito/La Grande Brasserie. 5 Mi Ranchito. 6 Le Tutti Frutti/ La Petite Faim/A Cloche-Pied/La Grande Brasserie/Le Nectar. 7 La Grande Brasserie.

B 1 Faux (no dress code). 2 Vrai. 3 Faux (by the manor gardens). 4 Faux. 5 Faux (no credit cards accepted). 6 Faux (oysters). 7 Faux (climatisation).

3 Tu prends l'apéro

A Pascale: Allô!

Annie: Allô, Pascale? Bonjour, **c'est** Annie.

Pascale: Ah, Annie, comment ça va?

Annie: Ben ça va! Ecoute, je t'appelle pour savoir si tu **peux** venir prendre l'apéritif samedi **soir** avec Philippe.

Pascale: Samedi? Non, Annie, je ne peux pas. Je vais **chez** ma belle-mère, c'est son anniversaire.

Annie: Ah! C'est dommage; et dimanche?

Pascale: Dimanche, oui, ça va, je **veux** bien. A quelle heure?

Annie: Vous **pouvez** venir pour midi. El vous **voulez** manger avec nous?

Pascale: Non, Annie, c'est très gentil mais je **dois** finir mon projet pour lundi.

Annie: Tu es sûre? Je **fais** un couscous…

Pascale: Et j'**adore** le couscous. Ecoute, d'accord … mais on ne restera pas tard.

Annie: Pas de problème. A dimanche alors!

Pascale: Merci Annie, à dimanche!

B 1 **e**, 2 **b**, 3 **g**, 4 **c**, 5 **i**, 6 **h**, 7 **f**, 8 **a**, 9 **d**.

C A Salut Michel(le), ça va?
  B Ça va! Et toi?
  A Ça va! Ecoute, tu veux aller prendre un verre avec nous ce soir?
  B Ce soir? Malheureusement, je ne peux pas.

A C'est dommage!
B Je dois aller chez Véronique, c'est son anniversaire.
A Elle peut venir aussi, si elle veut.
B D'accord! On se retrouve où?
A Au Café de la Mairie, à 20h00.
B D'accord. A ce soir!

A Bonjour Michel(le), ça va?
B Ça va! Et vous?
A Ça va! Ecoutez, vous voulez aller prendre un verre avec nous ce soir?
B Ce soir? Malheureusement, je ne peux pas.
A C'est dommage!
B Je dois aller chez Véronique, c'est son anniversaire.
A Elle peut venir aussi, si elle veut.
B D'accord! On se retrouve où?
A Au Café de la Mairie, à 20h00.
B D'accord. A ce soir!

4 Tu veux manger au resto?

A starter: **entrée**, main courses: **plats principaux**, dessert: **dessert**, fish: **poisson**, meat: **viande**, vegetables: **légumes**, homemade: **maison**, seafood: **fruits de mer**, chips: **frites**, included: **compris**.

B 1 6.40€. 2 5.20€. 3 11.90€. 4 12.50€. 5 9.30€. 6 5.50€.

C 1 S, 2 D, 3 S, 4 A, 5 A, 6 S, 7 S, 8 D, 9 A.

D 1 e, 2 c, 3 d, 4 f, 5 b, 6 g, 7 a.

5 Qu'est-ce que c'est 'shepherd's pie'?

A cuit au four: steak and kidney pie/ shepherd's pie; en croûte: steak and kidney pie; un plat froid: Ploughman's; de l'agneau haché: shepherd's pie; de la salade: Ploughman's; du pain: Ploughman's; des rognons: steak and kidney pie; des pickles: Ploughman's; des légumes. steak and kidney pie/shepherd's pie; du bœuf: steak and kidney pie; de la purée de pommes de terre: shepherd's pie; du fromage: Ploughman's.

C 1 Steak and kidney pie? C'est une spécialité anglaise. C'est du bœuf et des rognons cuits avec des légumes, en croûte. 2 Ploughman's? C'est un plat froid. C'est du fromage avec du pain, de la salade et des pickles. 3 Shepherd's pie? C'est de l'agneau haché avec des légumes et de la purée de pommes de terre cuits au four.

6 Quelle soirée!

A Blanca is **hungry**. They've been waiting for **one hour**. The waitress eventually brings a **medium-rare** steak for Thierry and a **sole** for Blanca. The waitress then puts some **vegetables** on the table.

Blanca is suddenly horrified as she sees a **hair** on her fish, and at the same time, Thierry notices that his steak is **too cooked**. Thierry calls the waitress. She apologises and takes the plates **to the kitchen**.

B 1 **b** There's a fly in my salad, it's disgusting! 2 **d** There's some lipstick on my glass. 3 **a** My fork is dirty, would you give me another one please? 4 **e** There's some chicken in it and I'm a vegetarian. 5 **c** There is a mistake in the bill.

La Francophonie

B winter, December, March, meat, vegetables, cheese, bread, week, butter, flour, main cities, kitchen, soup, main course, 10.37€, mother, child.

UNIT 6

1 Vous vous souvenez?

B Line 1: entrée, **fourchette**, plat principal, dessert. Line 2: bleu, saignant, **salé**, bien cuit. Line 3: saumon, thon, truite, **chèvre**. Line 4: **pommes**, poireaux, épinards, champignons. Line 5: cuillère, assiette, verre, **mouche**.

2 Qu'est-ce qu'il y a à faire?

A opera house, cathedral, canals, science museum.

B *Examples of answers:* A Paris, on peut visiter la Tour Eiffel. A Londres, on peut

faire le tour de la ville dans un bus à impérial. A Douai, on peut écouter le carillon.

3 Il y a un distributeur de billets près d'ici?

A *Dialogue 1:* près d'ici, en face, cinéma, là-bas. *Dialogue 2:* en voiture, à pied, rue. *Dialogue 3:* le syndicat d'initiative, désolé. *Dialogue 4:* cinéma, en voiture, derrière.

B 1 cashpoint, 2 cinema, 3 station, 4 Underground station, 5 tourist office, 6 square, 7 post office, 8 car park.

C 1 Vrai. 2 Faux. 3 Vrai. 4 Vrai. 5 Faux. 6 Faux.

4 Pour aller au stade, s'il vous plaît?

A 1 Vrai. 2 Faux (c'est à gauche). 3 Faux (prenez la troisième à droite). 4 Faux (c'est ici, juste à gauche). 5 Faux (prenez la troisième à droite). 6 Vrai.

B 1 Continuez tout **droit**. 2 Prenez la **deuxième** à **gauche**. 3 Oui, **prenez la troisième à droite**. 4 **Prenez la deuxième à droite**. 5 Oui, alors **prenez la troisième à droite** puis **la deuxième à gauche**. 6 **Prenez la première à gauche** puis **continuez tout droit**.

C 1 Le château. 2 Le supermarché. 3 La banque. 4 Le musée.

D When you arrive in Calais, **follow directions for Lille**. When you reach Lille, **follow directions for Valenciennes**. **Take junction 9**, and turn **right** towards Douchy-les-mines. **At the crossroads**, turn right and drive on to **the traffic lights**. Turn **left** and carry on straight on **for about 3 km**. Just **after the bridge**, turn left. The cemetery is **on your right**. Take the **third left**, rue Pasteur, number 26.

5 Quel temps de chien!

A 1 Vrai. 2 Faux (il fait froid). 3 Faux (il fait 8 degrés). 4 Faux (il neige). 5 Vrai.

B 1 Lille: fog, 12°C. 2 Brittany: rain, 10°C max. 3 Paris and 4 East

(Strasbourg): cloudy, 14°C. 5 Lyon: fine weather. 6 The Alps: snow (above 2500 m). 7 Riviera: sunny, thunder storms (tonight). 8 Pyrenees: windy and cold, 7°C. 9 Corsica: cloudy, rain (in the morning).

C 1 En hiver, dans le nord de la France, il pleut beaucoup et il fait froid. 2 Au printemps, en Bretagne, il ne fait pas froid mais il y a beaucoup de nuages et de vent. 3 En été, dans le sud, il fait très chaud et il y a du soleil. 4 En automne, il neige dans les Alpes. 5 Aujourd'hui, ici, il fait du brouillard et il fait seulement 11 degrés.

La Francophonie

A 1 Culture/Musées. 2 Restaurants. 3 Transports. 4 Education. 5 Vues de Liège.

B *First paragraph:* 1 The port is the third largest river port in Europe. 2 Liège is situated in the heart of trans-European rail/road networks. 3 Transport, biotechnology, space research, electricity, steel… *Second paragraph:* The river and the hills. *Third paragraph:* 1 **b** motorway network; **d** high-speed rail network (TGV Thalys). 2 Oui. 3 Restaurants, cinema, theatre. *Fourth paragraph:* 2 Religious art museum. 3 Glassworks museum. 5 Furniture museum. 6 Gun museum.

UNIT 7

1 Vous vous souvenez?

A 1 Il fait du soleil. 2 Il y a des nuages. 3 Il pleut. 4 Il neige. 5 Il fait de l'orage.

2 On y va comment?

A 1 **b** by boat/ferry, 2 **d** on foot, 3 **e** by motorbike, 4 **g** by bus/coach, 5 **i** by underground, 6 **a** by car, 7 **c** by plane, 8 **h** by train, 9 **f** by bike.

B 1 Perpignan, South of France: by car. 2 Montreal and Quebec, Canada: by plane and car. 3 Scotland: by ferry and car. 4 Brittany: by bike. 5 Tunisia: by plane and coach.

C 1 J'y vais tous les jours. 2 Non, j'y vais en train ou en bus. 3 J'y vais deux fois par semaine. 4 Non, il n'y travaille plus depuis un mois. 5 Non, il y va avec ses parents.

D 1 Faux (with his wife). Vrai. 2 Faux (will hire a car). Faux (for two weeks). 3 Faux (she has friends over there). Vrai. 4 Faux (cycling). Faux (two or three weeks). 5 Faux (for a month). Faux (they'll travel by coach).

E 1 Je reste à la maison ce soir. 2 Il va louer un vélo. 3 Nous allons vendre notre maison l'année prochaine. 4 Je vais aller à la banque demain matin. 5 Tu vas à Londres la semaine prochaine?

3 Je vais réserver le ferry par Internet

A

Crossing Calais-Dover: **Return**

Calais-Dover: Tuesday 17th **July**
11.15

Dover-Calais: **Tuesday** 19th August
13.00

Passengers: Two adults + **two children (4-15 years old) + one baby (under 4)**

Vehicle: **Camper-van**

B 1 **Seafrance:** Seafrance, bonjour! (1)
Client: Non, en camping-car avec cinq passagers. (14)
Seafrance: Oui, pour quelle traversée? (3)
Client: 13h30. (12)
SF: Oui, pour quelle date? (5)
Client: Pour le 17 juillet. (6)
SF: A quelle heure? (7)
Client: Bonjour, j'ai un problème de connection Internet, et je voudrais faire une réservation. (2)
SF: D'accord, et le retour, pour quelle date? (9)
Client: Non, deux adultes, deux enfants et un bébé. (16)
SF: A quelle heure? (11)
Client: Le 19 août. (10)

SF: Oui d'accord, et vous voyagez en voiture? (13)
Client: 11h15. (8)
SF: Cinq adultes? (15)
Client: Calais-Douvres, aller-retour. (4)
SF: Très bien, ça fait 490 euros. (17)

C 1 08h00. 2 05h30. 3 14h40. 4 17h30. 5 23h55. 6 03h45. 7 13h45. 8 12h15.

4 A la gare

A 1 Isabelle is going to Amsterdam **next week**. 2 She wants to go on **Tuesday**. 3 She has to be in Amsterdam by **6.00 pm**. 4 She's returning to Brussels on **Thursday**. 5 She'll be travelling **on her own**. 6 She wants to pay **by credit card**.

B See p. 18.

C 1 d, 2 f, 3 a, 4 e, 5 b, 6 c.

D 1 A quelle heure est le prochain vol pour Londres? 2 C'est quelle porte pour le vol AF541, s'il vous plaît? 3 L'embarquement est à quelle heure? 4 Il arrive à Edimbourg à quelle heure? 5 Je peux avoir une place fumeur? 6 Est-ce que le personnel de bord parle anglais?

4 B

Aller-simple: Bruxelles-Midi / Amsterdam / Mardi 23 / 14h28 / 17h07 / 1 / 0 / 0
Aller-retour: ✔ / Amsterdam / Bruxelles-Midi / Jeudi 25 / 8h56 / 11h32 / 1 / 0 / 0
Prix total: 117 / Carte de crédit ✔ / Isabelle Moutier

5 On peut louer une voiture …

A permis de conduire, clé, louer, vol, aujourd'hui, location, formulaire, kilométrage limité, emplacement.

B aider; voiture; quand; semaine; type; petit; 215,29; 2 000; comprises; 11h00; documents; gare.

C more/older, included, Theft, Damage, Young, Effects, Additional driver

E 1 **c** The engine's making a funny noise. 2 **d** The headlight's broken. 3 **a** I have a flat tyre. 4 **f** My car's broken down. 5 **b** My windscreen wipers are broken. 6 **e** The indicator isn't working.

La Francophonie

A Horizontal: maritime, entretien, routes, aerodrome, pays

Vertical: ferroviaire, reseau, aerien, bitumées, routiers

B 1 2500 FCFA. 2 Midnight. 3 Malick Sy Avenue. 4 Blue and yellow; green. 5 The green bus. 6 Every 10–15 minutes.

Looking forward

60 rooms in city centre: air conditioning, en-suite bathrooms, 6 French television channels, 'Canal satellite' channels, daily newspapers, fast food/snacks all day, launderette, private car park monitored 24/24.

UNIT 8

1 Vous vous souvenez?

A 1 Il est cinq heures dix/Il est dix-sept heures dix. 2 Il est onze heures quarante/ Il est douze heures moins vingt. 3 Il est midi/Il est douze heures. 4 Il est six heures trente/Il est six heures et demie. 5 Il est minuit/Il est zéro heure.

B 1 à l'aéroport. 2 à la gare. 3 à l'aéroport. 4 à la gare. 5 sur le ferry.

C 1 Faux (because of fog). 2 Faux (train from Paris). 3 Vrai. 4 Faux (Platform 12). 5 Faux (arrived in Portsmouth, passengers to go back to their vehicles).

SOLUTIONS TO EXERCISES

2 Tout d'abord, il faut chercher un hôtel

A 1 Proche de l'aéroport/climatisation. 2 Au bord de la mer/climatisation/chambres handicapés. 3 A la campagne/animaux acceptés. 4 Centre-ville/station de métro/parking. 5 A la montagne/restaurant.

B

Name:	Mme Michaud
Telephone:	03 13 56 51 00
Place/town requested:	Nice region (not in Nice)
Requirements:	Quiet area, spacious for children to play, full board, family room.

Name:	M. and Mme Jaubert
Telephone:	01 68 72 62 15
Place/town requested:	Cannes
Requirements:	Small hotel near beach and shops. Room on ground floor, wife in wheelchair

Name:	Mme Delannay
Telephone:	03 20 38 49 56
Place/town requested:	Mountain region
Requirements:	Comfortable hotel with air-conditioning, swimming pool and restaurant. Likes fish and provençale cuisine.

C 1 **d**, 2 **a**, 3 **e**, 4 **b**, 5 **f**, 6 **c**.

D Bonjour, je cherche un hôtel près de Monaco mais pas à Monaco même. Je voudrais un hôtel confortable avec piscine et beaucoup d'espace pour que les enfants puissent jouer. J'aimerais visiter la région et j'ai donc besoin de renseignements sur la région. Je préfère la demi-pension parce que j'aimerais aller dans différents restaurants et goûter les spécialités provençales. Pouvez-vous me rappeler. Je m'appelle ... et mon numéro de téléphone est le ... .

3 Cet hôtel a l'air sympa!

A étang, le jardin d'hiver, à 5 km de Saint Omer, baldaquin, (se) détendre, chambres, les affaires, siècle, hébergement, chambres familiales.

B compris, prix, séjour, lendemain, simple, nuit, gratuite.

C 1 160 euros. 2 No, breakfast is 12 euros per person. 3 Double/twin room + breakfast + bottle of champagne + aperitif + gourmet dinner + lunch the following day. 4 50 euros. 5 Free. 6 Leave his credit card details.

D 1 Je voudrais réserver une chambre double. 2 C'est combien une chambre simple? 3 Le petit déjeuner est compris? 4 Il y a une piscine? 5 La troisième nuit est gratuite. 6 Je peux confirmer ma réservation par fax?

E **You:** Bonjour, je voudrais réserver une chambre s'il vous plaît. ... **You:** Pour vendredi 27 juin. ... **You:** Pour deux nuits seulement. ... **You:** Non, pour deux personnes. Je voudrais une chambre double avec salle de bains privée. ... **You:** Parfait, alors avec petit déjeuner pour les deux jours. ... **You:** Bien sûr! Mon nom est...

4 Les adjectifs

A le vin – rouge; la plante – verte; les spécialités – italiennes; des films – français; un hôtel – confortable; un poisson – rouge; des devoirs – difficiles; un homme – heureux.

B 1 C'est un hôtel **spacieux** et **confortable**. 2 C'est une **petite** chambre **moderne**. 3 Il y a un **beau** parc fleuri. 4 Il y a un restaurant **chinois** près d'ici! 5 Je n'aime pas l'eau **plate**, je préfère l'eau **gazeuse**. 6 J'adore les **vieilles** maisons **romaines**.

C **véritable** studio; **grand** lit; ligne **téléphonique directe**; réveil **automatique**; matières **chaleureuses**; couleurs **gaies**; éclairage **modulable**; **grandes** serviettes.

D bed, sofa bed, phone line, socket, air-conditioning, washbasin, bath, shower, taps, lighting, hair dryer, towel.

5 Ça ne m'impressionne pas!

A **a** 3, **b** 5, **c** 2, **d** 4, **e** 1.

B Version **a**.

C 2 The hotel is too noisy. 3 The food was awful. 5 The room was stuffy.

D 1 Il n'y a pas de douche dans la salle de bains. 2 Le robinet fuit. 3 Il fait froid dans la chambre. Le chauffage/le radiateur ne marche pas. 4 Les gens dans la chambre à côté/voisine font beaucoup de bruit. 5 Je ne peux pas ouvrir la fenêtre, elle est coincée.

E *Model answer :*
Madame, Monsieur,

Je voudrais vous faire part de quelques commentaires sur la qualité des prestations offertes dans votre hôtel. Ma chambre est trop petite et il n'y a pas de vue sur le lac.

La nuit, il y a beaucoup/trop de bruit à cause de la boîte de nuit en bas. Au restaurant, les plats sont toujours froids. Je vous serai reconnaissant(e) de bien vouloir me donner une autre chambre et de vérifier la qualité du service au restaurant.

Veuillez agréer, madame, monsieur, l'expression de mes sentiments distingués.

La Francophonie

A 1 Madagascar is situated 700 km west of La Réunion. 2 Distance between Paris and La Réunion as the crow flies. 3 The 'cold' season between May and November. 4 This island loomed up/appeared from the sea 3 million years ago. 5 La Réunion has 30 km of beaches. 6 Reflecting diversity of La Réunion's population, coming from all over the world (here from Africa, Madagascar and China).

B coat hangers (cintres), bath towels (linge de bains), cutlery and plates (assiettes et couverts), bottle opener (limonadier), can opener (ouvre-boîtes), hair-dryer (sèche-cheveux).

Looking forward

J'ai mal à la tête. Je me sens fatigué(e). J'ai des courbatures.

UNIT 9

1 Vous vous souvenez?

A 1 Je cherche un hôtel à la **montagne**, je n'aime pas la mer. 2 Je voudrais **réserver** une chambre double, s'il vous plaît. 3 Je suis dans une chaise roulante. Est-ce que vous avez des chambres pour **handicapés** ? 4 L'ampoule de la salle de bains a **grillé**. 5 Il fait froid dans la chambre, le chauffage ne **marche** pas. 6 Veuillez **agréer**, monsieur, l'expression de mes **sentiments** distingués.

B 1 Il a un gros chien noir. 2 J'ai une petite maison à la campagne. 3 Ils ont une cuisine moderne et spacieuse. 4 C'est un beau vase bleu. 5 Je préfère le pain blanc.

2 A votre santé!

A 1 sport/physical activities. 2 your eating habits. 3 weight. 4 smoking. 5 stress. 6 medicines. 7 alcohol. 8 visit your doctor.

B 1 **a** cœur, **c** poumons, **d** muscles, **e** os. 2 **a** la marche, **b** la natation, **d** des étirements, **f** la musculation.

C préserver, perdre, améliorer, diminuer, prévenir, résistants, monter, porter, faire, remercie.

D Je vais faire plus d'exercices physiques parce que je suis trop gros(se) et je veux perdre du poids. / Je voudrais perdre du poids parce que je mange trop et je ne fais jamais d'exercices. / Je vais arrêter de fumer parce que je fume trop et c'est trop cher. / Je vais réduire mon stress parce que je travaille trop et je veux/vais sortir avec mes amis plus souvent. / Je vais boire moins parce que je sors trop et je ne devrais pas boire plus de 2 unités par jour. / Je vais changer mes habitudes alimentaires parce que je cuisine seulement des pâtes et j'ai besoin de manger plus de légumes verts.

3 Un rendez-vous chez le dentiste

A 1 a, 2 b, 3 b, 4 a, 5 c.

B **Secrétaire:** Cabinet dentaire, bonjour.
Annie: Bonjour, je voudrais prendre rendez-vous avec le Dr Démory, s'il vous plaît.
Sec: Oui, pour quel jour, madame?
Annie: Demain après-midi?
Sec: Malheureusement, demain ça sera difficile ... par contre jeudi matin, le docteur peut vous prendre à 10h00.
Annie: Oui, c'est bien, ce n'est pas urgent de toute façon, c'est juste pour un contrôle.
Sec: Votre nom, madame?
Annie: Mme Boutin, Annie.
Sec: Donc, jeudi 10h00, madame.
Annie: Merci, au revoir.

C **Vous :** Bonjour, je voudrais prendre rendez-vous avec le Dr Philippe, s'il vous plaît. ... **Vous:** Aujourd'hui si possible, j'ai mal aux dents. C'est très douloureux. ...**Vous:** Et demain matin? ... **Vous:** Oui, parfait. Est-ce que je dois apporter mon formulaire E111? ... **Vous:** Monsieur X/ Madame Y. ... **Vous:** Merci et à demain.

D Annie téléphone au dentiste car elle voudrait changer son rendez-vous. Elle voudrait en prendre un autre **la semaine prochaine** parce qu'elle **a une réunion à Londres** ce jeudi. Son nouveau rendez-vous avec Dr Démory est à **10h00**.

E 1 g, 2 b, 3 e, 4 c, 5 f, 6 a, 7 d.

4 J'ai une fièvre de cheval

A 1 e, 2 b, 3 g, 4 a, 5 h, 6 c, 7 f, 8 i, 9 d.

B 1 Aches everywhere: head, arms, legs and she's feeling tired. Throat's a little sore too. 2 Blood pressure is a bit low. 3 One tablet. 4 Two in the morning, two at lunchtime and two in the evening. 5 20 euros.

C **a** 4, **b** 1, **c** 6, **d** 7, **e** 2, **f** 5, **g** 3.

D 1 Je ne me sens pas bien. 2 J'ai très mal à l'estomac. 3 Vous avez quelque chose pour le nez bouché? 4 Je voudrais du sirop pour une toux sèche. 5 Vous avez une crème pour les verrues?

5 Je me sens déjà mieux

A **a** 4 (headache/tablets), **b** 2 (woman with sore throat/syrup), **c** 5 (insect bites/cream), **d** 1 (stomach ache/capsules), **e** 3 (man with sore throat/lozenges).

B 1 Faux (one tablespoon in the morning and one in the evening). 2 Vrai. 3 Faux (take one lozenge every 3 hours. Do not exceed 5 per day.) 4 Faux (take one capsule with lots of water). 5 Vrai.

C mouthwash, condoms, wasps, cotton buds.

D 1 Scissors with rounded ends. 2 Arnica is for bruises. 3 Biafine is for burns. 4 Cream for sunburn and spray for insect bites.

La Francophonie

A 1 80 volcanic islands and submerged volcanoes. 2 120 different languages. 3 Vanuatu is situated 2172 km north-east of Sydney. 4 Vanuatu is situated 5750 km south-west of Honolulu.

B 1 3.5 hours. 2 There are 9 active volcanoes. 3 Capital city. 4 English, French and Bichelamar.

C 1 Take a preventive treatment against malaria. 2 Because the preventive treatment for malaria makes the skin more sensitive to the sun. 3 GP, dentist and

SOLUTIONS TO EXERCISES

physiotherapist. 4 They will be transported to New Caledonia, New Zealand or Australia. 5 AIDS.

Looking forward

Rez-de-chaussée	1ᵉʳ étage
salon	chambre
cuisine	bureau
cellier	salle de bains
entrée	
WC	WC
bureau	
salle de bains	
salle à manger	

UNIT 10

1 Vous vous souvenez?

A head – la tête, eyes – les yeux, ear – l'oreille, nose – le nez, mouth – la bouche, throat/neck – la gorge/le cou, back – le dos, arm – le bras, hand – la main, stomach – l'estomac, legs – les jambes, foot – le pied.

B **You:** Bonjour monsieur/madame. … **You:** Je voudrais quelque chose pour le rhume et le mal de gorge, s'il vous plaît. … **You:** Je préfère quelque chose de plus fort comme des comprimés. … **You:** Non, mais j'ai froid. … **You:** Je dois prendre combien de comprimés? … **You:** Très bien. C'est combien, s'il vous plaît?

2 A la maison

A 1 *Not mentioned:* white, violet, black, pink. 2 *Not mentioned:* bathroom, entrance hall.

B 1 orange – helps digestion/security/comfort – dining room. 2 red – warmth – kitchen. 3 green – space/relaxation – bedroom. 4 blue – calm/space/relaxation/good for meditation – lounge. 5 brown – stability. 6 yellow – stimulates brain – study/office.

C 1 les annonces/ventes. 2 travaux. 3 locations. 4 ventes de prestige. 5 déménager.

D 1 House in Lille close to **Underground** station. Double glazing, shutters, **small** yard at the **front** of the house. Two bedrooms. 2 House in Douai with lounge, kitchen, two bedrooms, **attic** and garden. Needs decorating. 3 House in Tourtour. Wooded area. Stone house with fitted kitchen, lounge, fireplace in **lounge**, three toilets, bathroom. **One** bedroom upstairs. Swimming pool **in basement**.

E campagne, rez-de-chaussée, salle à manger, équipée, bureau, salle de bains, cabinet de toilette, étage, chambre à coucher, dehors, terrasse.

3 J'ai besoin d'un nouveau jean

A a 5, b 6, **c** 4, d 3, e 2, f 1.

B 1 manches longues / col / tour de poitrine. 2 rayé / poche / veste. 3 très tendance / boutons / chemise. 4 robe / coloris. 5 dentelle / jupon (or jupe). 6 laine / longueur.

C taille; cabines d'essayage; au fond; serré; chemise; celui-là; kaki; essayer; caisse.

D 1 J'aime bien **ces** costumes. **Lequel** préférez-vous? Je préfère **celui-ci/celui-là**. 2 J'aime beaucoup **cette** cravate. Oh non, moi, je préfère **celle-ci/celle-là**. 3 J'aime bien **ces** chaussures. **Lesquelles** préférez-vous? Je préfère **celles-ci/celles-là**. 4 Regarde **ce** jean, il est génial! Il n'est pas mal, mais je préfère **celui-ci/celui-là**. 5 **Cette** jupe est très jolie, non? Bof, je préfère **celle-ci/celle-là**. 6 Oh, regardez **ces** chapeaux! **Lequel** préférez-vous? J'adore **celui-ci/celui-là**.

4 J'ai passé un excellent week-end

A 1 **b**, 2 **a**, 3 **d**, 4 **e**, 5 **c**, 6 **f**.

B *Examples of answers:* J'ai commencé à 9h00. Nous sommes allés au théâtre. Vous êtes né(e) le 27 décembre. Nous avons lu le journal. J'ai été malade. Vous avez fait le ménage. J'ai eu un problème avec ma voiture. Vous avez pris rendez-vous avec le dentiste.

C Pictures 4,1,6,5,3,2.

D Annie **a passé** un bon week-end. Son mari et elle **sont allés** chez des amis pour un barbecue. Ils **ont mangé**, ils **ont bu** et ils **ont dansé**. Le lendemain, ils **ont eu** mal à la tête. Samedi après-midi, elle **a fait** du shopping, Daniel **a rangé** la chambre des enfants. Le soir, toute la famille **est restée** à la maison. Dimanche, Annie, Daniel et les enfants **sont allés** à la plage. Ils **ont joué** au football et au badminton. Annie **a pris** un coup de soleil.

La Francophonie

A 1 Nature, history and culture (forests, sea, mountains, caves, ancient remains, festivals etc.). 2 Seaside resort, a wonder of nature with thousands of rocks and magnificent caves. 3 Waterfalls, lakes, flower valleys and pastures. 4 Persimmons, plums, apples, pears and peaches. 5 The remains of the former capital Hué were recognised by UNESCO as cultural world heritage site.

B tunique (tunic), pantalon(s) (trousers), chapeaux (hats), jupes (skirts). *Also:* bijoux (jewellery), bracelets (bracelets), boucles d'oreilles (earrings), colliers (necklaces).

C 1 Faux (fine silk). 2 Faux (still very prized). 3 Vrai. 4 Vrai. 5 Faux (they have flower and animal patterns). 6 Faux (they wear bracelets, earrings and necklaces).